Kiplinger Forecasts:

THE
NEW AMERICAN
BOOM

Exciting Changes
in American Life and Business
Between Now and the Year 2000

By the Staff of the
KIPLINGER WASHINGTON LETTER

Published by
The Kiplinger Washington Editors, Inc.
1729 H Street, NW
Washington, DC 20006

Distributed by
Select Magazines, Inc.
8 East 40th Street
New York, NY 10006

This book is available in bulk quantities at discount. For more information,
contact the Circulation Department, The Kiplinger Washington Editors, Inc.,
at the above address.

ISBN: 0-938721-01-1

Printed in the United States of America

First Printing: May, 1986

Contents

Acknowledgements

A book of this broad scope calls for the labor of many hands and hearts. Authorship was a collaboration between Knight Kiplinger, editor in chief of *Changing Times* magazine and associate editor of the *Kiplinger Letters*, and Sid A. Levy, longtime associate editor of the *Kiplinger Washington Letter*.

They had the support of the entire staff of the *Kiplinger Letters*, who supplied valuable reporting and judgments: Editorial Manager Henry Earp, Editorial Director Phillip J. Kiesner, and Associate Editors Peter Blank, Melissa Bristow, Martyn Chase, Lee Cohn, Kenneth Dalecki, Leonard Fried, Richard Golden, Gene Goldenberg, Steven Ivins, Lloyd Kath, Dana Martin, James Mayo, William Senior, Charles Snyder, Marc Stertz and Dale Taft. Our thanks, too, to former Associate Editors Harry Lenhart and Janet Meyers.

We owe special thanks to the staffs of The Conference Board, Office of Technology Assessment of the U.S. Congress, Institute of Electrical and Electronics Engineers, World Biotech Report, Population Reference Bureau, and World Future Society, for reports and analyses we were able to draw upon.

Particular appreciation goes to Dr. Nestor E. Terleckyj of the National Planning Association, Washington, D.C., whose Economic Growth Model was most helpful in testing our own projections. And thanks to freelance writers Edith Roth, Patrick Gilbo and Michael Tully for special research and reporting; and to Dorothy Moorhouse for invaluable assistance in checking the copy for accuracy.

Our gratitude, too, to the dozens of others in business, government, universities, research organizations, scientific and trade groups, consulting organizations and the like who gave us their views and the benefit of their special knowledge.

The Kiplinger Washington Editors
Washington, D.C.
May 9, 1986

Introduction

By Austin H. Kiplinger
Editor in Chief, The Kiplinger Letters

Over the past three decades the U.S. has come through a period of enormous upheaval. A succession of alterations in business has moved us from the dominance of manufacturing to a preponderance of services. It has been an era that defies classification into any traditional category.

Was it a time of peace and prosperity or conflict and distress? Was it progress or regression, growth or contraction? It was some of all of these, but whatever else it was, it was NOT a period of tranquility. In just two decades we have had the Vietnam War and a struggle over civil rights. We have had turbulence on campus, riots in the streets, a social-sexual revolution in mores, a flood of female workers into the labor force, high inflation, and a surge of conservatism in politics. The anti-tax revolt was symbolized by California's Proposition 13, and a disenchantment with big government was accompanied by the efforts of a Democratic president, Jimmy Carter, to begin the deregulation of business.

Clearly, the growing suspicion of big government and governmental answers was broadly based—not just a murmur of nostalgia from old traditionalists and not just from the Republican side of the aisle. In fact, the movement against the expansion of big government may actually have been aided by the anti-war protests of young dissenters who—in their own irreverent way—

were emulating attitudes of their elders when they objected to what government was doing to their lives. So what is now commonly referred to as the Reagan Revolution in American politics did not originate with Ronald Reagan, but came as the culmination of a gradual shift in American political attitudes over a period of several decades.

With all this, we also had the oil embargo, resulting in a 1,000% increase in the price of oil, which is not only the world's basic energy source but also the most widely used raw material. As if this were not enough, the oil price explosion was accompanied by war in the Middle East, revolution in the Arab-Moslem community and worldwide terrorism. The U.S. added a little icing to the cake in the form of the high inflation, mounting federal deficits, and the highest nominal interest rates in its history.

Could any civilized government, any sophisticated industrial society survive such an incredible series of blows to its solar plexus? Would anyone of respectable credentials and acknowledged common sense have predicted such a scenario 20 year ago?

Had I indeed forecast such a scenario, I would have been ridiculed or pilloried. One author, Paul Erdman, did write a novel based on a horrifying collection of calamities, and as a novelist, he projected them into a huge collapse of the western economic system.

But the astonishing fact of our times is that we experienced the enactment of these events in real life without the consequences that he described. The system did NOT collapse. The world of the '80s has been wrenched and torn but not split apart. Our economies, despite unprecedented excesses and distortions, have not crumbled into a pile of statistical rubble. The *Crash of '79* did NOT occur.

Even as I am writing this, inflation is running at barely 3% a year, oil prices have dropped into the 'teens, and the U.S. economy is in its fourth year of strong recovery from a severe recession.

This suggests, cogently, that the world society, our political and economic institutions, have an almost limitless resiliency. Faced with necessity and adversity, our instinct for survival takes over. The adage reminds us that "necessity is the mother of invention." The adage also tells us that necessity is the prime mover in world political and economic affairs. When things get bad enough, people will take corrective action.

Which brings us to the present. As you may surmise, in the course of my work I talk with hundreds of people in business and government, in organized labor, in finance, in universities and research labs and think tanks. We talk candidly about the weaknesses that we all see around us. We don't gloss over the troubles and shortcomings we see.

I find a common element in their judgments these days, whether they have a liberal or conservative orientation. The common judgment is that the imbalances and distortions in our economic life are beginning to respond to treatment. I find a cautious optimism, a feeling that the U.S. is putting its house in order and correcting the flaws that have hampered its performance in recent years.

Look at some of these conditions—the minuses in our economic situation—and see what's happening to them:

Unemployment is still running around 7%—a waste of humanpower. But last year, 2,000,000 new jobs were created and filled. The demographics of the next few years will see a slowing of entrants into the labor force, leading to a more complete use of existing talent.

Overpriced labor and an overvalued dollar are both in process of correction, as unions recognize that competition is worldwide and American labor must adapt to that reality. Corrections will come slowly, since they are institutional in nature, but they are coming. The overvalued dollar is being adjusted day to day as our interest rates decline.

The U.S. trade deficit with the world is still running at more than $10 billion a month. This will not be corrected soon, but the gap is trending downward, and the rapid changes in the value of the dollar and the yen will contribute to improvement. Better marketing of American products will gradually spur the sale of U.S. goods overseas. Agriculture, for all of its current problems, will slowly adjust to lower world market prices and regain some of its former share of world food sales.

The U.S. federal budget deficit is trending downward—minor improvement, but the changes are in the right direction, and most importantly, the deficit will represent a smaller and smaller percentage of a growing national economy.

Overconfidence in ourselves during the heyday of our world dominance led to an under-investment in new techniques and a slack in our savings rate. The overconfidence is being corrected, but improvement in savings and investment is still ahead.

Lagging productivity is responding slowly, but it IS responding to automation, robotization, computerization, and loosening up of restrictive work rules that were put into effect when union labor dominated the workplace. The drive for survival is forcing a more realistic view of manning requirements on machinery. And with union membership remaining at just one-sixth of the workforce, new restrictive rules are less likely to succeed.

Overcapacity in agriculture: Here the solution will be painful, sometimes brutal, but inevitable after more than 40 years of subsidies which encouraged overcapacity in milk production, field crops, cotton, sugar, tobacco and other farm products.

Outmoded trade and antitrust policies: Once again, there is a growing awareness that many of our government policies were based on times long gone, when the bulk of our competition was within our own borders. Now we know that competition is worldwide, and our trade policy needs an overhaul. Until this happens, U.S. companies will have to struggle to assert themselves in foreign markets where nationalistic policies prevail. This remains one of the biggest hurdles for American industry, and in the short run it will require superior products and superior salesmanship.

We still have plenty of problems, but if my assessment of strengths and weaknesses is right, the U.S. is on the verge of a major resurgence in its economic fortunes.

After weighing the pros and cons with people on the firing line of research, technology, management and marketing, I believe this country is poised for one of its strongest periods of solid growth—based on new techniques and new technologies. Evidence is mounting that the U.S. economy, in the 1990s and extending into the 21st century, will raise American living standards to new high records for U.S. consumers and will increase the American share of business in world markets.

The advances will not come evenly. The progress will be accompanied by occasional slow-downs in growth. But in every case, the slow periods will be mild and will be followed by significant bursts of growth in new technology, new investment, and increases in the gross national product.

By 1990, U.S. population will be 250,000,000. It will be a more mature mix, with the median age rising. After the era of youth emphasis, the Baby Boomers will be approaching middle age—their most productive time of life.

In the decade of the '90s, the U.S. will emerge into a new era of growth in living standards, comparable to the period immediately following World War II. While the impetus then was catch-up, the impetus of the '90s will be go-ahead, as the U.S. plays its greatest trump card—its enormous supremacy in basic scientific research. Despite appearances, the U.S. has more research capacity—in education, equipment and talent—than any other nation on earth. Within the 50 states are the world's most powerful research laboratories. While other nations have made industrial and marketing inroads, the greatest basic research capacity is in this country.

If you doubt this, think for a moment about the lists of Nobel Prize winners in science, which—year after year—are dominated by U.S. scientists. The U.S. became the leader in world scientific progress following World War II, and has continued to draw the world's best brains to its laboratories.

But what we must do—and WILL do—is develop faster ways to transfer basic research into technological development, and then design marketable products. Product design and development must be—and WILL be—speeded up. Laws and production schedules will be modernized. Government deregulation started the ball rolling. Some further modernization of antitrust laws will enable American business to coordinate produce development, as the Japanese have been doing for years.

In 1925 Calvin Coolidge said, "the business of America is business." Today I say, "the business of America is EDUCATION." Education constructs the foundations of technology, and technology in turn provides the track for industry and commerce to advance into the 21st century.

This is the countdown stage. We are in it now. These are the times of development for the super computer, for biotechnology, for fiber-optic telecommunications, for robots, for theory simulation, for "artificial intelligence," for investment in new techniques of all kinds. In the decade of the 1990s, research and development will launch America into a high-technology orbit. To maintain its new role in technology, the U.S. will modernize on a massive scale, accompanied by a wave of capital investment and more friendly tax and antitrust policies.

So much for what will be happening in OUR country. What about the rest of the world?

The truth is, the coming era of technology will be global. It will be based on American science, but it will be applied worldwide. This doesn't surprise us any more, since we are accustomed to foreign labels in the market place.

International competition will be accompanied by new forms of international corporate cooperation. The implementation of all these new technologies will be carried out by consortiums of companies from all the industrialized nations. American, Japanese, German, French and British firms will participate in joint ventures. And one consequence will be the re-opening of many overseas markets to American products and services.

Europe will begin to catch the fever, giving American exports a better shot at overseas sales, laying the groundwork for longer-term gains from 1990 to 2000, and across the century mark to 2005. Developing nations will be the basic providers of raw materials and the finishers of those materials into basic manufactured goods. They will be a growing market for our high-technology capital equipment, and the U.S. a market for their manufactures and consumer goods.

These changes will bring tensions and social crisis, of which the U.S. will have its fair share. New ways may or may not be better, depending on your point of view, but new ways are coming.

And now, having recited this litany of change, let me step back from the subject and ask the question that is probably on your mind. How strong are these prospects? How likely are they to come about?

In my judgment, these developments are definitely in the cards for the next 15 to 20 years. The foundation work for them is already happening in the laboratories, plants and offices around this country. The changes will be spread around America, not concentrated in any one region, despite the visibility of some of the fast-growing areas of the South and West.

None of what I have described is a guarantee of happiness. But it IS a guarantee of activity, vigor and a strong resurgence of growth in this country over the next two decades. To the extent that these have been qualities of life on the American scene in the past, the American future will, once again, depict the qualities that have made it great.

Austin Kiplinger

Washington, D.C.
May 9, 1986

1

Threshold of a Boom

Americans will surprise themselves before long with a technological boom that will take off in a steep upward curve.

This technological surge will trigger a period of sustained economic growth that has few parallels in American history. Relatively few people see this coming. Some scientists, engineers, investment risk-takers and entrepreneurs do, but most consensus economists don't. Given their profession's recent forecasting record, we'll go with the scientists, engineers and risk-takers.

The road to the year 2000 won't be free of occasional bumps—short intervals of slow growth or mild recession—but unlike previous overheated booms, it will not carry within it the seeds of an eventual bust.

This will be a transformation as sweeping as the Industrial Revolution, and it will take place in a far shorter period of time. Like all earlier economic transformations, it will have its victims as well as winners—a sort of "creative destruction" of the outmoded and inefficient in favor of the innovative and productive.

The new boom will be accompanied by relatively modest inflation—which is only one distinction between this and previous ones; there are others, which we will lay out as we go along.

It will be a private-enterprise affair, fueled chiefly by the ingenuity and investment of the private sector; the current and continuing upswing in corporate research and development spending will pay off big, as it always has. The government's role will be a background one—helping with basic research and development but otherwise standing aside, with gradual removal of regulatory impediments, especially in the field of antitrust and exporting.

Government regulation is in a long-term decline with little prospect of major reversals. Growth of the federal government will level off, but this will put more pressure on state and local government. Congress will probably maintain some sort of automatic-pilot mechanism for restraining budget deficits—not necessarily today's Gramm-Rudman-Hollings scheme, but something like it that the courts can accept.

The political appeal of protectionism and government manipulation of the economy via "industrial policy" will fade as our involvement with the world economy grows and spreads. But this will take time and struggle, and there will be pain involved, as there has been in the past—jobs "lost" to foreign competition. Still, substantial progress toward more open trade will be made.

The New American Boom will take place in a climate of low population growth in the U.S. and in most of the industrialized West. In this country, one effect will be a steady improvement in the productivity of the work force, which will be made up increasingly of older, more experienced and better-educated workers, with a declining proportion of the young and unskilled. This could be a mixed blessing; many employers will have to bid high for skilled labor in a slower-growing labor force. But higher investment in various forms of automation will more than offset rising labor costs and give a further boost to productivity.

These productivity gains will enable our economy to enjoy both rising real incomes and a new competitiveness in world markets, while holding inflation down at the same time.

With inflation low and disposable income rising, an increasingly affluent, increasingly middle-aged society will generate enormous economic opportunities for entrepreneurs and marketers with ideas for products and services.

New, small firms will provide most of our employment growth. Bigs will grow more slowly and will increasingly become venture capital centers themselves, helping to nurture new firms and new products within their own ranks and reaching out to attract others. In both giant corporations and small businesses, there will be a spreading internationalization of ownership—foreign investors buying into American business, American firms buying up or into foreign companies.

OLD PROBLEMS

A lot of old familiar problems will still be around in 2000—some worse than now, some better: Tense relations with Russia, the arms race, the threat (though diminishing) of nuclear war, spreading political terrorism. Poverty and stagnation in much of the Third World (but less than now). Deterioration in many older inner-city areas. High unemployment among minority youth. Urban sprawl and traffic congestion. Incipient breakdown of municipal infrastructure in older cities. An explosion of illegal immigration. Increasing strain on our veterans'-care system. An upturn in numbers of the very old, with accompanying special-care requirements. The rising cost of maintaining water quality and supply in many parts of the country.

But energy won't be one of the worsening problems. Conventional fuels will be plentiful and cheap throughout at least the next 15 years, while we make great strides in developing alternative energy sources to phase in when fossil fuels become dear. Exotic new fuel cells and batteries will revolutionize the generating and storing of electricity.

NEW INDUSTRIAL POWER

The principal components of the coming high-tech takeoff include these:
▶ Automation, robots and flexible manufacturing
▶ New-generation computers and microprocessors
▶ Biotechnology
▶ Energy generation and storage
▶ Fiber-optic laser communications
▶ Commercial ventures in space
▶ Growing internationalization of corporate ownership

U.S. industry will transform itself along fresh lines. It will continue to yield dominance in many basic industries—carbon steel, rubber, petrochemical processing, electronic components—to developing countries that can do these things less expensively. But in many sophisticated fields, American productivity, already the highest in the world, will zoom. Some of the greatest increases in productivity will come in services of central importance to growth of the entire economy, which will confound the traditional wisdom that says productivity in services is hopelessly low.

Growth in such lines as communications, data processing, financial services, education, and biotech research will have multiplier effects across many others, expanding their productivity and profitability. And these effects will spread out through the economy in a fashion still not apparent to most people. It's called "synergy," and it stands for the way systems interact in support of each other.

These interconnections are already at work and they are nearly impossible to map in any neat, orderly way. The force lines of synergy go off in all directions, knitting an almost random web. They are part of an entrepreneurial revolution that is sweeping through and transforming the economy—not only with the creation of whole new industries, but also by helping to revitalize older, basic lines.

Reindustrialization will come through the application of high technology—automation and robotics—together with enhanced management, financial and data-handling techniques. Contrary to current myth, manufacturing is not shrinking in America. Its output is growing, and it will become steadily more competitive with the rest of the world.

In most hard-goods and production-line industries, flexible manufacturing techniques will become dominant. Employing "intelligent" robots, "expert systems" and related technology, such plants will be small and highly integrated with the ability to turn on a dime, using computer-directed routines to shift from one product to another in a fraction of the time conventional factories require, and with vastly greater rates of productivity.

JOBS AND LABOR

Along with a rapid rise in job creation, we face a sharp slowdown in the growth of the labor force, which by the mid-'90s will have altered the basic aspect of this country's unemployment problem. There will be some labor shortages in high-tech lines, and unemployment will trend downward toward some minimum representing theoretical "full employment," leaving only the virtually "unemployable" without jobs. This minimum rate could be 5% or even lower, depending on how well this country meets the challenge of training and upgrading the unskilled. Many low-skill jobs will be filled by "off-the-books" illegal immigrants, leaving native-born Americans on the official jobless roles. This points up the importance of education, social-service programs, and job training in preparing this country for a high-tech future—an issue that government and business will have to deal with at all levels.

Manufacturing employment will grow more slowly than in the rest of the economy. To those who measure growth and evaluate change only by employment numbers, this appears as a threat—even a calamity. But this view is already out of step with the times. The fact is that overall employment is expanding steadily, with the non-manufacturing sectors leading the way. This is one of those transitions we referred to earlier, but it has been underway for several decades. Only the pace of change will be different.

The gap between the median earnings of white and racial-minority workers will continue to narrow, virtually disappearing early in the next century. (Note that we say "workers"; unemployment will remain higher among non-white Americans, so the median incomes of racial minority groups will still be lower than for whites.)

Unions will continue to lose membership and clout, especially in hard-goods lines where automation will take over. But also in other, service-oriented lines—the bulk of the economy—where employers will act almost as if unionized, offering wages and working conditions that will leave little for unions to improve on.

Growth in fringe benefits will slow for a decade or so, then accelerate again as companies find themselves competing for highly skilled workers in a tight labor market. More and more companies will permit, or even encourage, employees to "telecommute" to the office—work at home and keep in touch with headquarters over a home computer.

Career choices facing tomorrow's generations will be keyed to technology, but not technology alone. While industry and business will need specialists of many kinds, they also will be looking for management talent among those with good communications skills, a broad educational background, and the imagination to see ways of reaching new markets.

Management styles will change with the times, impelled by the working habits of a new generation of young entrepreneurs. Old structures will be challenged by new "lateral" systems. And agility will be the key to keeping up with the competition.

GROWTH LINES

High-growth fields over the next couple of decades include a mixture of the old and new. Here's a sampling:

Aerospace. Plastics, composites, ceramics. Epoxy-fiber laminates. Bioengineering (in health, agriculture, industry). Pharmaceuticals. Space manufacturing and processing. Computers, microprocessors, office machines. Data-processing software. Health-care services. Surgical and medical equipment and devices. Electrical equipment. Electrical storage (batteries and fuel cells). Robots, automation. Industrial controls. Lasers. Fiber optics. Financial services. Travel. Publishing. Telecommunications, electronic mail. Advertising. Home appliances. Wholesaling, retailing. Broadcasting. Adult education, retraining. Water and waste-treatment systems. And others.

Some lines will undergo further shrinkage and will manage to stay afloat only to the extent that they can automate: Steel, which will become an industry of small specialty producers. Petrochemicals, in transition from commodity to specialty chemicals. Glass. Nonferrous metals and mining.

Others will stay about as is for a while, picking up again only around the turn of the century: Oil production and refining, for example. Housing.

Some of the high-tech lines that are the basic industries of the new boom are already fairly well developed, while others are still in their pre-takeoff stage, gathering strength for the growth to come. In this phase, progress at times is bound to seem painfully slow or even nonexistent—but not to people who know where to look and what to look for, which is what this book is about.

It's important to keep a base line in mind for purposes of weighing future growth: Just about all the technology that will be taken for granted in the year 2000 already is either in being or about to leap off the computer screen or out of the laboratory. All the people who will be employed then have already been born. It is estimated that 90% of all scientific knowledge has been generated in only the past three decades or so. Roughly the same proportion of all scientists and engineers in the world's history are now alive and working.

It's probable that both their numbers AND the base of scientific knowledge will double by 2000 around the world.

The net of it is that companies and individuals who cling too long and too hard to their old ways are almost sure to be left behind, as—to cite just one example—the machine tool industry is finding as it scrambles to keep up with the robotics revolution.

A FORECAST SAMPLER

Here is a sampling of sector-by-sector forecasts that you'll find throughout this book in greater detail:

Computers: Knowledge growth will be exponential—meaning that it will double and redouble, not simply add to what we already have. It will have a huge beneficial impact on productivity in all lines, including business in general. "Expert systems" will become advisers and assistants in many fields, and the advent of the truly "user friendly" computers—including some with voice-activated operations—is at hand. The U.S. will continue to be the leader in computer technology, but not in manufacturing, which will shift increasingly to low-labor-cost Third World nations.

Communications: Enormous growth in capacity will make other kinds of growth achievable in business, financial services, entertainment, defense, personal services, international relations and trade. Fiber optics will be the main vehicle of transmission, in competition as well as interconnection with satellites.

Office automation: Transformation of the office will go into high gear, taking advantage of advances in networking to link computers and communications on both a local and wide-area, even worldwide, basis. An enormous amount of paper-handling will be eliminated via improved electronic storage systems. Office productivity will grow by leaps and bounds.

Education: Teaching at all levels, especially the younger grades, will undergo a computerized transformation with great improvements in quality and effectiveness—and labor savings in a traditionally labor-intensive field. Students will be able to learn at their own pace, guided by their computerized curriculum and monitored by the teacher.

A new generation of parents, raised on computers, will be receptive to this kind of revitalization in public schools. Corporations will do even more "educating" than the schools, and most executives and professionals can look forward to frequent refresher courses during their careers.

Space: Orbital laboratories and factories will provide new kinds of commercial prospects with great promise for improvements in human health, industrial materials and processes and communications—plus some surprises. Many business and investment opportunities will result, along with potentially staggering profits.

Defense: Spending growth will slow, but the sheer size of the defense business will continue to make opportunities for innovative firms in high-tech lines. The next 20 years will see a transformation of conventional weaponry, making warfare more automated and less labor-intensive. Relations with Russia won't allow for any relaxation of our overall defense effort.

Biotechnology: Commercial applications of genetic engineering will be an area of explosive growth well into the new century. It is in a buildup stage, during which the public may lose interest, only to be caught napping by a sudden expansion of this multifaceted industry in the '90s. Big changes are ahead in agriculture, medicine and health, industrial applications and others—all with great profit potential. Newly engineered genetic substances will be in common use for such tasks as neutralizing sewage, increasing farm yields in arid climates, making low-cost fuel alcohol from vegetation, extracting more oil from seemingly exhausted wells, and making plastics derived not from petroleum, but from vegetable fiber. In sum, we'll see revolutionary results from an evolutionary process.

Farming: Agriculture is in for another round of modernization through technology in which commercial farming will swallow up many smaller, family farms. Production and productivity will climb, and there is hope for substantial cuts in government subsidies. Fewer people will make their living in farming, commodity prices will stay low, and our export markets will be curtailed by rising farm productivity in the developing nations. A critical long-term issue will be the competition between development and agriculture for dwindling water supplies, with development usually winning.

New materials: In plastics and new ceramic materials, you'll see rapid growth in the use of stuff that not only substitutes for, but also improves on, conventional metals and other materials. They'll be lighter, stronger, cheaper. We'll even have plastics that can conduct electricity, for the ultimate solid-state computer parts.

Health: Costs are at long last within sight of a ceiling. The drain on public and private resources (and on individuals' pocketbooks) caused by rapid inflation in this sector will be at an end. Blame it on a new miracle drug called competition. There will be less hospitalization. There will be fewer hospitals, but they'll be big, for-profit, multipurpose medical centers. Most people will get their medical care from a prepaid medical plan, and most of the physicians will be salaried, not self-employed.

Computer technology will greatly improve the lives of physically handicapped people, and people with mental illness will be the beneficiaries of advances in behavior modification with new drugs.

The bottom line: better health care for more people, at lower real cost.

Financial services: The cashless and checkless society that has been prematurely forecasted for years will become a reality over the next 15 years. Banks and kindred institutions will become automated money-and-credit factories with lines out across the country and the world. Instant crediting of payments at the point of sale in stores will create a high-speed financial environment in which every dollar is earning interest for someone, without even momentary idleness. Some employers may even begin paying employees daily via direct electronic deposits in the employee's bank account.

Transportation: Our modes of moving goods and people about will automate as much as they reasonably can, given limitations of cost and physical space. Major changes—magnetic levitation trains, hypersonic airliners and such—will take more than a couple of decades. But commercial and business aircraft will benefit from new structural and engine materials, adding greatly to their fuel efficiency.

The automobile will still be the principal mode of personal transport, but it will increasingly become a pleasure machine full of advanced gadgetry. New engine technology will bring great mileage improvements, and new materials will extend car life and cut maintenance costs. We'll find our way from point to point with computer-screen maps and automatic navigation and homing devices. And the electric car, around for years in primitive forms, may at last become practical.

Construction: With low population growth and fewer new households forming, new residential construction will slow. But smart builders will take advantage of rising affluence among an older population by moving into remodeling, second-home construction, and specialized commercial construction. High land costs in sought-after regions will encourage clustering of new homes, and the homes themselves will be smaller, more efficiently laid out. New homes will participate in the high-tech boom, with central control systems for home entertainment, cleaning and security.

Home appliances and entertainment: Appliances and gadgetry for home use will undergo design and component changes that will make them more reliable and longer-lived—and more thrifty in their use of electricity and water. Improved batteries will turn up in more and more portable applications.

Home entertainment will become fully computerized, with instant access to an ever-widening range of recorded music, film, live performances and the like. Record shops and VCR rental stores will turn into automated data banks for electronic shopping. Signals will come into the home either by satellite or over phone lines, and pay-by-use will be standard for billing.

Marketing: Retailers will find big profits in carefully calling their shots—finding the right niches in the demographic and market transformations that are just ahead. There will be pinpoint targeting of customers and much more direct selling to consumers, through mail order and "teleshopping," ordering on a home computer from an array of choices available at local stores and in catalogs. Consumers will be better heeled but tougher to please, and computerized national shopping will make price comparison much easier than it is now.

Publishing: Print publishing will thrive despite the growth in electronic communications and electronic media, in part because an aging, better educated population will naturally gravitate towards reading matter. Newspapers will still be hot properties, and new magazines to fit every imaginable kind of audience will come and go. Productivity in printing and publishing will zoom. We may even see the advent of computerized "books"—a book-sized device that would play a disk or tape holding an enormous amount of text and display the words on a small screen.

Lifestyles: Changes in the way we live will be guided by a number of trends, including the aging of the population, growing middle-class affluence, and increasing leisure time to enjoy that affluence. We will see sustained booms in leisure travel, the arts (both for spectators and participants), and sports that cater to the middle-aged.

Regional growth patterns: We will see a continuous spreading-out of economic opportunity, which will tend to limit and then reduce regional differences in growth rates as time goes on. Internal migration will continue to favor the Sunbelt, but this trend already is slowing, while older parts of the country are resuming their own growth.

Factors in an eventual flattening of Sunbelt growth rates will include overcrowding in the more sought-after areas, rising taxes, and persistent problems of water supply for development, agriculture and waste treatment.

Among the states, California, Texas and Florida will continue to be the fastest growing, but there will be changes in both their population and economic mix. California will benefit from its relationship with the booming "Asian Rim" nations; Texas, suffering from the decline in energy prices, will exploit its potential for high-tech and health-care development; Florida will continue to draw a heavy influx of tourists, but also a rising proportion of job-seekers, and its share of national employment growth will be 10 percent or more.

International trade and finance: Bit by bit, barriers will be lowered, and world trade will flourish. The dollar will remain the world's premier currency—strong, but at levels below its recent unprecedented heights. Foreign investment in the U.S. will remain heavy, helping to finance much of our high-tech expansion.

The developing countries will take over most of the world's basic manufacturing, and with the earnings of those sales, become major purchasers of high-tech goods and services (financial, communications, education) from the U.S. and other developed nations.

Asia will be a growing trade partner, perhaps beginning to overshadow our traditional partners in Europe. And more of the Third World will turn to private foreign investment to supplement U.S. aid programs and World Bank assistance for development. There will not be a collapse of the international credit system or massive repudiation of Western loans by Third World borrowers.

Domestic politics: There will be a continuation of the current trend toward moderate conservatism—essentially middle of the road, but slightly to the right side of the middle. Demographic and economic factors point this way and reinforce the prospect of a warm climate for private enterprise.

There won't be much tinkering with the processes of government, with the possible exception of eliminating the electoral college. We see this happening only if, as has almost happened twice in recent decades, the winner on popular votes gets fewer electoral votes than his opponent and is denied the White House.

A SOCIETY IN FLUX

The transition this book describes will be far-reaching but not so abrupt or wrenching as were the upheavals of the late '70s and early '80s, when a combination of bad luck and bad planning caught up with a number of basic U.S. industries. That wave of layoffs and collapse is now behind us, while ahead lies a period of rising worldwide competition.

To maintain its lead, the U.S. will have to automate and modernize on a massive scale. Our comparative advantage in world trade is technology—the higher, the more advantageous to America. But what challenges our lead is the rapid spread of technology throughout much of the rest of the world. Capital investment in plant modernization will continue strong in America, stimulated in large part by federal tax and antitrust policies which, on balance, we believe will continue in the years ahead, although with some modifications.

Keeping up with the change and growth just ahead will call for fast footwork. The leeway for adjusting to change is shrinking year by year, as the speed of technological development picks up and as product cycles shorten.

2

A Changing Population

A wave of change sweeping through the American population is going to have wide-ranging effects on the way we live, work, spend money, pass our leisure time—and exert our political will.

Notwithstanding the current baby boomlet, we see an indefinite continuation of generally low birthrates and small families at least through the year 2000, caused by later marriage and more female employment. These trends are being driven equally by the dual forces of female career aspirations and the high cost of rearing and educating children.

Native-born Americans will continue to reproduce at less than replacement level. Population growth, coming to a total of barely 12% over the next 15 years, will result almost entirely from a high level of immigration and from the higher-than-replacement birthrate of new immigrants. These mostly Hispanic new Americans, added to the high-birthrate population of black Americans, will give the U.S. a steadily rising percentage of racial minorities.

With the overall birthrate low, the median age of the American people will march steadily upwards, with profound effects on the economy, especially consumer marketing. An aging labor force will be more experienced and thus more productive, with less unemployment and less productivity drag from absorbing so many young employees.

And this will be a highly affluent older population, spending its money in new ways and posing new challenges to marketers.

While all this is happening, the population center of the U.S. will be moving relentlessly to the Southwest. The geographical center of the population today is just west of the Mississipi in Missouri; by 2000 it will be somewhere in the Ozarks of Arkansas.

By 2000, our population—which now numbers near 240 million—will have grown to 268 million. Over-65s will outnumber teenagers by a third; just now, the ratio is about 50-50.

But the large in-between group of middle-agers—the Baby Boomers born during the high-fertility era from 1945 through the mid-'60s—will be the predominant trend setters.

Their characteristics include a higher average level of education; little or no involvement in past wars and the attitudes they leave behind; small inclination to unionism; friendliness toward business, free enterprise, entrepreneurism; skepticism toward big government as the engine of social betterment; and more inclination to regionalism and decentralized regulation. Most of this reflects the attitudes of the Sunbelt and West, to which they are moving in heavy numbers. Like all generalizations, these are bound to have exceptions, but they'll hold for broad planning purposes. Keep them in mind in reading the rest of this book.

The over-45s will outnumber the rest of the population by close to a fifth at the turn of the century, putting the presidential election of 2000 pretty much in their hands. Unless their political leanings undergo some sort of upheaval between now and then, the outcome will favor conservatives; in fact, the choice is likely to be among variations on conservative themes.

Which is another manifestation of the increasing stability of society in general. After two decades of social turbulence, mass sweeps from one side of the road to the other aren't in the cards. It's a wide road, and most of us will be trooping somewhere down the middle.

BIRTHS AND RATES

There's a baby boomlet going on right now—the so-called Baby Boom Echo—but it won't make much of a lasting impression. Total births in the past couple of years have been running just slightly ahead of the 3.6 million born in 1983, which was the total in 1950. In the '50s and '60s it jumped to well over 4 million (the peak of the Baby Boom), then slowed to about 3.2 million in 1975 and picked up again to 3.7 million in 1982.

The current boomlet, which will peak in about three years at 3.9 million births, reflects a small jump in the number of women of childbearing age, but by 2000 total births will be down to about 3.5 million, because there will be fewer women in that age group.

These are small fluctuations but they make a big difference. For example, grade schools will begin to bust at the seams again in the next several years (and already have in some metropolitan areas). But not for long; by 2000, the number of children under 10 will be at an all-time low. Makers of kiddie gear and grade-school stuff, take note. In the meantime, high schools and then colleges face declining enrollments.

GRAY POWER

The era of a youth-dominated culture in the U.S. is ending. The "mean age" of the population today is about 35, give or take a few months. That's what statisticians use as the midpoint between zero and the oldest living Americans, with appropriate weight being given to numbers in each age group. By 2000, the average will rise to 37. And ten years later it will be nearly 39. That doesn't sound like much change, but to nudge the mean age that much requires enormous shifts in the size of age groups.

The 14-to-17 age group is 6.2% of the population today; by 1990 it will be 5.2% and by 2000, 5.7%. This uptick at the end is a brief anomaly; the percentage will fall again in the following decade, to about 5.3% in 2010.

The 18-to-24 group will follow the same pattern, only more so. Right now they are 12% of the population. By 1990, 10.3%; by 2000, 9.2%. Those are fairly drastic declines, especially in terms of market share for goods and services. It means big bucks lost for makers and sellers of all sorts of teen-oriented-or-influenced stuff. It also mean headaches for military recruiters.

The retirement-age group will rise from about 12% of the population now to 13% by 2000; not a huge jump, but combined with the decline in youngsters, it adds up. By 2010, the number of over-65s will nearly double again, when the Baby Boomers hit retirement in large numbers.

Of the 65-and-over group, the over-85s will nearly double in number by 2000, a reflection of improving life expectancy—71 for males and just over 78 for females now, 72.9 and 80.5 by 2000.

Communities everywhere will awaken to this trend as 2000 nears—especially those in outlying parts of the Sunbelt, where retirees will continue to swarm. Effects on local economies will be substantial. Housing, medical care, retailing, transportation, etc., will be affected, to say nothing of social security and retirement plans in general.

MORE IMMIGRANTS

At 1.9 babies per woman on average, the native-born fertility rate is running below replacement levels. The U.S. population would level out and then begin to fall sometime in the early part of the new century were it not for the newcomers.

Immigration both legal and illegal will run as high as a million a year on average between now and the year 2000—a total slightly above levels of recent years.

Even without a liberalization in our immigration laws, the influx will grow year by year, mostly Hispanic and mostly from Mexico. The U.S. is and will remain the magnet for the world's displaced and dissatisfied ("We're the bottom of the funnel," says one government official), and no other prosperous countries—not Canada nor Australia, for example—will take more than a fraction of the total.

So far, the economy has absorbed the newcomers fairly well, but there are strains ahead. In the mid-'90s, Mexico's proportion of young job-seekers is due to about double from present levels, while the kinds of entry-level jobs they are seeking at home will shrink drastically. This will create enormous pressures at the border. (See our chapter on high-growth regions and states.) But it will also help alleviate the shortage of American-born youngsters in the labor force; low-wage employers will welcome them.

THE RACIAL MIX

It will be a long, long time before today's racial minorities—blacks and Hispanics—become majorities; no reader of this book can live to see it.

But the non-white component of the American population is steadily growing. In 1980, whites were 80%, blacks 12%, Hispanics 6.4% and others 2%. Today, all minorities total about 22% of the population; by 2000, they will be about 28%.

The black fertility rate is over 30% higher than white and expected to remain so; the rate for Hispanic immigrants is even higher than for blacks. If total immigration averages a million a year between now and 2000, our population then will be 72% white non-Hispanic, 13% black, 11% Hispanic and just over 4% Asian and other. By 2020, white non-Hispanics would be down to 65%, blacks up to 14%, Hispanics to 15%, and others, 6.4%.

The lion's share of those "others" are, and will continue to be, Asians. The 1980 census turned up the fact that the number of Americans from Asia and the Pacific islands was up 140% from 1970. Chinese were the most numerous, followed by Filipinos and Japanese. But the single largest increase was among Koreans— 400%. Vietnamese became a recognizable minority for the first time in 1980.

By 2000, assuming little change in current immigration rates, Filipinos will be a larger group than Chinese, who will come in second. Koreans will be third in size, moving ahead of Japanese. Vietnamese will outnumber Indians. By 2030, the Japanese will have lost third place and moved down to sixth.

California is where a third of all Asian Americans live, and this proportion is likely to continue. In 2000, there will be some 2.7 million in the state, Filipinos being the largest group, Chinese second. New York follows California in the number of Asians, Hawaii is third, Illinois fourth, Washington fifth. These five states are home to about three-fourths of Asian and Pacific islanders in the U.S., says the Population Reference Bureau.

WORLD POPULATION

A big factor in immigration pressure on the U.S., of course, is world population growth. It's slowing in the industrialized, developed countries, but rising rapidly almost everywhere else.

While the Western world sees zero population growth on the horizon, China, India and other Third World countries are struggling to contain near-explosive growth. Mortality rates have been declining while birthrates zoom.

Fortunately, major gains in agricultural productivity will alleviate some of the food pressure. Jobs may be another matter, though. By one estimate, the developed world now employs fewer people (roughly a bit more than a half billion) than the net number of NEW jobs that will be needed to employ the working-age population of the Third World in 2000.

In our own world neighborhood, Mexico, Central America and the Caribbean basin countries will probably double their working-age population in 15 years. Before the middle of the coming century, Mexico's population alone is expected to more than double—from just above 70 million now to 174 million or so.

Today, the world holds about 5 billion, with 75% of these living in the less-developed countries. By 2000, the number will be about 6 billion, the Population Reference Bureau estimates, and if this rate of gain continues, world population will have doubled by 2034.

Despite Third World government plans to keep people in rural areas, there will be continued growth megalopolises like Mexico City, Shanghai, Seoul and Sao Paulo, as rural populations crowd in in search of a better life than in the countryside.

We will see more "expansion migration"—whole groups spreading out in search of work or simply escape. For example: Turkish "guest workers" no longer needed in W. Europe; Middle Easterners fleeing the fading job market in Saudi Arabia; Hong Kong residents moving as the takeover by China nears; and political and economic refugees in general.

CHANGING U.S. LABOR FORCE

Fewer young workers, more middle-aged—that's the broad picture for the American labor market over the next few decades.

Growth is due to slow in the native-born labor force, but it will be the best labor force we've ever had—better educated, skilled, trained, and serious about working. It will be weak at the low end, where big-city blacks and recent immigrants (especially illegals) will compete for a shrinking number of openings for low-skilled labor. A big education and training challenge awaits us there.

The 25-34 age group is due to fall 22% between now and 2000, while the group 35-44 will rise 22%. In the 45-to-retirement age group, a rise of about 21%. By the mid-'90s, the number of people between 31 and 56, prime working years, will be up by 21 million and rising. And by 2000, there will be a 23% decline in the 18-to-24 age group compared to today.

This is a reversal of the trend in the '70s, when productivity sagged in large part because the labor force was relatively young and unskilled. The opposite will be true in the fifteen years just ahead.

Another plus: declining unemployment as labor force growth slows down. The labor force grew three million a year in the late '70s, as an expanding economy struggled to absorb the waves of Baby Boomers and adult women entering the job market for the first time, plus high-wage manufacturing workers diplaced by foreign competition. As powerful as America's job creation was during the '70, there still weren't enough jobs for everyone, and unemployment rose to double digits for the first time since the Great Depression.

Today, in the mid-'80s, work force growth is about 1.3% per year, about half the annual growth rate during the '70s, and the outlook is for continued slow growth during the next 15 years. By the early '90s, new entries into the labor force will run only about a million a year. Many will be racial minorities. And if present patterns hold, they will be inadequately educated and trained.

Women will account for most of the growth in the labor force between now and 2000...two-thirds or more of it. Their participation rate—the proportion of working-age women who have jobs or are in the job market—continues to grow, but is likely to level off in the mid-to-late-'90s. An increasing proportion of women will be college-educated, at a time when older, less well-educated men are taking early retirement...another productivity plus. For many women who wish to combine a career with child-rearing, "telecommuting"—working on a computer at home, linked to the office by telephone—will help accommodate them.

More and more jobs will be "unisex," and the "comparable worth" doctrine of pay equality will have become more widely accepted by employers—not because of legislation, but under the pressure of labor market conditions. If the trend to early retirement continues, the percentage of men over 55 in the labor force could drop from 42% or so at present to as low as 35% in the mid-'90s.

For women workers over 55, the percentage could fall from the 40% range to as low as 20%, the Bureau of Labor Statistics estimates. More and more firms may be looking for ways to attract and keep older workers on the job as the new century nears, with such inducements as flexible hours and retraining.

In the prime age group of mid-20s through mid-50s, employers will have excellent pickings. These are the Baby Boomers heading into their most productive years between now and 2000. Their ranks will create a bulge in coming years, the largest group of prime-age workers in our history; nearly half will be working women. There will be, in fact, something of a buyer's market, and competition for middle-management jobs will get rougher.

HOW WE'LL SPEND

Middle-class, middle-aged affluence will be rising, steadily and steeply, over the next several decades. Households headed by the middle aged will expand by about half by the mid-'90s, and their income levels will rise about three-fourths. A third of such households are likely to have incomes of $50,000 or better in constant dollars. Those with incomes under $30,000 will be fewer than at present—about 40% vs. over half in the early '80s.

The American standard of living has tended to double every 30 years in this century, and there is reason to think this cycle is speeding up. If long-standing patterns continue to apply, spending will rise along with incomes, while the savings rate—the amount of money Americans put aside in investments of all kinds—is likely to soften.

All of which should be important news to producers, sellers and merchandisers. These will be sophisticated consumers—better educated and work-experienced than those of today, and thus not necessarily easy pickings. But the markets will be there for businesses that target their customers astutely.

People of retirement age and up will be more affluent than their predecessors, and they will be a larger population group than now. Free of most impediments that characterize the early years of families—big mortgage payments, children to raise and educate—these households will have income to dispose on themselves. Good news for travel, leisure and luxury lines.

The rate of new family formation, now showing an upward blip among the last of the Baby Boomers, will decline in the '90s, but average income per household will continue to rise, due to the working-wife trend that has by now become the norm. Growth among two-income families will slow down toward the end of the century, however, as the number of women entering the job search tapers off at some unprecedented high point.

Spending patterns will continue to shift toward services—not because purchases of things will slow, but because most people will have more money left over to go into services, such as financial advice for working households and travel and health care for those headed by the elderly.

3

The Economic Outlook

We expect the American economy to expand at an average annual rate approaching 4% for the rest of the 20th century, starting well under that rate today but accelerating through the 1990s.

This means the gross national product will double by about 2004, and double again early in the third decade of the 21st, around 2022. That's REAL growth, figured after inflation averaging roughly 4% a year over the same period.

This achievement will be an extraordinary record of sustained growth. To put it in perspective, consider the average growth rates this economy has recorded in recent decades. So far in the '80s, we're running average real growth of only 2.3% a year, with that figure dragged down by the severe recession of 1981-82. During the '70s, the nominal rate of GNP growth was very high, but after discounting for high inflation, average *real* GNP growth rate was only 2.9% per year.

To find a post-World War II decade that provides a benchmark for the level of sustained growth we're talking about here, you have to go back to the 1960s—a time of low-inflation prosperity that we at the Kiplinger organization dubbed "The Soaring Sixties." And yet the real annual growth rate of the '60s—3.9%— is likely to be eclipsed by the technology-driven boom that we foresee between now and the year 2000.

During the next several years, real GNP growth will continue to average less than 4%. But we project it to begin a steepening rise in the early '90s, and by the end of the '90s it will be running well above the trend rate, pushed by the cumulative effects of technological synergy.

This will not be a perfectly smooth upcurve; it never has been. There will be interruptions, but they will be brief and shallow compared to boom-and-bust business cycles of the past. They will be mostly "growth recessions"—not actual recessions, with declines in GNP for two or more quarters, but periods in which the rate of increase is so slow that unemployment rises.

The engine driving the New American Boom will be rising productivity. It will be on an even stronger uptrend and will probably achieve record-high rates by the mid-'90s.

Our projection is average annual productivity growth of close to 3% into the mid-'90s, then rising to 5% or more into the new century. Note that these are estimates of what the official, conventional indexes will show; the actual increase will probably be considerably greater.

Official measurements of productivity change are admittedly patchy. They have consistently understated the impact of high technology and are particularly inadequate in keeping up with non-manufacturing productivity. Because the economy is growing faster in the latter than in manufacturing, the "official" productivity trend has thus appeared lower than it really is.

Inflation will continue at rates that we have come to regard as "moderate," averaging 4% annually between now and the year 2000. (Back in the '60s, remember, 4% was considered almost runaway inflation.) The biggest reason inflation will behave: high productivity, resulting from a more experienced work force with better tools at its disposal. Others reasons will include moderate (and occasionally restrictive) monetary policy, heightened world-wide competition, and low prices for basic commodities, especially petroleum and foodstuffs. Yet another reason, just as crucial, is that now, in the latter half of the '80s, Washington is finally coming to grips with the budget deficit.

Personal incomes will be rising fairly steadily for the rest of the century along with employment levels, and in no small part because of the spreading-out through the economy of the benefits of expanding productivity. There will be room for substantial, noninflationary wage-and-salary increases at a time when unemployment is dropping and shortages of skilled labor are likely to bring some competitive bidding-up of pay.

There will be no shortage of capital for business expansion, and it will be available at interest rates generally lower than today. Much of it will be generated internally—the retained earnings of a growing American economy. But a lot of it will continue to come from overseas. The Bureau of Labor Statistics estimates that investment in equipment will rise to more than 10% of GNP by the mid-1990s, up from 9% in the mid-'80s and 7.6% in 1977.

PRODUCTIVITY BOOSTERS

In addition to the multiplier effects created by such factors as computers, automation, flexible manufacturing, speed-of-light communications, biotechnology and others, productivity will be enhanced by these trends:

▶ A maturing, better-trained work force.

▶ Increased saving and investment.

▶ Expanded research and development.

▶ A leveling-off or lessening of federal regulation.

▶ A sharp reduction in the restraints on cost-cutting imposed by union work rules and wage scales.

▶ The heightened impact of competition both from imports and from new, innovative firms and products in the domestic economy, all of which forces management to take a "lean-and-mean" attitude toward controlling costs and boosting efficiency.

Other countries may from time to time register higher rates of productivity growth, as they have in the past. But keep in mind that they are building on much smaller bases. It will be a long, long time—if ever—before they can challenge the total U.S. economy on a one-to-one basis.

LOWER DEFICITS

Our growth and inflation forecasts are based on the conviction that by the end of this decade the annual federal budget deficit will have been brought down sufficiently to convince the world that American interest rates and inflation are going to average lower during the '90s than they did in the '70s and early '80s.

And even though the deficit may still be relatively high for a non-wartime period, it will be moving downward while GNP is moving up. The continuation of these two trends is crucial, for it means the deficit will be a steadily declining proportion of the total economy.

At the growth rate we foresee, nominal GNP will be just over six trillions by 1990. If the annual budget deficit is reduced to $100 billion in that year (still far higher than Gramm-Rudman-Hollings targets would mandate), the deficit would equal 1.6% of 1990 GNP, which is just about the same proportion of GNP that annual federal deficits consumed between 1947 and 1980. It would be a substantially lower proporation of GNP than during the Great Depression (about 3%), the 1970s (2.3%), and the first half of the 1980s (4.5%).

The process we have sketched is not exactly "growing our way out of the deficit," as some supply-siders have predicted, but it would be significant progress, enough to dispel talk about imminent crisis—a deep recession, an explosion of inflation, or both.

The point is that with inflation no longer offsetting much of the effect of growing deficits—that is, paying off federal obligations in cheaper dollars—the impact of further big increases in the deficit (given the current anti-inflation leanings of the Federal Reserve) would be to push interest rates back into double digits again and plunge the country into a recession comparable to the period of 1981-82. Our national will to avoid such a recurrence will be the biggest stimulant to budgetary restraint.

Bringing federal spending down to livable levels—with deficits being just an occasional device for stimulation in slack times—will be painful. Many domestic programs will have to be cut more than they already have been, either by attrition or outright spending reductions. Defense spending will bear a big share of the spending restraint. Fewer dollars will be spent on defense for several years to come, even with the heavy research and development expense of Reagan's Strategic Defense Initiative, the so-called "Star Wars" antimissile defense. In the early '90s budget growth will resume, but only at the rate of inflation, given some progress with arms-controls talks.

Memories of near-runaway inflation usually die hard, so it's surprising how quickly high inflation was dethroned by recession as Public Enemy Number One—at least in man-on-the-street perception. But inflation is still considered by many policy makers in Washington—especially at the Federal Reserve—to be a sleeping giant that could be awakened by persistently high deficits and sloppy monetary policy.

In the meantime, fiscal policy will be considerably more cautious than in the '60s and '70s. No extravagant new social programs, fewer add-ons to existing ones. More reliance on markets and less on government use of the budget and tax system to achieve broad social goals, which goes for the government-led "industrial policy" or "reindustrialization" programs that befogged economic debate in the early '80s.

TAXES

The overall tax take is going to rise, naturally, as the economy expands. The tax impact will tilt in favor of saving and investment vs. spending and borrowing. The income tax will remain the mainstay of federal revenues, despite recurring and inconclusive debates over a "value-added tax" and other forms of consumption taxes.

Marginal tax rates will be lower across all brackets. But the concept of stiff minimum taxes will spread, and many high-income individuals and families will wind up paying a higher percentage of their income in taxes, as minimums are imposed and deductions are trimmed or eliminated in periodic waves of tax code overhauling.

The biggest growth in the tax burden will be in state and local taxes, to pay for activities that will continue shifting from the federal government to jurisdictions closer to home.

For business, a mixed bag of changes that will help service-sector firms the most, but won't hamper capital investment much either. You'll see lower marginal rates but higher minimum taxes. The credit on new equipment will die, but depreciation will be sweetened for many kinds of capital goods. Some deductions—such as for business entertaining—will be trimmed.

Tax "reform" will be a lengthy process, taking up the rest of the '80s, possibly continuing into the '90s, as Congress and succeeding administrations tinker with transition rules and readjust rates to fit changing conditions.

Indexing of tax brackets for inflation will be a permanent feature, saving taxpayers plenty and limiting the revenue windfall that

Congress used in the '70s to boost federal spending in many fields. However, indexing may be modified to limit adjustments to a couple of percentage points below the inflation rate. Figure on annual "fixes" of about 2% or 3%, given an average inflation rate of 4%.

MONEY AND CREDIT

Financial institutions and their borrowers will have ample access to short-term funds from rapidly growing corporate cash flows. An ample supply of ready cash—and confidence that inflation will remain generally low—should help hold down both short and long-term interest rates.

We foresee the cost of money averaging lower than today over the next 15 years. The reason: Nominal interest rates might seem low today, compared to the late '70s and early '80s, but "real" interest rates—the difference between nominal rates and the inflation rate—are still very high, relative to historical norms. Real rates have tended to run about 3.5% over many years, but at present, with inflation down to about 3% in the spring of '86, the real interest rate on 30-year Treasury bonds is a rather high 4.5%, and 10% fixed-rate home mortgages are costing the homeowner a very heavy real rate of 7%.

Lenders are still adding a bigger inflation premium to real interest rates than they need to, but a few more years of mild inflation will bring nominal (and real) interest rates down to more traditional levels.

For this reason, we believe adjustable-rate borrowing makes a lot of sense today for those willing to accept a modest degree of risk. In the longer-term future, as interest rates settle into the generally lower range that we foresee, most borrowers will be satisfied with fixed-rate financing, and it will be the dominant credit mode, as in fact it has been during the hot home mortgage market of 1986.

Federal monetary policy—meaning manipulation of money and credit in the banking system—will continue to be driven more by fear of inflation than of recession. There will less inclination to experiment with monetarism. Federal Reserve policy will be "pragmatic," resorting to whatever seems to work, rather than ideological or mechanical.

But events may move faster than the Federal Reserve can keep up with. Progressive deregulation of our financial-service systems is going to feed an increasingly large supply of credit and near-money into a fast-growing economy, and some of this will be outside the Fed system. Conventional restraints on bank credit and the money supply may thus have a declining impact.

This high velocity of money would bring a considerable expansion of credit availability, which could spell inflation. This inflationary pressure will be moderated, but not neutralized, by factors described above, including productivity gains, the price restraint of competition, budget restraint, and low world commodity prices.

SOCIAL SECURITY

The social security system will be left largely untouched. The annual cost-of-living hike for recipients will be trimmed to something less than the rate of inflation, but with the CPI behaving well, this capping will lack the economic (and political) pain once feared.

Anxiety about the future of the system will be quieted by the fact that it will be running a surplus well into the new century. Financial pressures on the system will be eased by high employment (hence high rates of participation) and a likely slowdown in the early-retirement trend, as more firms encourage older workers to stay on at least part time.

Political pressure for expanded benefits will be moderated by several factors, not the least of which will be Congress' memory of the near-disaster that resulted from constantly hiking benefits without raising payroll taxes—a favorite election-year trick of congressmen during the '70s.

More importantly, the spread and sweetening of private pensions plans, plus the taxpayer's own IRA, will relieve the burden on social security of being the principal retirement income for most Americans.

SHRINKING GOVERNMENT

The size of government will taper off and rise little, if at all, between now and 2000. We expect federal outlays to be a declining proportion of GNP for the rest of the century, with the growth rate of the budget steadily declining—barring sudden, unforeseen emergencies and shifts in policy.

A substantial part of this tapering-off in federal outlays reflects the end of revenue sharing with the states and reductions in other grants to states and local government. There is likely to be little if any real increase in these transfers in the period just ahead, and the shifting of burdens to the states will put pressure on their tax rates.

An enormous amount of state and local fix-up and replacement work needs to be done on roads, bridges, water-and-sewage systems and other elements of infrastructure. Borrowings for such purposes are likely to rise fairly steadily. Congress is putting restrictions on private-purpose industrial revenue bonds and exotic offerings designed to turn a profit on interest, but none of these tightenings will cripple a lively municipal bond market.

THE FOREIGN ROLE

The downward drift of interest rates in this country will erase some of the differential between our levels and those of other industrialized countries, continuing to moderate the value of the dollar without any sudden shocks to our own or world markets. This will help the competitiveness of American products abroad and narrow the severe trade imbalance that has brought record-high deficits in our foreign-trade accounts.

Still, the dollar will remain strong and will continue its role as the premier trading and investment currency of the free world.

Foreign capital has been a boon to America during the turbulent mid-'80s, playing an instrumental role in financing both our soaring federal deficits and our recovery from recession, without refueling inflation.

This reliance on foreign capital will gradually diminish, due to lower trade deficits, greater domestic capital resources, and lower American budget deficits and interest rates. But even with interest rates in the U.S. about the same as in other developed countries, foreign capital—both loans and equity financing—will continue to flood into America, because of international confidence in our political stability and the prospect of making a high real return on investment here. There will be an increasing number of mergers and joint ventures between American and foreign companies.

Capital markets are already on their way to total internationalization. U.S. business will be operating in world markets where competition will be fierce and where access to credit and financial data will be instantaneous and everywhere available. Transborder transactions will be on a continuous 24-hour basis.

LABOR FORCE

Labor force growth will taper off to less than 1% a year on average during the '90s. That's lower than the 2.4% a year in the '70s and about 1.3% in the '80s, but still a healthy figure for an economy with low population growth. The reason: The participation rate—the proportion of the employable population either working or looking for work—will rise from about 65% now to nearly 70% by 2000. Prospects of good pay will bring out a higher percentage of people who might otherwise stay home or take early retirement. Record-high immigration will help offset some of the decline in numbers of youth entering the labor force and will fill most of the available low-end jobs.

The proportion of employable women coming into the job search will continue to rise but will tend to taper off at some high point before 2000, chiefly because the supply of them will be nearly exhausted; the rest will be homemakers or otherwise occupied.

Unemployment will decline very slowly over the coming 15 years or more, with minor interruptions, reaching 5% or less by the turn of the century. That's still well above the sub-4% rates we ran during the late '60s, but it's about as close to "full employment" as we are likely to get, in an economy moving from basic industries to high technology, with the extra challenge of absorbing high immigration.

CORPORATE RESTRUCTURING

There are two significant trends in the structure of American business today, and it's unclear which will dominate during the next two decades. Perhaps the answer is that neither will, but that they'll continue to move in parallel.

One trend is the development of super-conglomerates, resulting from the merger of giant companies with other giants. The other trend is its opposite: an amazing surge in entrepreneurship, the creation of new small businesses. (See our chapter on Managing Business.)

We believe corporate restructurings will continue at a brisk level, but the frenetic merger mania of the mid-'80s will cool off. There will be a variety of reasons for this slowdown, but renewed antitrust vigor won't be a factor. The government will keep its hands off all but the most blatantly anti-competitive mergers, and recent tax changes and Federal Reserve moves against junk-bond financing of mergers won't be much of a discouragement, either.

The biggest drag on corporate acquisition activity will be prosperity and a rising stock market. The recent merger binge resulted largely from the depressed stock prices of many solid companies. Acquirers saw it was easier to buy good assets cheap than increase earnings through traditional market expansion. The run-up of the stock market in 1986 has left far fewer bargains, so acquisition activity will wane.

Another big factor restraining acquisitions will be the stock market's growing awareness that the future belongs not to companies adept at the financial trickery of acquisitions, but to those that are investing heavily in the R&D that will produce tomorrow's high-profit products. The stockpiling of earnings in a cash war chest for corporate raiding generally precludes, or at least restricts, high investment in R&D and capital equipment.

But corporate restructuring—mergers, acquisitions, and spin-offs—will remain a temptation to boards of directors with a keen eye for short-run shareholder interests, if not for long-term benefits. Many stockholders will still be eager to sell to anyone who holds out a higher price than the market has previously offered. The New American Boom of the '90s will be spearheaded by new, relatively small firms, and many of these will be takeover targets, willing and unwilling.

The long-term effects of corporate restructuring are unclear. At their worst, corporate raiders are greedy profit-takers who wreck healthy companies, liquidating assets and slashing long-range R&D programs, hurting future productivity and earnings.

At their best, takeover artists can serve the same useful function in the economy that hawks and vultures serve in nature, eliminating weak, inefficient firms. Divisions without a chance of growth are sold or shut down, and the bloated ranks of management are trimmed. The results can be traumatic for individuals and communities, due to the temporary loss of employment and, in some cases, the long-term reduction of personal income. But capital is reallocated to other higher-return uses, and the net effect on the general economy can be anti-inflationary. Some would argue that keeping American business competitive in low-cost world markets will require the freedom of combining, recombining and dismembering corporate pieces to find the most efficient forms and sizes.

One of the most healthy side-effects of the merger boom has been its opposite: the DE-conglomerizing of some mammoth corporations, many of which have proved to be unwieldy in size and unimaginative in management. Either as a defense against a takeover or in the wake of a successful raid, many corporations are spinning off divisions into separate companies. Some of these new firms may someday enjoy the innovation and flexibility of management that are the strengths of the small company.

4

Abundant Energy

Energy is not going to be a problem in the next few decades. There will be more than enough oil, gas, and coal to fuel accelerated economic growth at reasonable prices.

But the important point about the distant future of world energy, beyond the year 2000, is that it won't be dominated by fossil fuels. The hydrocarbons of today—coal and oil and gas—are already an aging technology, and the same can be said for conventional nuclear power. The future belongs to energy sources now in their infancy of research and development. Technology will work several small miracles between now and 2000, and "enough" energy may even turn into "too much."

In the short run—the next 15 years—the U.S. can get by just fine, even if oil supplies from the Middle East are interrupted by political unrest or war. With oil so cheap, our reliance on imports is rising, but we're not at OPEC's mercy.

Americans used to use electricity like water. Now they treat it like a scarce commodity, and this isn't likely to change. It applies across the board—from homefolks turning off the light switch to manufacturers of appliances, autos and heavy equipment who have found ways to use a lot less energy in producing goods that do the same.

Sudden oil scarcity woke everyone up to the possibilities of coal and newer alternate energy sources. Even though oil is abundant again, so much progress has been made toward perfecting several of these that there is no turning back now.

OIL APLENTY

There will still be surplus oil capacity in 2000, even with anticipated increases in oil consumption. Most of this excess has piled up in the OPEC countries, and OPEC will continue to be torn asunder by its conflicting needs to restrict production in support of price and to increase individual market share in support of national economies.

In fact, OPEC has been reduced to the role of "swing producer." Its members now are falling over each other to supply only a third of world needs; it used to be more than half. A third of U.S. oil imports comes from OPEC, and we could find substitutes for that third within two years in the event of a full cutoff—and even less than two years, the closer we get to 2000.

The oil shock of the '70s brought a lot more oil onto world markets. Any future shock will have the same effect, a fact the OPEC countries must take into account before they try to jerk the rest of us around again. Many non-OPEC producers could expand their output rapidly if the market were there. And many industrial and commercial consumers are equipped for rapid switchover to gas or coal—to say nothing of other energy sources coming along.

But the same oversupply that has unseated OPEC also has effects at home. The U.S. oil and gas industry will be in the doldrums for years to come.

Most forecasters see a resumption of price increases by the early '90s, accelerating modestly as oil consumption grows here and abroad. But there is another scenario: Prices might continue to fall in "real" terms (that is, with allowance for inflation) well into the '90s, as new discoveries rise in step with demand. Vast areas of the world have yet to be thoroughly combed over by oil prospectors...China, for one. Mexico has great reserves which it may yet put onto world markets. OPEC countries will sell every barrel the market can take.

Biotechnology might do startling things to oil reserves, either late this century or early in the next. New strains of microorganisms are being developed that, when pumped underground, could loosen up old oil deposits not recoverable economically by conventional means. Ditto for oil shale and tar sands. Result:

billions of additional barrels of oil. If the U.S. ever does have a viable synthetic fuels industry, it is likely to be biotechnical, not chemical or heat-retorted.

COAL

Growth in coal demand will be dampened by low oil prices, but improved ways of burning it with less pollution are coming along and will be adopted by utilities. Some involve the use of powdered coal in slurry and other forms of suspension. Others use preliminary retorting (or cooking) of coal to break it down into semi-liquid form before combustion.

But forget about interstate coal-slurry pipelines for piping powdered coal in water from western strip mines to power plants. Congress has said "no" too many times in recent years for there to be much hope in the time span we're talking about. Backers of such projects, some of which put up millions of dollars, have written them off.

NUCLEAR POWER

How about atomic power? Some 35 conventional (fission) plants are under construction now, most of them too far along to be canceled; but just about all have taken much longer and much more money to build than promised, and public and investor confidence had waned, even before the Soviet reactor accident in 1986.

The future of atomic beyond those 35 plants is uncertain. Unless the industry can come up with a simplified standard design that is convincingly safe and won't exceed cost estimates by leaps and bounds, there will probably not be any new ones begun for some time to come. Even with an improved design, which is being worked on at present, the need for A-power in the future remains to be established. If current forecasts of power demand and of fuel supply are within a reasonable ballpark, the power industry should be able to get along without it until well into the next century.

The key issue is that of cost, once the issue of operating safety is taken care of. Any accurate assessment has to take into account the ultimate costs of nuclear waste disposal, including the "decommissioning" (i.e., dismantling) of worn-out reactors, a problem that has yet to be faced squarely. More than 10,000 tons of high-level waste already are in storage at nuclear sites, a total which may grow to over 45,000 tons by 2000.

No agreement is in sight as to where this stuff may ultimately be put into permanent storage, but one government plan under consideration calls for an outlay of a billion dollars for a "repackaging" depot at Oak Ridge, Tenn., which could process 15,000 tons of waste starting in the late '90s for eventual transfer to permanent disposal sites elsewhere; places in Texas, Nevada and Washington State have been suggested.

Some 15 nuclear plants will have to be decommissioned in the next 15 years, with another 55 coming up in the first decade of the new century.

There also is speculation about the possibilities of safe storage in ocean depths, at costs that have yet to be estimated. But how much of the expense of disposal is to be borne by the taxpayers and how much by utility stockholders is far from settled.

The time may yet come when nuclear power turns out to be cheaper than other energy sources, but that may also be considerably further off than most atomic-energy advocates believe. Until then, nuclear power's long-deferred boom remains elusive.

And electricity from nuclear fusion? It would be the greatest thing since the electric light, completely upsetting all forecasts by providing the cheapest kind of power imaginable without the dangers of nuclear fission. But three decades of research here and abroad have yet to produce a workable fusion reactor, and experts concede that none is within view as yet. Put fusion down for the 21st century; with luck, the first half of the century.

NEW SOURCES OF POWER

Then there is solar power. Or is there? So far, no amount of research and development has brought the cost of photo-voltaic cells down to levels competititive with conventional (i.e., oil, gas or coal-fired) electricity, although there have been important improvements. Thin-film technology now under development may bring even more, but a significant breakthrough might come just in time to be eclipsed by the improved fuel cell. Solar will continue to be marginal, except in special situations where cost is a secondary consideration—military and space applications, for example—and in areas with lots of sunshine and limited access to conventional power.

A number of other fuel sources will continue to be investigated but will remain minor: Biomass (combustible organic waste), ethanol (an alcohol useful as a gasoline additive, distilled from grain or sugarcane), methane gas (which can be tapped from buried waste dumps, manure piles and old oil fields), geothermal heat (from underground sources), and so on.

Finally, consider this: Suppose somebody comes up with an energy source so cheap, so plentiful and so simple and nonpolluting that all other fuels suddenly become obsolete. Sci-fi? No. The answer is our old friend hydrogen, the lighter-than-air combustible gas whose prospects went up in flames with the zeppelin Hindenburg many years ago.

Hydrogen could be that perfect fuel. But first, ways have to be found to produce it cheaply and safely in large volume and then to pipe it around the country. Production calls for a cheap energy source, perhaps a nuclear reactor in an isolated spot on the Gulf Coast. The raw material is water; the process has been known for years. Hydrogen could be used in every kind of engine imaginable—from go-carts to airliners.

It's under intensive research right now in the Defense Department, NASA and elsewhere. Contracts for further development by industry may be let in a year or two. There are many obstacles yet to be overcome, and not all authorities have high hopes for it. But if it works, you can forget about just about every other energy technology.

GENERATING ELECTRICITY

Over the next 15 or so years, while we move ahead on alternative energy sources, the U.S. will be using energy in much the way we do today. And we will use about the same amount of oil and gas as now, despite GNP growth, thanks to design efficiencies in motors and burners and in new homes, which will be all-electric, with wider use of heat pumps, which are in effect reversible air conditioners that draw heat from the air in one location and discharge it in another.

Electric utilities estimate that their load will rise some 3% a year for the next 10 or 15 years. Other estimates range all over the lot, depending on the policy viewpoint of the estimators.

Three percent probably isn't a bad guess, given the fact that consumption growth has been running at about that level in recent years—on average, with ups and downs. The kind of economy we are moving into will be a bustling and prosperous one, but electricity demand isn't going to rise in lock step with GNP the way it used to. High-tech is not energy-intensive. Manufacturing plants will use a lot of power, but their automated processes will be energy-efficient. And many may produce a large part of their own power needs.

Utilities have been badly burned by optimistic demand fore- casts that have left them with overpriced and underutilized capacity, including nuclear. They're trying not to make that mistake again, if they can help it.

And they can help it in a variety of ways—by diversifying into small power units, for example; there won't be any more monster plants. By purchasing power from small independent sources, as they are required to by law: mini-hydro plants, windmill farms, etc. By turning to battery and fuel-cell technology. And by going to the incremental approach when demand threatens to outstrip capacity. Perhaps by upgrading existing plants (say, by installing turbines, which are rapidly becoming more efficient) rather than building new ones.

RECYCLING ENERGY

One reason the U.S. will have enough electricity for coming growth is that industry is going for cogeneration in a big way. Note that word well; you'll hear a lot about it. It means using waste or byproduct heat to produce electricity. It's simple, and it's an old practice, popular around the turn of the century, before large central utility plants came along.

Factories are recycling the heat they use in their processes to run generators and produce electricity. Some have done so well at it that they are selling power to nearby utilities. Just now, this is most common in such lines as pulp and paper, refining, food processing and chemicals, where large-scale operations require a lot of heat. But it is also beginning to turn up on a smaller scale as more efficient equipment is developed—in fast-food outlets, for example, and before long, perhaps in shopping malls, schools and hospitals.

More heat-recirculating systems, probably in combination with heat pumps, will be used in large buildings and apartment complexes to take advantage of the warmth given off by the occupants and the lights and office equipment they use. Dairy farmers have known this principle for ages; cows are warm animals—it's one reason houses used to be built over barns.

Municipal governments are getting into this act too. And more and more municipalities will be looking at building their own power plants, reviving another idea that faded out years ago; some will use new technology to sell power at cheaper rates than utilities can offer.

And an old technique known as district heating may become new again, as this country's energy conservation efforts grow more sophisticated. It involves the placing of small power stations at strategic locations in areas of dense population concentration to heat and cool a neighborhood or complex of buildings. Such systems were common early in this century and some are still functioning, mostly in old cities in the Northeast. They are well advanced in Europe.

Such plants can achieve high levels of efficiency compared to large conventional plants when combined with new technology, including improved heat pumps. By the '90s, they could be operating at 80% efficiency, compared to only about 66% in conventional plants today, energy experts tell us.

Builders and developers as well as managers of large institutions such as hospitals, housing projects and universities are already interested, as are manufacturers of heat pumps, boilers, heat exchangers, heating and cooling monitoring and control devices, and the like.

CONSERVATION TECHNIQUES

Air conditioning is a bigger gobbler of electricity than heat in most areas, but this also may change in coming years. Designers are building in refrigeration units that will take advantage of relatively cheap off-peak power to cool water reservoirs at night and over weekends. Then the cold water will be used during the day to cool the building.

Improved heat pumps are coming along that will be far more efficient that today's models. Powered by gas instead of electricity, they will produce efficiencies as high as 180% of present heat pumps. These should be available in the early '90s for residential and commercial use.

Eventually, say around the turn of the century, we will have fallen into the habit of viewing communities as integrated heat sources. Neighborhoods or districts or entire towns will be engineered to take maximum advantage of available heat via recycling and other conservation measures. Examples already abound in Europe. Sweden, for example: Heat pumps draw heat from the discharge of sewage treatment plants where bacteria that are used to degrade pollutants create warmth as they work.

Utilities already are experimenting with intermittent cutoff of power to home air conditioners by remote control. These brief interruptions reduce energy use without noticeable effect on interior temperatures. Systems like these can be operated by central computers linked to sensors that make it easy to deal with each customer individually. This technique is certain to spread.

Cities will begin watching for opportunities to install new heating and cooling systems as they open up the streets for rebuilding of water and sewer systems. Sooner than that, current materials research may have come up with new kinds of flexible pipe that can be snaked through existing worn-out pipes. That could open up all sorts of possibilities.

Meanwhile, the utilities themselves are undergoing vast changes. They are moving into what may be a sort of competitive market, one in which power will be auctioned to the highest bidder. This is becoming possible via techniques that facilitate "wheeling" power through a large network—switching it from surplus areas to deficit areas in a flash. These switch-overs are usually brief, perhaps a matter of hours, and the use of computers to keep constant tabs on the most economical and efficient use of power within a large net helps make them work.

There is even talk of deregulating the utility industry sometime in the years just ahead, but we think it is only that—talk. Politicians are leery of it, especially in places where overexpansion, especially of nuclear power, has left consumers holding the bag while utilities try to pass on the cost via rate hikes.

BATTERIES AND FUEL CELLS

There are many ways to generate electricity, but one thing we haven't yet developed is a cost-effective battery for storing large amounts of it for later use.

New kinds of storage batteries now in development will someday be used by utilities for "load leveling" and "peak shaving." This could lead to generating stations running full blast 24 hours a day, which is the most efficient way to run them. Power generated at night, when demand is low, could be stored in batteries and then fed back into the system to help meet peak demand during the day. The batteries would also ease the burden of costly standby equipment needed to take over in the event of a generator breakdown.

And batteries of this kind may be installed in office and commercial buildings to store power pumped into them at reduced rates during off-hours.

Batteries might reinvigorate the prospects for such marginal sources of power as windmills and solar cells, making it possible to accumulate and store electricity cheaply when the wind blows and the sun shines for later use on calm and cloudy days. They might also dampen utility industry interest in such alternative storage schemes as compressed air caverns and stored water potential; these are feasible but very expensive.

Military interest in high-performance batteries runs wide, deep, and quiet—as in submarines. The British are working on a system that would combine nuclear power with batteries strong enough to run a sub silently for long periods of time, a modern throwback to the days of subs with combinations of diesel engines and batteries.

And battery-driven electric vehicles are high on the U.S. military's wish list. Work is underway on what could turn out to be a true "super battery" capable of outperforming the best of those mentioned above and even of competing with conventional internal-combustion engines. It's military; it's classified. It may surface within five to ten years.

If it's as good as its developers hope, cars and trucks might someday be able to run 1000 miles or more without recharging, achieve high speeds and never need a drop of gasoline. The internal-combustion engine would become a museum relic.

While batteries just store electricity, a kind of chemical reactor called a fuel cell uses fuels fed into it to actually generate electricity, in large amounts disproportional to cell size. The idea has been around for some time and has been less than a resounding success. But it might be on the verge of becoming just that. Several government and private laboratories are working on designs that could offset oil demand by millions of barrels a year, perhaps hundreds of millions, if the optimists are right.

Just now, the leading edge of fuel cell technology is the lithium-air concept, in which an electrode bathed in air produces huge amounts of energy, can run for years, and has an indefinite shelf life. It has drawbacks too; nitrogen is produced and must be vented or isolated in some fashion to avoid explosions. But this is a technical problem, not an insurmountable roadblock. Experts think early fuel cell versions will turn up within the next two or three years as power sources for emergency equipment of various kinds, including military, then will be scaled up for other applications.

Other kinds of metal-air fuel cells, some using aluminum or zinc, also look promising, along with phosphoric-acid systems, still in the very earliest stages, which could turn out to be even more powerful. Another kind of fuel cell might use hydrocarbons—natural gas, alcohol, oil, etc.—to produce electricity directly, without needing a motor-driven generator. Out of these and related technologies may soon come devices that could put out "a megawatt in a beer can."

Fuel cells the size of a compact car could be trucked to installation sites and be set working in a matter of months. They may come in increments of 5000 megawatts and could be used to beef up conventional utility plants in almost any location.

By 2000, perhaps a bit earlier, we'll see fuels cells and batteries used as neighborhood substations for utilities in big metropolitan areas where construction of conventional stations is too expensive.

5

Incredible Computers

For some idea of where computers are now and where they are heading, compare bicycles and racing cars. Or better still, racing cars and jet planes.

Today's best computers are faster and more powerful than anyone dared imagine 20 years ago, but they're still bicycles compared to the jet planes they will turn into. In another 10 years, they will be many times faster and more powerful. Today's best computer will be as obsolete as those of 20 years ago are now.

Sooner than that, improvements now being made in computer and software design will contribute a powerful extra wallop to productivity in every aspect of the American economy, on top of the huge gains they have already imparted.

While the U.S. will remain preeminent in computer research and development, it is questionable whether this country will continue to be a major manufacturer of basic computer goods. As semiconductors became a commodity over the past several years, low-labor-cost countries have taken over their manufacture. Now Asian firms are becoming tough competitors in the assembling and marketing of basic business and personal computers. This trend is likely to continue.

The U.S. has a wide lead in the production and marketing of software, but the lead is narrowing and faces a growing challenge from abroad. France and Japan are particularly strong competitors, but so also will be a number of other countries in the developed world and—perhaps surprisingly—the Third World.

Writing computer programs doesn't require much overhead: A reasonably agile computer, native smarts, plus mathematics ability and perhaps some courses in computer science are enough for starters. And such technical and intellectual equipment can be found all over the world. Singapore, Korea and India are growing competitors, and other countries will be entering the market, including mainland China.

Governments can protect and sponsor home-grown software producers in much the same way they do any other native industry, and many already do, via restrictions on imports of competing products plus various kinds of subsidy and export assistance. The picture is complicated by the lack of strong international protections for software copyrights, a problem our government will have to work on. In fact, protecting a proprietary program already is difficult enough in our own market.

Demand for customized and "tailored" software will be one of the strongest elements of that market in the years ahead, as the exponential growth of computer capacity makes new approaches possible. Companies will go for software that gives them any sort of competitive edge, and programmers will be in demand on company staffs, among software producing firms and as independents. We already have a vigorous, home-grown "cottage industry" in software, and many other countries will soon have their own.

Over the next 15 years, computer manufacturing will follow the pattern of virtually every other industrial enterprise. The U.S. will maintain its strength in R&D, while other nations will come along in our wake and take over basic production at a lower cost. Even American companies will do their manufacturing and assembling overseas, to remain competitive. This will reduce the demand for low-skill American labor, making it imperative that American education provide enough skilled labor to maintain our technological superiority.

Computer security will remain a troublesome but probably fading issue. The more powerful and complex computers become, the easier it will be to design safeguards against illegal entry into computer systems. Of course, the would-be data thief will have collateral advantages if he has access to equally powerful machines. But in the end, sheer complexity and the enormous amount of data being stored and processed may be as good a protection as most users can hope for. These factors won't prevent security breaches but will make them more difficult and, in many cases, more trouble than they are worth.

THE CHANGES AHEAD

Within a few more years, a single silicon chip the size of a postage stamp will incorporate all the power of a 1986 state-of-the-art mainframe computer with its hundreds of chips, the sort of large central processing machine that serves as a corporate or institutional data system. Such a chip may contain as many as 100 million memory bits.

Today's large systems will shrink to the size of a small personal computer, capable of executing many billions of instructions per second. This kind of compression not only makes it possible to pack an incredible amount of data processing capacity into a small space but also permits the packing of multiples of that power into larger units to take on jobs that are quite beyond the very biggest computer we have today. That has been the history of computers from the beginning, and it continues to open new possibilities.

It will lead to the creation of "thinking" robots with something approaching, or at least patterned after, human intelligence; expansion of "expert systems" of computerized knowledge; analysis of the molecular structure of proteins for use in developing new enzymes; and the solving of very complex or large-scale problems like the design of entire aircraft or a dam or weapon system via computer simulation. These are just a few examples.

It seems especially fitting that some of the advances in computer design and capabilities just ahead will be the direct result of commercially funded space research, a development that could not have come about without the computer. This is a rather neat example of the way various branches of high technology come together to form a whole greater than the sum of their parts.

EXPERT SYSTEMS

Expert systems are spreading out into more and more fields, becoming machine assistants to a range of professions and occupations, from surgery to auto repair. Expert system is the

name given to a computer program that compresses knowledge—
and, if it's a comprehensive expert system, ALL the knowledge—on a given problem.

This information is arranged in a branching array ("if this or
that, then what?"), so that it can discard possibilities one at a
time until it comes up with a correct answer. In this way it leads
an individual through a step-by-step process while taking account
of unexpected variations and adapting to them. This is pretty
much the way a physician, for example, conducts a diagnosis.
(Expert programs will become sufficiently detailed for individuals
to do a great deal of self-diagnosis before consulting a doctor or
psychologist.)

Systems of this kind will help run automated factories, assist
designers and engineers, act as consultants and economic mod-
elers to corporate management, supervise arbitrage and other
short-term investment programs for corporations, advise investors on managing their portfolios and even execute buy-sell-hold
orders, help design planes and cars, speed up the creation of
customized computer software, act as tutors and teachers, manage autonomous operations in space or on the battlefield, inter-
view loan applicants to determine their eligibility, interpret geological data for oil and mineral exploration, help surgeons run
pathological tests during surgery, coach lawyers and judges on
the law and precedents, play detective for police departments,
watch bank accounts for abnormal behavior, allow parents to
assess their children's development, give tax advice and help
prepare returns. They will assist wherever any body of knowledge can be reduced to a system of rules and methods, which
means the possibilities are almost endless.

A few such commercial computer programs are already on the
market. These will become a flood as computer capacity doubles
and redoubles and as software designers come up with new ideas.
Such programs will be a particularly powerful tool for all kinds of
businesses.

TALKING COMPUTERS

Voice-activated computers will add a new dimension to the
entire expert-system scene. Instead of having to communicate

with the program via a keyboard, individuals will be able to talk to the computer and it will talk back, for no-hands interaction. The surgeon, for example, won't have to turn away from the operating table; he will have a tiny mike at his lips. The fighter pilot will talk to his airplane in combat. A composer will be able to sing to his computer, which will discern pitch. (There are already computers attached to keyboards that will print out the notation of whatever one plays.) Police officers in patrol cars and executives too proud to type will love voice systems. "Talkwriters" will begin to replace typewriters and word processors in some applications.

One catch, and it's not a small one: The computer will have to be carefully taught, and so will the speaker. Voice input-output systems already exist but can recognize only a few hundred words read methodically into their memory by a single speaker. The computer answers back in a tinny, uninflected voice that takes some getting used to. But such admittedly primitive systems already are helping blind authors to produce their own manuscripts, complete with punctuation.

Within about five years, voice activation will be able to handle vocabularies of several thousand words. And within 10 to 15 years, it may be able to respond to more than one voice, although a machine that can answer ANY voice seems unlikely until well into the new century. There are problems arising from accent, inflection, voice quality and—let it be noted—sobriety; some 21st century cars may not start if the driver's voice can't be recognized by the built-in computer, for both security and driving safety.

And there seems to be a tradeoff between size of vocabulary and the number of voices accepted; if one rises, the other falls. Current research into machine sound-pattern recognition may break this bottleneck, drawing on the expanding capacity of computers to sort through millions of information bits per second, but it will take several more years to find out.

INTELLIGENT COMPUTERS?

Artificial intelligence is the mountain range that lies beyond the expert-systems foothills. The term stands for a computer capacious and clever enough to emulate processes of the human brain —for example, reasoning by analogy, meaning the ability to recognize similar patterns and put them together to work out a result.

The ultimate goal would be computers clever enough to solve problems with little more to go on than an instruction to do so. Or smart enough to translate from one language to another with a human feel for nuance and subtlety, or to react to rapidly changing conditions—in the air, in space, on a battlefield or on a highway—and make the right decisions.

These are things that humans do with varying degrees of success but which computers cannot and may never be able to do. "Never" is a word computer experts abhor; perhaps we should say "not for a long time." But the fact is that computers are still less "intelligent" than your average grasshopper and may not work their way up to ant level in our lifetimes. So take with several grains of salt the extravagant talk you may hear about the wonders of artificial intelligence. Expert systems are the best we will have around for a long time to come.

So-called parallel processing will bring AI closer, just the same. In computer terms, this means using multiple processors to work out a problem in mass fashion, each processor handling some part of it, with all processors reporting to the finish line simultaneously.

This sort of operation can produce incredible speeds but is difficult to manage—rather like controlling a herd of charging buffalo. It is being done today on a few massive computers. Within five years or so, it is likely that parallel processing will have been brought to the point where it can be used in relatively small machines. This will replace the old-fashioned "linear," one-step-at-a-time principle that has dominated computing since computers were invented.

OPTICAL AND BIONIC

Optical computers could set the entire computing world on its collective ear. These would substitute photons—that is, submicroscopic flashes of light—for electrons, whereupon the world's fastest computer would be operating at the speed of light, the absolute limit so far as conventional physics knows, and three times faster than electrons. This development depends on fiber optics, which is making rapid progress, and on the optical switch, which exists only in the imagination of a relatively few engineers and scientists. Commercial research in space may hold the answers, but most experts put this prospect down for the early 21st century, if then.

For those who really want to let their imaginations run wild, consider the bionic computer, which would make even the optical computer look slow. The principle here—and it has yet to prove itself in even tentative fashion—is that chemical reactions at the molecular level would touch off atomic impulses that could be translated into computer language. This is the closest theoretical approach so far to the functioning of the human brain, but it is also the furthest away from any kind of practical demonstration. "But," says one biotech-industry official, "who would have said 15 years ago that today we would be able to splice genes and make entirely new ones?"

Back to the here and now, there is bubble memory—a physicist's term for a new kind of computer chip on which data can be stored in magnetic form and are not subject to loss in cases of power interruption, which is a highly vulnerable aspect of computers.

Bubble memory will probably take over the storage function in the small computer field—the minis, micros, desktop and personal computers—within 10 years or so, whereupon floppy disks and disk drives will disappear or be relegated to backup status and low-tech home use in video and audio systems.

With bubble memory, computers will no longer need mechanical parts in their routine operations and thus will break down less often. This kind of storage is far more capacious than most present varieties; the average small computer will be able to store a thousand pages of text on a single chip. And access to this mode of memory is much faster. It eliminates the need for program and document disks, meaning that the average home or office user of a computer won't have to be feeding disks in and out of the machine.

And most important of all, such a development will speed the availability of the truly "user-friendly" computer—the sort of nice, understanding machine the industry has promised for years but has yet to deliver. By the early '90s, personal computers will be ready to accept instructions in plain English—simple menus to choose from, no computer jargon—and will perform far more complex services at greater speeds than are possible now. The variety of software programs will double and double again. Complex and highly artistic 3-D graphics will be available to home-computer buyers as well as to designers, engineers and architects, along with more sophisticated business accounting and spreadsheet systems.

Advanced bubble memory techniques are under development in this country and Japan that might make all the foregoing obsolete around the year 2000 by producing a chip capable of storing one MILLION pages of text on a single small chip.

SUPER COMPUTERS

At the other end of the scale is the "super computer," which is still a label more than a concept. It is being pursued by scientists in the U.S., Japan and Europe. The race—for that is what it is—was touched off at the beginning of the '80s by the Japanese, who announced their objective to the world: the development of a "fifth generation" of computers powerful enough to move the world into an entirely new phase of automation and, not incidentally, to move Japan into the forefront of computer science. For this the Japanese government together with industry has targeted physical and manpower resources on a scale unmatched anywhere else, even in the U.S.

The American response has been to launch several projects, each of which is aimed in the same general direction but with different specific objectives. One is the Microelectronics and Computer Technology Corp. of Austin, Tex., sponsored by 21 U.S. computer and chip makers; it is working under an antitrust exemption to develop jointly owned designs for high-powered commercial computers and software.

Other projects of similar scope are being carried forward by the Department of Defense, whose interest is primarily in battlefield and intelligence applications of super computers; by a consortium of microchip makers; by the National Security Agency for encryption and code-breaking purposes; and by several universities in collaboration with private groups.

Japan has set itself a mid-'90s target for establishing leadership in the super-computer field—leadership now held by the U.S. Our own conclusion, after talking with a number of experts in the field, is that it has a better than outside chance, but that the U.S. is more likely to maintain its lead if present research and development programs are continued at least at their present levels.

Whoever comes out ahead, the noncommunist world will profit mightily from super-powerful computers in both commercial and military applications. The Soviets claim to have their own similar program but are starting from so far behind that their habitual dependence on borrowed or stolen Western technology is expected to continue.

The road to super-computerdom is not yet clearly staked out, but one likely route is called "data flow," a concept now undergoing testing and development here and abroad. It would prepare a large-scale computer to do calculations via an enormous number of separate built-in processors, each of which would be programmed to do its task as soon as data reach it. In this fashion, a problem would flow through the computer in a broad flood rather than in a gushing stream, as at present. The principle is a highly refined version of parallel processing. American scientists working on it believe it has great promise and hope they get there ahead of the Japanese.

THE NEW LOOK

Design and other innovations will change the outward appearance and style of all computer monitors. The cathode ray tube, essentially a TV tube, will give way in both computers and television to flat screens, an inch or two thick, using liquid-crystal displays that will produce much higher definition and color sensitivity.

Keyboards can't shrink much, given the average size of the human hand, but there may be fewer keys to worry about as increasingly detailed and "friendly" software takes on more of the choices now foisted onto computer users. So-called peripheral items—extra disk drives, special storage units and the like—will be incorporated into the computer itself or even eliminated by some of the developments we have discussed above.

Portable computers will flourish—lap-sized, hand-held and voice-activated—for use in all sorts of away-from-home situations. Combined with cellular radio, which will be available everywhere within a decade, portables will make it simple to do business with the office no matter where the individual is. Greatly improved batteries will help slim down the portables and extend their service life. One effect of all this will be that "work" no longer will be a matter of a desk and a fixed location, if the computer user prefers another mode.

Computer prices in general probably won't fall steeply, but content and quality will rise so dramatically that the computer buyer of 1990 or 2010 will be getting a great deal more bang for the buck. The temptation to wait for something better to come along ought to be resisted, however. If a computer can be of value now to a business firm or individual—and it is hard to imagine a business that could not benefit from one—the purchase should be made now.

The history of the computer age, now roughly 40 years old, is consistent on that point: Those who hung back ate the dust of those who didn't, even if they saved some short-term expense by waiting.

6

Communications Flood

What's happening in communications is forcing us to reconsider what we mean by information. It is not simply data, but knowledge, and the knowledge component of almost everything important to our future is increasing at a startling pace.

If knowledge is power, the U.S. is and will continue to be the most powerful nation on earth—indefinitely. This is power in more than the military sense, which, not incidentally, is increasingly becoming a knowledge as well as hardware affair.

Our ability to assemble, analyze and communicate data out of which knowledge can be constructed is expanding at a staggering rate—faster in some cases than we can digest.

The next couple of decades will see enormous gains in communications capacity via computers and new transmission and broadcast technology. This growth will create new businesses and bolster many existing ones, while making others obsolete. For the successes, the growth potential is out of sight. It will help make new jobs, improve living standards and both complicate our way of life and make it more enjoyable.

Computers will have a central role in the era of explosive communications growth just ahead. The single biggest impetus of growth will be fiber optics, a technology that has already produced amazing changes but still has some surprises in store.

FIBER OPTICS

Fiber optics is a cheaper and more efficient means of moving information over long distances than any other known technology—satellites included—and it will gradually take over the communications marketplace.

A single hair-like fiber already can carry more traffic than a copper cable thick as a thumb—90,000 conversations or more. A multi-fiber cable no thicker than a spaghetti strand delivers information the way a fire hose carries water, in a gushing stream.

Here's how fiber optics works: Computers translate information (sound, video, written messages, whatever) into digital impulses, the same binary form that computers employ. Lasers convert these into pulses of light called photons and fire them by the millions per second into minutely fine glass threads. The photons zip along at the speed of light and at the other end are translated back into original form.

All communications will soon be digital, meaning that the content of any message, whether words, numbers, voice or music, will be translated into computerese. Digital is replacing so-called analog transmission, in which information is converted into electrical impulses, and it means enormous increases in capacity, speed and clarity. A good example is the digitally recorded compact disk, which is already well on its way to taking over the record business.

All that the fiber-optic technology needs to establish itself firmly is a series of developments that already are underway:

Improved glass fibers, clear enough to permit transmission over transatlantic distances without need for repeaters or other intermediate amplification gadgetry. This improvement is likely to emerge from the laboratory within a few years. (See our chapter on space.)

Optical switching and control systems, to increase the speed (and hence the capacity) of fiber-optic networks to the speed of light. These also will stem from space-based research and will create an enormous market. Many small firms already have invested in this prospect and some will grow into bigs.

Laser refinements, to improve the definition and efficiency of transmission over fiber-optic cable. The laser is the source of light, the engine that drives a fiber-optics system. Scientists believe today's laser technology is crude compared to what is coming by the year 2000.

The net result will be so much growth in communications capacity that parts of it will seem almost "free." Conventional copper wire electronics will be phased out, and sometime early in the new century will probably disappear in most communications.

With fiber optics doing the carrying of data, homes and offices will be able to order up movies and music from central libraries; consult data bases; do electronic shopping; buy and sell stocks; arrange travel plans and tickets; call up specialized news programs; send and receive electronic mail and computer data; link up computers anywhere in the world for exchange of data or combined processing; participate in teleconferences; receive graphic and printed materials on their own printers and more—in addition to the usual telephone services we're already used to.

Fiber-optic technology is moving so fast that it surprises even its promoters. A cable installed only four or so years ago along the railroad right-of-way between Boston and Washington already is obsolete compared to improvements that have come since. Within a few years, today's best will look primitive. "The trend in capacity," says one scientist deeply involved in fiber-optics development, "is exponential, meaning it doubles every year—the rate of transmission. And the physical limits are so far away that the potential is mind-boggling. In theory at least, we can give everyone a voice channel on a single fiber as thin as a hair."

One of the attractions of this technology is that there is no leakage from the individual strands the way there is with copper; so unauthorized interception is harder, and glass fibers don't have to be insulated from each other, which shrinks the space they require in a cable.

Another appeal of fiber optics is that it produces a very high degree of fidelity with little or no energy loss. With the improved fibers that are coming along, a transatlantic telephone conversation will be as clear as one to next door—no echo, no lag, no noise.

A one-piece transatlantic fiber-optic cable will probably be in place by the early '90s. Chances are it can simply be fed out of a low, slow-flying airplane; it won't need any expensive line-laying equipment. Fiber cable is already in use under the seas for relatively short hops—in the Caribbean, for example, and to offshore islands—and a new link is planned from Hawaii to Japan in the next few years. Each of these will eventually be replaced or supplemented with the improved variety.

FIBER VS. SATELLITES

Fiber optics and satellites are in a race for dominance in continental communications, and particularly in entertainment. Direct-to-dish telecasting is bound to grow as the cost of receivers comes down. Satellites already are feeding dozens of channels to home dishes in large areas of the U.S. beyond the range of most TV stations or cable. The real boot for satellites will come from high-resolution "Ku band" transmission, now just getting started. Hundreds of movies will probably be made available to dish owners that way. Fiber optics can do the same, but the cost of laying cable to thinly populated rural areas will probably remain prohibitive for a long time. So chalk up the TV market to the satellites.

But satellites, given their capacity limitations, may not be able to compete with fiber optics in many other applications, including transmission to metropolitan areas and across the Atlantic. They will still be good for broadcasting to fixed ground stations anywhere in the world and across areas where fiber cannot be laid. Good also for emergency situations, such as the restoration of communications in disaster areas. A mobile ground station can be installed fairly quickly.

So we shall probably wind up with a mixed system...satellites AND fiber-optic cable, and they will work in tandem as well as compete. For example, semi-rural areas where cable might pay off could receive TV via fiber-optic lines from a common dish antenna aimed at one or more satellites. And satellites will become important in such applications as truck-fleet control, mobile communications, cellular phones and the like, not to mention their growing importance in military roles.

CHANNELS FOR ALL

Within a decade or so, there will be enough capacity so that almost any group that wants its own channel can have it for special broadcasts...religious programs, sports, intellectual content, hobbies, political appeals, home service, exercise and health, even all-advertising channels.

Just the same, the satellite business already is developing a surplus-capacity problem, and investors are getting nervous. As fiber-optic cable expands, this surplus may worsen and could even reach a glut in ten years or less, given expected achievements in optical switching.

And that could mean a severe shakeout in the industry, with mass communications pricing reduced almost to a "commodity" basis, in which market bidding determines who pays how much for what. And when capacity gets that cheap, more possibilities open up.

The chief one is indicated by the fact that cable will have sufficient "band width" to carry ALL kinds of communications—telephone and videophone, TV, radio, computer data, teleconferencing, etc. And it will proceed to do so as fast as the cable can be strung. First to offices and then to homes. The office phase is already underway; new buildings are being made "fiber ready" with internal connections for the new cable. This will become the standard.

REPLACING COPPER

Rewiring into homes will take longer. Replacing the copper telephone connections that now extend to virtually every building in this country can hardly happen overnight or even in a few years, given the enormous investment involved. But the attraction of fiber cable will grow to such a compelling point that it will become economical to do so, and several companies already have announced plans for fiber cable systems in various parts of the U.S. and under the Atlantic.

Inter-city cables could be laid along power-line and railroad rights-of-way, or along highways. And in cities they can be strung along with electrical wires to eliminate multiple connections for telephones and TV. Promoters haven't yet figured out what to do in cities that require cables to be buried, but a solution is bound to turn up one of these years as the profit potential swells.

The cost of such service is likely to rise no faster than the cost of living in future years and quite possibly less, given the vast productivity improvements that are coming along. Five years from now, the current furor over increases in local telephone charges to offset the decline in long-distance charges brought about by competition will probably have been forgotten.

TELECONFERENCES

Teleconferencing—a bright idea whose time comes and goes—will finally blossom with the coming vast increases in communications capacity at low rates. Ditto for electronic mail.

What has held teleconferencing back so far is that it is expensive and cumbersome—plus the fact that people still like face-to-face gatherings, a preference that probably will never be completely shaken off. Still, hotels and conference centers are being equipped with connections for teleconferences, and more and more trade and professional associations, trade fairs and business firms will put them into use.

With wide-band fiber optics, teleconferencers will have access to greatly improved voice, graphics and video capabilities. It will be easy to display charts, graphs, photographs and films in several locations at once, along with TV eye contact and voice communication.

Such technology will supplant the conference call by which executives have usually kept in group touch. It will become easy to set up and run a full-function teleconference in a matter of minutes. Large companies will use this technique to confer with far-flung branches, to share results and to deliver the latest word from On High.

Some in the travel and transportation business worry that this will cut into their trade. We think it may to some small extent—but not enough to hurt. There is an equally good chance that business travel will grow for other reasons, chiefly the expansion of the economy itself, meaning more branches, subsidiaries and areas of interest.

Besides, it's doubtful that any of the technologies we're talking about can really substitute for a personal look-see when there are tough questions to answer.

ELECTRONIC MAIL

As for electronic mail, it's sure to expand greatly but more as a business tool than a substitute for the personal letter. Networking among computers will make it easy for any computer owner to communicate with another if he has the wire address and the right connections. This already is happening on a relatively limited scale via computer "bulletin boards," dozens of which have sprung up around the country.

You won't have to own a fancy computer to get in on the electronic mail circuit: Electronic typewriters, word processors and telex machines can be used, so long as you have a telephone "modem"—a gadget that digitalizes and transmits your message via today's analog phone lines. And when that phone line is a fiber-optic cable, the flow of such communication will probably balloon.

Messages can be stored at either end as the occasion demands. Say you prefer to have the letter go out during the night; your "smart" telephone will accept it and send it at the proper hour. Or say your correspondent's line is busy or he or she isn't answering. The phone at that end will store the message until it's accepted. This applies equally to "voice mail," which is simply a telephoned message stored until the sender is ready for it to go or the recipient is available to receive it.

Some messages will consist of huge blocks of statistical data, sent by one computer for processing by another. These heavy chunks can be put into the electronic mail circuit during the day for delivery to others during off-peak hours at lower rates.

Systems like these will compete directly with facsimile transmission in years to come, particularly after the advent of full-scale fiber-optic transmission. It may well be cheaper and faster to move graphic information as electronic mail.

Neighborhood networks may begin to turn up before long—neighborhoods in the sense of both geographic proximity and shared interests. Households equipped with mini and microcomputers will be able to trade information on hobbies, work, health care, personal relationships or whatever comes along. There may be a great deal of computerized chatter going on, as there used to be on rural telephone party lines. (If you don't know what a party line is, ask someone over 50.)

POSTAL PLANS

The U.S. Postal Service has given up on electronic mail, at least for now. Its flier into that business was a flop and won't be repeated unless and until a clear need for it appears. That's unlikely, given the probable boom in electronic mail via privately owned computers and mail systems.

Instead, the PS will concentrate on better ways to do its regular job of delivering conventional mail while reducing its extremely labor-intensive operating costs. Look for increased concentration on the use of OCR (Optical Character Recognition) devices, meaning scanning machines that can read typed addresses.

The Service is financing considerable research and development into faster and more versatile OCRs than exist now, in hopes that someday they will take over most of the routine sorting and routing operations in post offices. Multi-line readers will allow the Service automatically to sort most letters down to the 9-digit zip code and imprint a bar code on the envelope so it need never be touched by human hands until it gets to the letter carrier. OCRs might even be able to read handwriting some day, but we wouldn't count on it.

As automation expands, the Postal Service may be able to trim costs enough to ease up on postage-rate hikes, perhaps even stretching them out to every five years or so.

Private use of electronic mail and of overnight delivery services will boom and probably cut into Postal Service volume, but won't eliminate the traditional mail carrier, who will still be plodding the routes in 2000 and beyond.

MOBILE PHONES

It will become increasingly difficult to escape the reach of communications in the years ahead, and this may bother people who treasure their privacy. Mobile phones will be everywhere, helped along by major improvements in cellular broadcasting, satellite communications and small batteries. Ditto for pagers, which will be merged into mobile telephones so that everyone who has a number is within reach of everyone else, even at long distances—so long as he or she is carrying the device. The only way to escape will be to leave it home, which may take more willpower than some people can muster.

Mobile phones may in fact become more common than the wired-in kind, given the developments we expect in small batteries. They will need only occasional recharging and will cut the phone-wire tether that now sends people rushing back to their desks to take a call. Separate paging systems won't be needed in large organizations; everyone will have his or her own phone along at all times.

People who want to be kept track of and who want to keep in touch will rely on the mobile phone. Within a few years it will be possible to use the phone as a monitor and beacon, reporting via satellite on one's geographical position for rescue purposes or on one's state of health in medical emergencies. Such gadgets will become a standby for the elderly living alone.

But with the growth in mobile communications goes a security problem—the relative ease of tapping into over-the-air communications. The problem hasn't been solved but probably will be, via computer-operated scramblers and other systems made possible (and unnoticeable to the user) by speedier, roomier computers.

The videophone will make a comeback—for those who are interested. Abundant cable capacity will make such service easily affordable. Whether individuals will ever go for it in any volume is speculative at best; not everyone wants to be visible to the other party to a phone call. But businesses may find the service useful for conveying visual information along with conversations.

Picturephones also will become popular for sending single pictures or other still graphics along phone lines. These too will compete with facsimile for such transmissions. The equipment costs several thousand dollars a throw just now but is sure to come down before long.

Individual telephones will become compact terminals for getting voice information from data banks, making it easy to pick up the latest stock quotes, for example, at any time or place. Or to check airplane arrival-departure times at the airport or make a quick credit check. The possibilities are open-ended; new ideas are coming along faster than we can track.

INTERNATIONAL ISSUES

Communication across national boundaries is running into some political problems that will take time to unravel. Flows of data, entertainment programs, voice messages, etc., leap invisibly via satellites across borders with the greatest of ease, and this bothers a number of foreign governments. Western European governments and several elsewhere, including South America, already have taken steps to restrict this free-flowing flood via regulations and taxation.

The major issue is really one of who controls the processing and thus makes the profits from its international movement. Widely distributed data flows are making it possible for companies in the U.S. to operate subsidiary facilities abroad; location loses importance. Up-and-coming technology allows instant credit checks, access to research and development data bases, financial clearing operations and so on.

But governments fear loss of revenue and loss of control over what goes on within their borders. Brazil, for example, is clamping down by requiring that data processing within its boundaries be done by Brazilian firms using Brazilian equipment. European countries may be heading in the same direction.

The U.S. opposes this trend and will try to negotiate open-sky rules via such instrumentalities as the International Telecommunications Union and the General Agreement on Tariffs and Trade. We have some domestic problems of our own; labor unions are objecting to what they see as the "export" of jobs via telecommunications—data processing being done abroad that could be done here. It's a sort of international "domestic content" quarrel, and it may be several years before it is settled—probably by means of agreements to share ownership and work in each country.

If this can be done, international communications links may begin to produce some minor economic miracles in a number of Third World countries that now lack their own communications infrastructure. Countries that allow in private data processing and communications companies may be able to build their own telephone systems as well as create new jobs. That at least is the sales pitch American negotiators are making.

In any event, this much seems clear: In the year 2000 and thereafter, country-by-country control over communications will simply not be possible. It will have to be international. The flow of information is advancing too rapidly. American TV already is found virtually everywhere via satellite or imported cassettes. Broadcasting of all kinds is undergoing explosive growth.

COMMUNICATING FREEDOM

Quantity becomes quality; sheer volume makes it increasingly difficult and finally impossible for any country to close its borders to information—not even the Soviet Union or other controlled societies. Russians already know a lot more about the U.S. than we know about the USSR, thanks not only to the Voice of America or Radio Free Europe but to the growing clandestine inflow of information via audio and video tapes and players.

No matter how hard the Soviet government tries to seal itself off, it will not be able to stem this leakage completely—in fact, it probably already is getting out of hand—and no one can begin to foretell its outcome. But at the center of every controlled society sits a government that fears for its stability if the people know too much about the outside world.

The spread of communications is having vast effects even in open societies like ours—as witness how our political campaigns have changed and how our ways of working and studying are being altered by the increasing access to information.

The controlled societies are going to be left in the dust of the information revolution. Our own intellectual freedoms allow vast numbers of our citizens to be part of that revolution and to use information in new and creative ways. Computer whiz-kids, not simply in this country but in every other free society in the world, are coming up with all sorts of unforeseen achievements.

Computers are giving the U.S. and other free nations the capacity to process and exchange incredible amounts of information. Only an open society such as ours can take full advantage of the new technology. And this will lead to unprecedented growth.

Controlled societies can either join up or fall behind. China seems to be moving in the direction of more openness for its citizens, even adopting a new copyright law based on our own. Will the Soviets join the 20th century before it becomes the 21st? And could they do so without allowing the healthful virus of individual freedom to infect their society?

Those are among the most intriguing questions posed by the information revolution.

7

Manufacturing by Robot

Factory automation is about to accelerate, after a couple of decades or so of fitful development. It will bring long-range improvements in American productivity that almost boggle the imagination.

Automation will not have the dire effects on total American employment that pessimists predict, and it will keep the United States competitive with less-automated overseas firms that enjoy substantial advantages in labor costs.

Development of the factory of the future is about five years away. It will take that long to break through the major remaining bottleneck to full coordination of computers, machines and management.

This factory will work like a single large machine—a continuous flow of production, 24 hours a day, machines fed by robots, the entire complex managed by computers that will spot trouble at the moment it develops, reducing waste and rejects down to near-zero. It will take up roughly one-third less space than a conventional facility of like capacity and employ far less labor.

Productivity will leap by at least 100 percent in most manufacturing situations. In some, it will go substantially higher.

Most of the components needed for this new wave of automation—the "second industrial revolution," as automation experts are calling it—already exist. Numerically controlled machine tools, for example, are an old story by now. Robots of many kinds already are at work in factories here and around the world (a larger number of them in Japan than the U.S., in fact). Computers of course are everywhere, or will be soon.

What is just ahead is a series of changes that will bring a sudden, exponential takeoff, meaning that efficiencies will double over and over again.

Robots are on the verge of several improvements in dexterity and vision so that they will be able to distinguish among parts and components with far greater accuracy. They will be more mobile and will be able to undertake more complex jobs with less specific programming. Instead of having to build in every minute step of a complicated operation, engineers will specify objectives and leave it to the robot and its computer to get there.

Robots also will be equipped with greatly improved sensors able to operate in hostile environments—heat, cold, chemical processes, space—and provide a constant, sensitive feedback of data on operating conditions.

Methods for networking computers into an integrated system are now available so that the progress of complex distributed operations can be constantly monitored by management, whether machine management or human.

And finally, we are about five years away from new machine-language standards that will make it possible for conglomerations of machine tools and robots to be fused into a single operating system under common control. This will work even with machines made by different manufacturers.

BUSINESS OPPORTUNITIES

That's the technical side of automation. On the entrepreneurial side, there will be plenty happening too.

More and more large manufacturing firms are positioning themselves for the takeoff by acquiring small machine tool companies. From more than a thousand such companies today, employing an average of fewer than a hundred persons, we will probably go to about a dozen within a few more years. But these will be high-powered companies, capable of producing new kinds of computerized machine tools at volumes and rates of productivity never seen before.

A related development is the burgeoning of dozens of new "incubator centers," most of them established by limited partnerships, to undertake the development of new products and components of others. These will be highly automated mini-factories, most of them located at or near a university, to draw on the capabilities of engineering faculties. And some will have tie-ins with the Department of Defense to provide military items and standby "surge capacity" to meet special defense needs, including those of an emergency.

Such centers are going to be increasingly instrumental in the development of products made from new composite materials—epoxy fibers, ceramics and the like—in addition to metalworking, and in biologicals as well.

This sort of development is beginning to attract growing attention in the venture capital market, and some of the larger brokerage and investment banking establishments are setting up special funds or divisions to promote it.

Washington has taken steps to encourage consortiums of firms in related fields, with relaxing of antitrust restrictions on the freedom of companies in various lines to join in cooperative research and development programs. A trail blazer is the Micro-electronics and Computer Technology Corporation of Austin, Tex.; another is the Semiconductor Research Corp., sponsored by 13 chip-and-computer companies.

Efforts to establish similar ventures in other lines will probably make considerable progress in the next decade and should contribute to the chances of a strong comeback for U.S. industrial technology. Consortiums of firms already have turned up or are likely to soon in aerospace software, steel, pumps, household appliances and wiring and high-tech ceramics—among many other lines.

In the process, the face of American industry will change dramatically. There will be a continuing wave of mergers and acquisitions. Large corporations are diversifying in new ways—not simply to pick up profitable subsidiaries in conventional lines but to equip themselves to branch out into new fields of technology and production.

Economies of scale will no longer be the exclusive advantage of large-sized production lines. They will be achievable in relatively small, integrated and automated plants, and this will lead to a dramatic expansion in smaller firms, many of them allied with bigs but also many new independents. These flexible-automation centers will be placed strategically close to end markets, thus cutting down on transportation costs and adding to productivity.

REMANUFACTURING

In the midst of this transition to high-tech automated manufacturing, another trend—almost antithetical—is taking shape. It's remanufacturing, a growth business you'll be hearing more about. Essentially it is the making of new products out of old by rebuilding them. The idea has been around a long time—in auto parts, for example.

Now it's set for faster growth as more and more entrepreneurs try their hands at it. They're buying up entire lots of worn-out equipment, such as industrial valves and fittings, boilers, generators, machine tools, even contents of whole plants, and rebuilding them with new parts and components as needed. Washing machines and other consumer durables could be grist for this mill as well.

Perhaps incongruous at a time when high tech is taking over the scene, but it makes sense from more than one point of view. The "raw material" is cheap, bought at salvage or junk value. The remanufacturer thus can undersell similar new products by 40% or even 50%. Consumers get a price break. Industrial users find they can build on their original capital investment by extending the life of equipment at modest cost.

And small firms just getting started might find this a way to get needed equipment together at cut-rate prices.

Over the longer run, say, well into the next century, these attractions may fade as automated manufacturing brings about economies of both scale and technology. Yet the prospect of rising materials, energy and production costs in older lines leads some proponents of remanufacturing to think it has a bright future.

FLEXIBLE AUTOMATION

Flexible automation, meaning the ability to retool with a minimum of fuss, is going to work major changes in the time it takes to introduce new designs and new products. Under conventional methods, a change in specifications—to say nothing of a jump in orders—has usually required a time-consuming changeover. What used to take months or weeks will now take days or hours.

The auto industry, for example, used to shut down once a year to retool for new designs. Even automated engine-block assembly lines have to be virtually rebuilt when designs change, as they did when four-cylinder engines came in, a process that took months. Flexible automation will wipe out those delays.

Resetting machine tools will be done on a computer keyboard. The skilled machinist who used to do this work will be a computer programmer.

In addition to much shorter turnaround times, flexible manufacturing will bring a dramatic reduction in costly inventories and in scrap and wastage, via networks of sensors and feedback loops to notify the computers when error appears—say, a slight deviation from design tolerances. Inventories, as the Japanese have demonstrated, can be held to a minimum by scheduling "just in time" delivery of materials and components; this requires continuous computer monitoring of production and computerized linkage among suppliers, all of which are on the way.

In effect, we will be stockpiling manufacturing capacity rather than finished goods.

And great savings in energy consumption will be possible by more sensitive computer controls over time-of-day loads and over choices among available sources, including ambient and byproduct heat. (See our chapter on energy.)

Techniques of this general kind already are being employed on a limited scale in factories here and abroad in what are called "automated cells"—sections in factories set aside for computer-controlled tools and robots. These installations have produced dramatic cost reductions but are still only a sample of the full potential.

New factories will be vertically integrated, most of them incorporating many stages of production into a single plant, from raw materials to finished products. The efficiencies and profits that can be realized from such operations will make it worthwhile for manufacturing companies to gut and rebuild old facilities or start over again with totally new "green field" plants, as GM is doing with its Saturn auto project in Tennessee.

The efficiencies are such, in fact, that some authorities see a good chance that the U.S. can attract back home some of the plants and industries that have gone abroad to take advantage of lower labor costs—textiles and clothing, for example.

ROADBLOCKS TO CHANGE

The transition to full automation will take time, however. Even though important breakthroughs will come in the next few years, the factory of the future will not sweep from one end of the country to the other overnight. Automation is too expensive for that. And there is considerable resistance being put up both by industry itself and by coalitions of labor unions, industries and political forces.

But competition is increasingly worldwide, and it is hard to see how the U.S. can shut itself off from the forces of technology that are bringing the competition directly to our doorstep. Lower wages abroad are a major competitive factor, but shielding our own wages from such competition may only mean a higher domestic price level and eventual loss of jobs anyway.

In fact, a strong argument can be made that more jobs will be lost via protectionist measures than by foreign competition in the long run. Industries that can't compete in world markets will fail, sooner or later.

Which is why the wave of flexible automation that is bound to come in this country can't come any too soon. Our major comparative advantage in the world is no longer manufacturing capacity—it is technology. By taking advantage of that lead, we probably can rebuild our lead in manufacturing.

IMPACT ON LABOR

The employment impact of factory automation is going to be a lot less severe than most people fear. For one thing, automation will proceed in a deliberate sort of way, without massive and sudden displacements of the kind the country saw in the early '80s. That wave of layoffs was caused in good part by automation—but NOT American automation. Lower-cost imports produced in automated plants abroad were a chief cause of the drastic shrinkage of employment in autos, steel and other basic lines during the recessions of 1979-1982.

We are not likely to see such large-scale displacement again unless our own industry fails to put itself on a more competitive footing. Prospects are that the computer and automation wave will itself make a large number of jobs, both in production and in the servicing and repair of equipment. That has been the experience in Japan, where factory automation is more advanced than in the U.S.

At the same time, the effects of rising profits and income throughout the economy that will stem from the growth of productivity and profits will make for additional employment, as growth always has before. Service lines will expand, but so will many kinds of manufacturing. And as American products grow more competitive on the world market via the productivity effects of flexible manufacturing, more jobs will be created.

The new technologies coming along will create whole new industries and greatly expand opportunities in existing ones, including not just manufacturing but also construction, farming, oceanography, mining, tunneling and space.

At the same time, growth of the American labor force will be slowing down, and by the middle to late '90s there will even be labor shortages, as we noted earlier. There already are, for that matter, among skilled and trained technical personnel, as well as among the teachers needed to turn out more of them.

By the time the pinch begins to hurt—as the factory of the future has begun to take off on a steep up-curve—our manpower problems will have changed from surplus to shortage. And most of the skilled workers displaced in the early part of this decade will have either retired or found other jobs.

The major problem will not be finding jobs for the jobless but training them to take the jobs that need filling. This will have to be a large-scale undertaking and it will be difficult.

There will be increasing demands for government to step back into the training picture on a large scale. But there are countervailing budget pressures and also much less inclination, at least for now, to see a government solution for the retraining problem, in light of the mixed-to-poor results from previous experiments. Voter attitudes on this point may change in the next decade or two, but our reading of the outlook doesn't hold much hope in that direction.

That is why much or most of the burden is going to shift to the states—and to industry, which is going to get more and more deeply involved in training from the entry level on up. Retraining programs are becoming an integral part of corporate human-resources policies and will be a growth area for many years to come. Employers will see these as a necessary investment in man-and-woman power needed for future growth.

THE ROBOT

Industrial robots are a disappointing sight. They don't at all resemble the endearing or fearsome humanoids the movies and science fiction have taught us to expect. For the most part, they are simply gawky mechanical arms with rotating and clutching devices designed to manipulate objects, moving them from one location to another, feeding them into machines and taking them away, or to perform such routine industrial duties as spray painting and spot welding.

Robots of the future will probably be even uglier but a lot more adept. In a few more years they will gain mobility and be employed in such construction jobs as building commercial structures, ship hulls and airplane bodies; crawling around and doing welding, riveting, wiring and other tasks in hard-to-reach locations and in environments where humans would rather not have to work; constructing walls, pouring cement, laying pipe, painting.

This will require some important breakthroughs in mobility systems. Wheels and articulated tracks may eventually be replaced with walking legs. Developments of this kind have a way of turning up without warning.

Most industrial robots will be machine controlled—that is, computer programmed and monitored. Others will be under human control via computerized sensors and feedback loops, plus television, so that operators will be able to run complicated jobs from remote sites. Mining underground, on the ocean bottom or on the moon, for example, will be run from a console on the surface of Earth.

Ultrasensitive controls can be built into a kind of "glove" or a helmet which will give the operator the feel of the job as though he or she were running the machine directly on the spot instead of from somewhere else. Moving vehicles, for example, can be guided via TV cameras which turn as the remote operator turns his head, creating the equivalent of on-the-spot vision. A coal miner in a white shirt will be able to run digging equipment below ground without leaving his office.

The computers that make all this possible become in effect "transparent." It will be difficult to tell the difference between operations by means of computer and operations by direct feel.

Another likelihood is that such technology will make possible the operation of several machines at once from a single control center—a prospect of great interest to the armed services, which are financing a good deal of robotic research and development on their own.

The computerized controls that all this requires are being progressively "hardened"—that is, made more reliable, less fragile, less accident prone and more resistant to rough conditions. Again, this meets military requirements but also will be important in many civilian applications, including commercial projects in space.

NEW USES FOR ROBOTS

Housekeeping robots will turn up before long, first in commercial applications and perhaps later for residences. These will be programmed to vacuum large areas and to perform such other tasks as emptying trash containers and restocking supplies. Chances are that these will be practical at first only in buildings designed for them—that is, with layouts open enough for easy access and with built-in wires and sensors to control the robots' behavior. It's likely that it will be simpler to assign a robot to each floor rather than teach them to ride the elevators.

As time goes on, the major shift in robot design will be toward specific applications rather than general-purpose machines. They will develop qualities that are even more important than precision (and the need for precision can be a drawback where microtolerances are involved), including the ability to adjust to changing conditions and to sense their environment through touch and sound as well as vision.

Software designers and engineers are working on "knowledge modules" which will give robots a kind of primitive reasoning ability. When told, in effect, to "pick this up and put it over there," they will do so without the need for the kind of intricate, step-by-step programming needed with current-generation robots. And if the "over there" turns out to be a bit out of position, the robot will adjust instead of grinding to a halt or dropping its load in the wrong spot.

And as computerized "expert systems" improve, robots will be able to make on-the-spot decisions under changing conditions. This is likely to happen within another decade or two.

Robots don't have to be big to be big money-savers. Mini- and micro-robots will be taking over a lot of routine bench work in tight environments, such as the assembly of electronic parts. And, for that matter, many of the tiny sensing and control devices that are going to be turning up in auto and aircraft engines, among other applications, are really a variety of robot.

Other applications for robots include guard duty—patrolling the perimeter of a factory or the rooms and corridors of buildings, checking locks, sensing intruders; filling and delivering orders in warehouses, factories and storerooms; making the rounds in hospitals with trays, supplies, medicines, etc.; providing mobility for the handicapped via special robotic prostheses and wheel-chairs; preparing and delivering fast foods; running gas stations; and doing other things no one has yet thought of. Thousands of business opportunities are sure to develop out of these.

Over time, robots will be building more robots; automated factories will be replicating themselves, but with incremental or even exponential improvements at each stage. Before the end of this century and well into the next, this kind of growth will contribute mightily to the coming American boom.

And in the process, enormous wealth will be created. Individuals and groups will become robot owners, a form of investment that is likely to develop and grow as robots spread. It is even likely that individual small investors will be able to buy shares in robot-leasing companies. The wealth will spread widely, and looking back from the early years of the 21st century, the old anxieties about the effects of robots on employment and income will seem rather quaint.

It is probably going to turn out that American industry is looking at the wrong set of concerns, to the extent that it drags its feet in automating. Business probably cannot afford to wait and see. Robots already are capable of producing major gains in productivity; ditto for computers and automation in general.

Companies that catch the wave now instead of waiting for the next one will wind up well ahead of those that lie back. It has been that way with each new wave of technology, from steam through electricity and internal combustion engines to the microchip... and now, with flexible automation.

8

Business in Space

The commercialization of space is just beginning to take off. Its development will be quite different from the government-contractor space enterprise that has grown up over the past quarter of a century around NASA and the Defense Department.

Many of the pioneers and future participants in this new space industry are likely to bring home enormous profits. Just how big and how soon won't be clear for a decade or so, but informed investors already are lining up to grab a piece of the action, while everybody else is distracted by the Challenger disaster of early 1986 and its aftermath—another example of a "sleeper" industry that will provide some surprises.

Venture capitalists, aerospace firms, banks and brokers and others are already forming new consortiums, corporations, limited partnerships and the like to push on into space commercialization. Most are doing so in the knowledge that profits may be slow in coming.

It will take a decade or so for the new space industry to establish itself; in the meantime, many of the new venture firms may fold up, while others persist. But it may take only a couple of early successes to point the way to what's coming.

The commercialization of space will progress in stages, more or less this way:

NASA will continue to launch both manned and unmanned Shuttle flights in coming years, after recovering from the Challenger setback, and American and foreign companies will rent space on them to carry out further experiments. Meanwhile, financial consortiums will be forming to underwrite commercial ventures, from launching rockets to acquiring a foothold in the space laboratories to come.

In the mid to late '90s, NASA will launch our first permanent orbiting space station. American and foreign firms will at once begin installing manufacturing and processing facilities in the station, which will expand steadily as new units are attached to it in orbit.

The commercialization of space will be a going venture, and the profits will start flowing in volume. Chances are that at least some of the companies already involved won't have to wait that long to turn a buck.

RESEARCH IN SPACE

The value of a space-lab environment to researchers lies chiefly in the virtual absence of gravity. Experiments can break loose from the earthbound pull that interferes, even at the micro level, with experiments aimed at producing pure compounds, crystals and the like without the settling and layering effects gravity causes on earth. Large vacuum chambers can be and have been built on earth for experimental purposes, but until someone comes up with an anti-gravity device, space is the best environment for gravity-free work.

Discoveries have been multiplying on each Shuttle flight, and some of them may turn out to be bigger than even their backers had hoped. Some examples:

New vaccines and other pharmaceuticals: Using space as a laboratory for finding cures for earthbound diseases and hereditary disabilities could open enormous markets. The "value-added" component of only a small amount of such substances could be staggering. Several dozen are on the list for space experiments, and sooner or later there is bound to be a winner, probably several. (See our chapter on biotechnology.)

Improved crystals: Researchers think microchip materials worth $50,000 a pound in current dollars can be produced in space in sufficient volume (it doesn't take much) to meet the growing demand for improved chips for computers and other applications. Other crystals may lead to development of an "optical switch," in effect a communications switching and routing device that uses light impulses instead of electrons and is therefore much faster than even the most advanced equipment now in use.

Glass fibers: Space research indicates that ultra-clear forms of glass can be developed there that will enormously boost the capacity and efficiency of fiber-optic cable, probably enough to span ocean-sized distances without loss of power or clarity.

Chemical catalysts: These are the key and often secret ingredients in the making of plastics. New ones discovered in space could lead to the development of greatly improved proprietary compounds.

Metal alloys: Researchers expect to come up with improvements in strength, lightness and durability for new applications on earth.

To comprehend the nature and potential of commercial space processing and manufacturing, you have to give up seeking comparisons with conventional factories and laboratories.

Space industry will be devoted only to small-batch, high-value work, no high-volume or bulky stuff. There won't be room for the latter even though the space station (and later versions of it) may grow to fairly substantial size. Once the basic facilities have been established in orbit, additions lofted into the same orbit can be nudged into place by "space tugs" (manned, maneuverable satellites) and bolted on. The result won't look anything like sleek, science-fiction "2001" concepts, but more like something that fell off an oil refinery or was welded together out of old boiler parts. In any event, space stations won't replace, but will supplement factories on earth.

At the same time they will lead to the building of another kind of space enterprise—the supplying of services to firms working in space. Companies have already been formed to design, build and launch rockets for delivering people and materials to and retrieving them from space stations. The design and construction of the manufacturing and processing equipment will be another part of this industry, along with production and operation of the space tugs to maneuver equipment in space and of power packs to provide energy for all these operations.

CHANGES FOR NASA

NASA's civilian role will shrink as time goes on, until by the mid-'90s, when the space business is about ready to fly on its own, it will have reverted to its former status as space explorer and provider of launch services to the military.

NASA would take a leading role, however, if the government finally decides to go ahead with proposals to establish a permanent base on the moon, which would probably begin around the turn of the century. Plans to establish space colonies on permanent platforms in higher orbit or to send manned expeditions to Mars and perhaps other planets may also begin to take shape about that time.

But first you can anticipate a lengthy and heated debate over this country's role in space. For the next several years at least, the debate will be dominated by President Reagan's so-called Star Wars proposal—the Strategic Defense Initiative—which is going to soak up more than the lion's share of space spending. SDI may yet go down the drain as a result of arms-control agreements reached with the Soviets or be held to a research-and-development level for several years in hopes of such agreements. But even so, its demands will put a strain on both the federal space budget and the supply of scientific and technical manpower.

The other side of the debate is the opinion that military and commercial uses of space should not be allowed to sidetrack space exploration for its own sake. The scientific community argues that invaluable lead time is being lost on probes that could be ready to explore the solar system and beyond in the early decades of the new century. Mining operations could be established on the moon and asteroids as a way of supplying future space stations and colonies, it is argued; this would be cheaper than ferrying materials to them from earth.

How this fight over priorities will be resolved is difficult to say at this stage. It is really a struggle over allocation of federal spending, and until the budget-and-deficit battle of the '80s is settled, the nonmilitary, noncommercial side of space will probably have to live on short rations.

But this could begin to change dramatically in the '90s, when the technological boom we have described is gathering force and freeing up additional resources for new ventures.

SHARING SPACE

In the meantime, prospects for international cooperation in the establishment of future space stations are improving. Britain and West Germany have already announced that they want to participate in the establishment of the first station, thereby assuring themselves a hand in the commercial potential of space, and other governments are likely to do the same. The European Space Agency, made up of members of the European Economic Community, is already well along with development of its Ariane rocket series for delivery of commercial loads to a space station. Japan also is developing a similar project but is somewhat behind the U.S. and the ESA.

Even the Russians, who are at work on a station of their own believed to be closely patterned after ours, may want in on some limited basis. A cooperative agreement between the U.S. and USSR on peaceful uses of space, which expired in 1982, might be renegotiated.

NEW COMMERCIAL USES

The objective of all these endeavors is the building of a follow-on generation of launch and delivery vehicles to take over and improve on the Space Shuttle, along with space tugs to maneuver and help assemble orbiting facilities and the development of new energy sources for space experiments and production.

Expansion in satellite communications will continue. Space shuttles have already demonstrated their capabilities for launching, retrieving and repairing satellites. New fortunes will be made in providing highly advanced relay facilities on satellites for communications, broadcasting, earth mapping, mineral exploration, weather forecasting and other uses. This will be a growing industry well into the new century, limited only by the crowding of stationary orbits and of transmission bands, problems technology will probably be able to solve before they become severe.

In communications, watch for the launching within the next 10 years of enormous antennas that will provide cellular radio service for far wider areas of the earth. These also could be used for worldwide broadcasting by government and private organizations.

Look too for the interconnection of communications satellites via laser beams that could speed transmissions between widely scattered points on earth, reducing the minute but troublesome delays inherent in present satellites.

Companies already are looking into the possibilities for building "public utilities" in space to supply power to orbiting stations via new kinds of fuel cells and batteries or by beaming energy from earth via microwave—techniques that may turn out to be cheaper than solar cells.

And researchers are at work on concepts for orbiting gardens to supply oxygen and edibles for space crews, some of which may spend months at work in stationary orbit 22,300 miles above the earth.

A network of suppliers will grow up around these core industries, much as it happened long ago in the auto industry or the military rocket-and-missile business. These will be smaller firms making and testing parts and components, supplying research and development facilities, particularly in energy, and providing specialized computing and software capabilities.

9

Booming Biotech

Biotechnology—the manipulation of organic processes to make new products—will be the hottest new line in the '90s.

It is going to revolutionize health care, agriculture, fuel production and parts of our industrial complex. The overall result will be an enormous contribution to American productivity and prosperity—something on the order of what computers have done and will be doing at the same time.

No one can now say what this contribution will amount to in percentages of GNP or other basic economic statistics; it is only clear that it will be huge. Some industry insiders believe that biotech sales alone will go from today's almost-nothing level to a few billions of dollars in the early '90s and to 40 billions or more by the year 2000.

The reason is that the industry will be producing pharmaceuticals, agricultural chemicals and pesticides, growth-promoting hormones for plants and animals and a number of industrial items all with very high valued-added potential. Markets for them will be elastic—as prices of the new products fall and the return from their use rises, demand will grow by multiples rather than simple addition. In the field of health care alone, consumers will pay almost anything within reason to get some of the new products coming along.

Financially, biotechnology already is a growth field, but the profits will take a while to build up, after some false starts. And when they do, the sky may be the limit.

Some 300 companies are in the field just now—a mixture of new starts, most of them small, and of well-established bigs in chemicals, pharmaceuticals, energy, agriculture and other fields that have either set up their own biotech divisions or are busily acquiring the smalls as a hedge against the future.

This process will churn around a lot—much as the friendly new microbes do in the fermentation vats at biotech factories—and by the early '90s may have simmered down to only a few dozen firms...meaning that many of today's "biotech boutiques" will have disappeared or been swallowed up.

There is great business potential in serving the biotech industry, as a supplier of equipment and components. A whole network of satellite companies will probably grow up around it to compete for the demand for laboratory equipment and new and improved fermenting, purifying and extraction systems.

Venture capital has been the name of the game in the past 10 years or so, during which the biotech industry jumped from almost zero to its present state. The essential building-block for the new industry dates back only to 1972, after all, when recombinant DNA was discovered.

It took a couple of years for early fears of what tinkering with genes and micro-organisms might do to the environment to well up and quiet down again. Then the new start-up firms began to proliferate like microbes and the venture capitalists leaped in, took firms public, and as their new high-tech stocks zoomed, grabbed the money and ran. Investors got impatient waiting for promised earnings, and stock prices plummeted. Now real products are finally coming to market, and biotech stock prices are being bid up again. The rest of the '80s will be the period of consolidation and takeoff, with the '90s becoming increasingly exciting. Biotech will be the leading science in the new century, taking over from chemistry and physics, and some of today's small firms will be among tomorrow's bigs.

There is an interesting parallel building up, in fact, between the micro-organism business and the microchip business: Biotech is today roughly where computers stood 15 or 20 years ago—on the threshold of a takeoff so steep that it left most of the early prophets (and profits) in the dust.

WHAT'S COMING

Here are some examples of what is in store in each of the major (and some minor) biotech fields—each product, keep in mind, derived from living substances, rather than chemicals:

Health: Human insulin (already on the market). Interferon, which will help treat cancer, several other diseases and perhaps even prevent the common cold. Clotting hormones to arrest bleeding. Unclotting hormones to prevent or arrest heart attacks. Human growth hormones. A wide range of vaccines for viral diseases, including malaria and hepatitis. Eventually an all-in-one vaccine, both to prevent and to cure. Monoclonal antibodies to treat most forms of cancer, plus advances toward gene manipulation to prevent cancer. A foolproof diagnostic kit for AIDS, perhaps later a cure. Improved means of testing the fetus for genetic diseases and malfunctions, including sickle-cell anemia and some forms of retardation. Later, perhaps a means of averting or treating retardation. Hormones that control pain and regulate blood pressure. A substance that lubricates joints, for treatment of arthritis. And many others, still only conceptual— such as laboratory-grown tissue for artery and joint replacement.

Agriculture: Safe hormones to speed the growth and increase the size of meat animals and raise the milk output of cows. Advances in hybridization. Genetic modifications of plants to improve photosynthesis and yield, build in natural pest resistance and create natural nitrogen-fixing abilities that will, in effect, fertilize plants. Plants that will thrive in arid or salty soils. Plants that resist chemical buildup and are frost-resistant. Improved strains of trees. A wide range of animal vaccines. New animal feed additives to replace chemicals. Speeded-up ways to test genetically altered seeds and animals. Conversion of potato starch into high-fructose syrup. New diagnostic means of testing for animal diseases. A synthetic biological factor to speed cheese-making. In aquaculture, improved strains of fish and shellfish and new means of detecting disease and pollution in those found in the wild.

Chemicals: Biological production of specialty (i.e., expensive) chemicals and food additives such as amino acids, vitamins, steroids, enzymes, sweetener ingredients, aspirin and others. Innovations in processing techniques including enzymatic conversion to increase speed and volume of output. Gradual replacement of petrochemical feedstocks (and dependence on oil) with biologically based processes for large-scale production of commodity chemicals used in industry and agriculture. New kinds of antifreeze and high-performance adhesives. Substitution of biological media for chemicals in papermaking.

Environment: Specialized micro-organisms to degrade (render harmless) pollutants and chemicals including dioxin, others to consume oil spills. Still others to leach out minerals and precious or strategic metals from low-grade or hard-to-reach geological deposits. Biological waste-treatment processes to remove harmful components such as heavy metals, requiring little energy input and producing useful byproducts. Removal of sulfur from coal to prevent acid rain. A biodegradable plastic that won't stay around to litter the landscape.

Consumer goods: Nonchemical drain cleaner (already on the market), detergents and other household cleaning products. New kinds of biological plant foods and fertilizers for home use. Safer insecticides and pesticides. Bacteria, already on the market, that make fluffier, higher-volume artificial snow at ski resorts. Later on, improved strains of home-garden vegetable and flower seeds.

Fuels: Substances to aid in the recovery of oil reserves from depleted fields, oil shale and tar sands. Low-cost methods for producing large amounts of industrial alcohol and fuel additives from the cellulose in biomass—meaning all sorts of vegetable matter—with minimum energy input.

Military: Biosensors to detect chemical weapons and vaccines to protect troops from them.

Computers: Possible development of biochips to replace conventional microchips with enzyme-activated molecular conductors, theoretically capable of replicating themselves.

These of course amount only to a showing of the directions biotech development is taking—hardly a complete road map.

WHO'LL LEAD THE WAY?

For now, the U.S. is the world leader in all this, but other countries are pounding hard on its heels—with Japan ahead of the pack. Japan and several European countries have "targeted" biotech programs, meaning that government subsidies and protections are being concentrated on them. Israel also has a number of innovative firms at work.

The U.S. provides some subsidy in the form of research grants to universities and private organizations, and these—plus the investor's dream of great gains—are what have brought the biotech industry to life. The level of government support is substantial, but probably will not be growing much due to budget restraints.

The regulatory climate could become a problem for American biotech firms. For the present it is more or less benign and is weighted more to promotion than restriction. Several agencies each have a piece of the action—FDA for drugs, EPA for environmental hazards, USDA for plant and animal research, NIH to review medical research and applications, and so on. A complicated review and monitoring procedure is in place to ensure that no proposal goes too far without its risks and drawbacks being thoroughly explored. As it is, FDA requires several years of testing before approving a new pharmaceutical.

But there is a lingering feeling in Congress that biotechnology may be too important to leave to the biotechnologists—a feeling that despite the assurances to the contrary, some altered micro-organisms might not be suitable for release into the human body or the environment. This is based in no small part on the uncomfortable precedent set in atomic energy, where environmental risks were severely underestimated and, at the outset, regulation and promotion competed with each other, promotion often in the lead.

Private environmental groups still have a deep mistrust of genetic engineering, and campaigns have been waged against everything from substances that prevent frost damage on vegetables to germs that make fluffier artificial snow.

Chances are that Congress will impose a review procedure of its own atop what now exists. And it wouldn't take more than one or two small "accidents" to convert that into more rigorous regulation.

Still, as the congressional Office of Technology Assessment has pointed out, "the relative freedom of U.S. industry to pursue a variety of courses in the development of products has also given the United States a comparative advantage. The flexibility of the U.S. industrial system and the plurality of approaches taken by entrepreneurial new biotechnology firms and established companies...have facilitated the rapid development of biotechnology in the United States."

It's unlikely that Congress will want to hamper this lead without very good reason. Gene-splicers already are taking great precautions to ensure that new strains of micro-organisms are incapable of reproduction outside the environment for which they are devised. Whether this degree of caution will persist when the industry later on becomes larger and ever more competitive remains to be seen.

HOW IT WORKS

The processes of biotech are both very old and very new. It was primitive biotechnology that invented beer—probably by accident; ditto for the discovery of what a little fungus could do for grape juice. Today, fermentation has been developed into a high art, employing sophisticated technologies and equipment that resembles a scaled-down oil refinery.

What is particularly new—and unforeseen except by dreamers until DNA was identified as a spiral helix in 1953—is the ability to break into the very basic chemical stuff of life and make alterations in the genes that determine characteristics of an organism. Today, bioscientists use these techniques to "operate" on the DNA in microbes to convert them to new functions.

One technique involves the monoclonal antibody, a means of bringing the body's own internal defenses to bear on tumors and cancer cells or, in the case of plant pathology, to identify and act on diseases caused by viruses, fungi or bacteria. The most commonly used micro-organism for human gene engineering is an old friend, Escherichia Coli, a resident of the lower intestine where it helps man and animals complete the digestion of food.

These, when treated with recombinant DNA, are reproduced in large quantities by means of a nutrient broth in a fermenting system. In some cases, production is vastly speeded up via a variety of fermenter called the bioreactor in which specific enzymes catalyze a continuing high-density reaction that may be capable of running for months. The same techniques can be used for mass production of cells from bits of tissue of plants and animals. Although these systems are complicated and require a great deal of research and investment, when they get going, overhead is low and productivity very high. There is still much work to be done, however, on the engineering of "downstream" recovery and purification devices, which can be an important cost factor.

GROWTH FIELDS

The outlook for biotech sales is strongest in pharmaceuticals, with agribusiness second. There are enormous profits to be made in the first category—virtually all of which will involve products to be dispensed only through physicians and hospitals. It's likely that pharmaceutical manufacturers will convert to the new biotech basis en masse but will not totally abandon current methods. The two will exist side by side for some time to come.

By the late '90s, the pharmaceuticals will probably have begun to level off, while agricultural-biotech products will be catching up and exceeding them in total sales.

The long-range implications of these two developments are substantial. Improved health-care products hold out the promise of bringing great reductions in the cost of health care, shortening of average hospital stays and further extensions of the average life span. Growth in the nation's health bill will be substantially reduced as time goes on.

Biotech will have similar effects in agriculture. Greater productivity can mean an end to world food shortages. The technology involved is adaptable everywhere and, once brought to market, is capable of being applied wherever it is needed—here and in the Third World—which may turn out to be a long-term threat to export markets for U.S. grains. It also could have profoundly beneficial effects on world politics by helping ease the potentially explosive effects of overpopulation in many areas.

The energy implications of biotech also are substantial. Just now, due to the abundance of cheap oil, the drive to find alternate sources is pretty much on hold. This is understandable enough; folks don't worry about a leaky roof when the sun is shining.

But biotech conversion of cellulose into alcohol is potentially so inexpensive and so productive that it may turn out to be economically feasible even while oil is plentiful. The same may be true for biotech recovery from nominally exhausted fields and of hard-to-reach heavy oils, shales and tar sands.

Environmental use of biotechnologies will be slower in developing, chiefly because of the cost of conversion—which most municipalities and state governments will resist as long as they can. Still, worsening problems of pollution, combined with evidence of economies available via biotech as compared to other methods, may speed the conversion. Put this down for late in the century. Sooner than that, however, the use of biological-degrading media for neutralizing dangerous landfills and waste dumps may become economical.

And this is to be said about pollution: Biotech advances that reduce the use of petro-based chemicals will also cut down on dangerous residues.

PICKING UP SPEED

The forecasts in this report cover the next 15 or 20 years—into the early years of the new century. But the forces of change in biotech are speeding up year by year, and the best estimates even by optimistic scientists may turn out to be overly conservative. For example, 15 or 20 years ago it took the equivalent of 50 man-years to replicate a single gene; today it takes three or four days. Tomorrow, who knows?

We've already pointed out that biotech may yet lead to an entirely new kind of super computer. The computer, whether bionic or electronic, will return the favor by helping to speed up the job of creating entirely new kinds of genes, which requires sifting through enormous amounts of data.

This is a form of synergy—the working together of different technologies to produce results greater than the sum of the parts. Take space research, too. Experiments under way on the Shuttle, and eventually in an orbiting space station, will help speed the development of new bio-pharmaceuticals for large-scale production on earth.

Quite literally, the sky is the limit.

10

Space-Age Materials

Exotic new materials and some old familiar ones in new guises are going to work wondrous changes in the next two decades, replacing such old standbys as steel, glass, lead, zinc and copper in a number of important applications.

For example: a kind of fiber-reinforced plastic stronger than steel but so light that it can be used for unsinkable boat hulls. Another strong enough to replace high-performance steel in auto drive shafts and leaf springs. And others to serve as bushings, gaskets, hoses and other auto parts that will resist fierce wear, high temperatures and corrosive materials.

And new kinds of ceramics will turn up in many uses requiring high durability and heat resistance, such as auto parts.

Most of the new plastics development will come in the field of polymers, a basic petrochemical technology that has been around for several decades but which is now undergoing a sudden burst of emergence into new forms and functions.

Auto body panels made of reinforced plastics aren't news any more, but they are still fairly rare and fairly expensive. By 2000 they will be the accepted way to go, replacing steel with laminated composites that will resist dents and scratches and have built-in color; no painting required.

Today's plastic panels are reinforced with glass fibers, which are cheap but relatively heavy. Tomorrow's will use plastic fibers derived from the stuff that goes into dry cleaners' garment bags but in a far tougher form. It will be much lighter as well as stronger.

Scientists in government and industry are coming up with ways to combine these fibers with ceramics and even such metals as aluminum to produce composites with superior strength-to-weight ratios, plus the ability to withstand extremely high temperatures.

These kinds of plastics are already turning up in military and aerospace applications, where cost is a minor consideration. As their cost comes down, they will become common in a wide variety of consumer applications...sporting goods (including bicycles), kitchenware, others.

One or more kinds of fiber-reinforced plastics will be widely used in construction, appearing first as large panels bolted together into modular units on site, later as beams and supporting members. In this field Europe already is ahead of us; American building codes will need revising before they are widely accepted here. But when they are, construction time and cost should shrink.

New kinds of adhesives will eliminate nuts and bolts and other metal fasteners which, in some applications, outweigh the plastic. Glues of this kind already are being used to assemble aerospace equipment, airliners and fighter-bombers from plastic panels. Cheaper versions will be needed for general use.

One kind of "ultra-oriented" polyethylene, six times stronger than steel but much lighter, will be handy for reinforcing concrete. We expect it to turn up in a lot of bridge-resurfacing jobs where freeze and thaw stress, combined with salt corrosion and rusting of steel reinforcing bars, has weakened concrete decks.

A kind of lightweight plastic that conducts electricity is in the offing. Already it has been used in experimental batteries that are in effect "solid state"—all plastic, without lead or electrolytic fluid. These produce a superior density-to-weight ratio and exceptionally long lives. They will probably be used in production-line autos before 2000 and in computers, as on-line or standby power sources.

These plastics will have a number of other uses when their conductivity has been improved through research now underway. They will form molded, built-in wiring that won't need insulation, in appliances, computers and other electronic items, for example. They will be used, perhaps, in heat-generating linings for outdoor wear and within building walls.

New polymers will be big in packaging. Before 2000 they will have replaced metal, glass and paper in just about all food and drink packaging...even beer. Campbell's already is marketing a line of soups in plastic containers that can be heated in a microwave oven and then used as tableware.

Mixed-media polymers can be tailored to all kinds of needs: special jogging-shoe materials; a heat-resistant plastic that looks like cast iron and can be used in trivets and hot plates; an especially slippery variety of plastic better than anything now known for bearings and bushings; flexible plastic armor for law-enforcement and military use; base materials for high-density laser-optic storage disks.

New applications will pop up year by year. Production and sales of the nonferrous metals such plastics will replace already are sagging and in years to come will hit new lows.

BIOTECH PLASTICS

All these plastics are based on petrochemical feedstocks, which could become a problem if we hit another oil-supply crisis. Although we doubt that this will happen, another technology a bit further down the road will help prepare us to laugh off any such development: plastics derived from biomass—virtually any living plant—via biotechnology. At least one such wrapping material has already been developed in Britain and is said to have several superior qualities.

Biotech is pointing the way to other exotic materials, including superstrong plastics based on derivatives of proteins combined with polymers and graphite fibers for use in aircraft and autos. Some of these can be used with other kinds of fibers, including metal and ceramic, to be molded into high-temperature gadgets and even into designer furniture—trendy, indestructible, pricey.

The use of proteins in such combinations is based on research into such prosaic questions as how come barnacles can stick so tenaciously to a ship's hull, or what makes old-fashioned cabinetmaker's hide glue so strong. The answer lies in collagen, a natural substance in human and animal bodies; through biotechnology, varieties of it are being developed that will lead to super-glues and super-plastics.

Another surprise from biotech is the discovery of a process using human blood products (cloned for production in volume) that serve in artificial human "gills" for breathing under water. It's a method of separating oxygen from seawater and will be important to divers and submarines.

Biotechnology is also likely to produce new kinds of high-performance lubricants for use in computers, delicate instruments and the like. The basis is a substance called hyaluronic acid, found naturally in the body as a gel in the eyeball and as a lubricating film in joints. Besides health applications it has important potential as both a precision substitute for oils, including whale oil, and a water-retaining or resisting coating for windshields, submarines and other gear.

Hyaluronic acid has the strange ability to act as an electro-repellant film under pressure. In contrast to oil-based lubricants, which allow surfaces to slide past each other, it creates a molecule-thin gap between surfaces so that they can function next to each other without contact or wear.

It also may turn out to be the way to develop optical switches, which in turn will open the way to optical computers, optical telephone and other ultra-high-speed communication systems and signal-boosting devices for military applications. This may be accomplished through the use of thin films of hyaluronic acid deposited on base materials, "doped" in such a way that they become light-sensitive conductors. It's theoretical now, but full of promise.

CERAMICS

Ceramics are a good example of the familiar turned exotic. Probably the oldest fabricated material known to man, clay fired into extreme hardness continues to serve in cookware, floor and roof tiles, ashtrays and those tacky souvenirs left over from your last vacation.

High-tech ceramics are derived from very fine clays, purified and augmented with other substances to produce ultra-hard pressings and moldings.

Japan already has come up with experimental versions of all-ceramic auto engines, and it may begin exporting them to this country in trucks and sports cars quite soon. Several American firms are deeply into similar research and development, and auto producers expect at least part-ceramic turbine engines to be in production within a few years. This technology has great potential for introducing unprecedented efficiency and performance into aircraft and truck engines. The U.S. Army has invested heavily in this prospect.

Advanced ceramic applications will turn up in instrumentation, particularly as sensors for extremely high-temperature, radiation or corrosion situations; industrial parts where heat and wear resistance are vital; and perhaps even in medical bone-replacement uses.

Consumers will encounter high-tech ceramics in new kinds of kitchenware but will not notice them hidden away within appliances and gadgetry where they will find many new uses.

Ceramics are based on cheap materials, which is an advantage to add to those described above. But they are brittle, as anyone knows who has dropped a clay pot on the kitchen floor. Science hopes to get around this problem via new combinations of materials. Bits of ceramic embedded in high-performance epoxies or polymers may be the answer. Stay tuned.

11

Good Health, Fair Prices

The next 15 years will bring startling changes in health care—better treatments for more ailments, provided in new ways, at a cost that will not increase as fast as it has in recent years.

New technologies in genetic engineering, computers, robotics, lasers and optics will give hope, and eventually relief, to millions of people now hindered by physical and mental diseases and handicaps. The boost in human productivity resulting from these advances will add lift to the American economy, not to mention the American spirit.

Between now and the year 2000, biotechnology of all sorts will have lengthened the average life span by more than in any comparable period in history.

The benefits will not be equally shared. There will be a kind of rationing according to income, with the well-to-do receiving excellent care; the poor, below-average; and the great bulk of the populace, adequate-to-excellent care. But the system will work well enough to bury any prospect of a national health system, which some call "socialized medicine."

As a business, after 10 or 15 years of high living, the American health-care industry is in for at least an equal period of slimming down and learning to get by on a tighter budget. This will be done with a diet pill called competition, and the impact will be far reaching.

Medical technology will expand and improve year by year, but the case for cost effectiveness will have to be made in each individual setting. Until their costs come down substantially, it is unlikely that the market for new devices will grow dramatically.

And patients outside major metropolitan areas will probably have to travel to take advantage of them.

Many hospitals will shut down, merge or convert to nursing homes, extended-care facilities or the like. Overall hospital usage will fall as much as 50%. For-profit hospital chains will continue to spread out across the country, snapping up many independents and nonprofits as they go. Some of these chains will become or be bought up by "supermeds," new health-care corporations dispensing a broad variety of services.

Doctors will increasingly band together in various kinds of practice groups to safeguard their overall bargaining power. But physician income and influence will level out or decline even so.

COST CONTROLS

The average annual rate of increase in overall health-care costs, which has outrun the Consumer Price Index for the past 15 years (10% vs. 7% in the past 10 alone) will finally begin to taper off. Within five years or so there is a good chance it will come down to about the rate of inflation.

Even though the rise in medical costs is going to slow down, overall spending will grow over the next couple of decades. This is because the public will be buying more care as the average cost eases, which in part will reflect the aging of the population—old people needing more health care than young—but also the growing affluence of society.

A decline in the growth rate of health-care costs would be no small accomplishment, and it won't come easily. The chief force behind it will be the cost controls imposed by Congress in 1983 under the rubric of DRGs, standing for Diagnosis-Related Groups. These are a schedule of fee ceilings for over 400 different medical procedures under Medicare and Medicaid, which account for upwards of 40% of hospital revenues today. Although subject to periodic adjustment, they already have put a sort of cap on medical costs and are beginning to force overdue management changes. And there will be more of the same. The DRG system is here to stay and if anything will grow more rigorous with time. Some version of it will probably be adopted by Blue Cross and other commercial health-plan insurers within the next several years.

Many more states will eventually follow the example of such states as New York, New Jersey, Massachusetts and Maryland in adopting all-payer control systems for hospital rates.

Other factors will also help hold down medical costs. One of these is the self-help approach to health. Americans are paying more attention to "wellness" via diet and exercise, a trend that is likely to expand as today's youngsters grow to adulthood and to persist among their Baby Boom parents who taught it to them. More and more employers will build such programs into their benefit regimes.

And this in turn will be reinforced by the trend to "cost sharing" in company health-care plans—meaning that employees will be picking up more of the tab with higher deductibles and special fees. Staying well becomes a better investment.

Another factor is that hospital usage will taper off substantially in favor of various lower-cost forms of care, including neighborhood clinics, group practices, home care, nursing and convalescent centers, hospices, outpatient surgery and so on.

And improved treatments and techniques, many of them stemming from biotechnology, will provide cheaper prevention and cure for many ailments that now require high-cost hospitalization and medication.

COMPUTER HELP

Computers also will hold down the rise in medical costs, using "expert systems" which will help physicians—and individuals on their own—to diagnose various ailments. Already in existence, these are "interactive" programs that lead to a diagnosis by a question-and-answer route. The software is written by physicians or other experts in a given field and is intended to reflect the best available professional information.

Simpler versions will be available for home use in diagnosing all sorts of conditions—including psychological upsets—and may cut down on resort to physicians and hospitals. At the least they will be helpful in directing individuals to the right kind of medical care, serving as a substitute for the fast-disappearing general practitioner.

Computers will also store treatment "protocols"—standard routines for various conditions and ailments which physicians and other health professionals will be required to follow. Via local and wide-area networks, doctors will be able to tap advice and knowledge from others and from large-scale data bases representing state-of-the-art experience in most specialties. Already in development are data banks of X-rays and microscope slides—digitalized images of every imaginable pathology—so a physician can compare them to the lab X-rays and slides of his current patient.

GROUP CARE

It is likely that the great majority of employed Americans will be served by one kind or another of prepaid group health practice within a decade—a health maintenance organization (HMO), individual practice association (IPA), preferred-provider organization (PPO) or other hybrid yet to be invented. Hospitals will set up their own HMOs; several already have. Ditto for some insurers.

It may take a decade or so for this mixture of coverage modes to sort itself out. Around the mid-'90s it is likely that a future presidential administration will move to put the entire health-care-reimbursement field on a new footing by requiring health-care providers to negotiate annual contracts for treating Medicare and Medicaid patients. These fees would be based on the diagnosis-related group ceilings and would be intended to cover the providers' estimated costs for the ensuing year.

This would require each of them to make careful actuarial estimates of their probable case load for the year ahead—meaning an analysis of the age mix and likely incidence of various ailments. Once agreed upon and contracted for, the annual fee would in each case relieve the government of its present burden of policing adherence to the DRG system, with all its paperwork and other overhead.

At the same time, it would give the health-care provider a clear idea of what its revenues will be for the contract year, which would put each insurer, HMO or other physician group under considerable pressure to hold down costs and stay within budget. And a few years of experience might result in a powerful restraint on the size of annual contract awards...depending on how tough the government is.

Meantime, state governments are taking their own hard look at ways to hold down costs for treating low-income individuals under Medicaid. Some already are experimenting with HMOs and fees negotiated in advance for the treatment of the poor. This system will probably spread throughout the country.

THE PROFESSION

In the long run, it is likely that independent practitioners will become a relative rarity, catering chiefly to the well-to-do who can afford a higher degree of medical attention than the average HMO member and acting as consultants and specialists on call by hospitals, clinics and HMOs. And a number of high-priced private clinics will continue to serve those who can afford them.

On average, physicians' real income is likely to slip as time goes on, because there will be so many of them and cost containment will restrain the rising of fees. The supply of physicians is nearing the glut stage, and medical school enrollments point to a worsening of the situation.

By 2000 or thereabouts, a majority of American doctors—although still on average the best paid in the world—probably will be on salary rather than self-employed. The right to practice various limited kinds of medicine will probably be extended to more non-physicians—nurses, paramedics, oral hygienists, acupuncturists, etc.

Salaried doctors will find themselves working under computer monitoring, too. Computers will keep track records on each, so that management can detect the under-achiever or the maverick who doesn't stick closely enough to the company guidebook on what treatment goes with what ailment.

SUPER HOSPITALS

Along with the consolidation of hospital ownership, the health business will see the rise of a couple dozen or so new nationwide corporations that some observers already are calling "supermeds." These will for the most part be vertically integrated, including in their stables HMOs, health insurance, hospitals, walk-in clinics, pharmacies, even facilities for dental care and mental illness treatment.

Such outfits will offer plug-in home-computer services, such as remote diagnostics and consultation. Remote monitoring too; patients' blood pressure and other vital signs can be checked without their having to report to the intake center in person. This will be a special convenience for old folks.

One area where cost controls will be especially tough is that of medical technology, where until DRGs came along it was assumed that any new device that could be purchased should be, at whatever cost the market would bear. The market—that is, the federal, state and private repayment systems—no longer is so willing to bear the multimillion-dollar cost of CT scanners, positron emission tomography devices, ultrasonic tomography machines and other state-of-the art inventions.

Because of the pressure to reduce hospital operating costs, the purchase of such equipment is shifting to group-practice organizations and the up-and-coming supermeds that will run many of them.

HIGH-TECH MEDICINE

New varieties of imaging machines are making it possible to zero in on disease, tumor and injury sites with far more accuracy and penetration than x-rays offer. Advances in understanding and treatment of such problems as Alzheimer's disease (premature senile dementia, now irreversible) and Down's syndrome (retardation, also irreversible) are expected in years to come, along with improved treatment of diseases and malfunctions of organs.

Other imaging techniques are under development that will operate at the microscopic level and even at the cellular level which, combined with electromagnetic devices, will facilitate gene engineering—the restructuring or combining of cells to treat a variety of diseases and genetic defects. This may in fact lead to the development of entirely new biotechnologies, extending even beyond medicine.

Biotechnology—gene engineering—is going to be the single biggest factor in improved health care. "Monoclonal antibodies" will increasingly replace radiation and chemotherapy for the treatment of cancer, tumors and other problems. These antibodies are genetically altered cells which carry the body's own anti-disease substances directly to the disease site. They also can be made to carry tiny radioactive charges to accomplish the same effect as radiotherapy, but with more impact and less body exposure.

Gene engineering will produce a variety of vaccines for different forms of cancer and other viral diseases and also will be used to deal with genetically caused conditions—i.e., inherited tendencies to disease or malfunction, such as Tay-Sachs disease and sickle-cell anemia. By 2000, it may also be effective against many kinds of retardation.

New or improved vaccines likely to turn up within five to ten years will deal with meningitis in infants, gonorrhea, whooping cough, influenza, several forms of diarrhea, types A and B of hepatitis, chicken pox, genital herpes, malaria and rabies.

One area in which it is sure to play a major role is that of brain and nerve-damage treatment. Within 10 years, researchers believe, they will have found ways to grow nerve tissue and replace damaged or missing brain tissue. Techniques are being tested on laboratory animals.

A key issue is the ability to isolate and manufacture special substances which occur naturally in the body, but in such tiny quantities that it is difficult even to isolate them. One animal experiment so far has promoted the regrowth of severed nerves in very thin implanted silicone tubes; another has spurred regeneration of brain tissue by employing implants of fetal brain matter.

Within a few more years it may be possible to replicate these results in humans on a wide scale, employing biotechniques to reproduce the required natural substances in sufficient quantity for general use; doctors at the University of Lund, Sweden, already have demonstrated this in a preliminary way with human patients.

And living brain and nerve tissues will be kept alive in special solutions to be ready for transplant and implant operations in treatment of stroke and other forms of brain hemorrhage and nerve impairment. New ways will be devised also to protect the brain during stroke until fresh supplies of blood and glucose can reach it.

Sometime around the end of the century it probably will be possible to regenerate parts of the central nervous system, including even the spinal cord. And treatment for back injuries and malfunctions, including nerve damage from ruptured disks, will be greatly enhanced.

Arthritis and related disorders are also in for dramatic new treatment. Researchers are working on ways to engineer changes in the body's immune system to get at the basic causes of many forms of arthritis. There are indications that a bacterium may cause rheumatoid arthritis and that genetic disease may be implicated in osteoarthritis. Cures are under intensive development, as are new materials and techniques for replacing joints and connective tissue, along with artificial materials for repairing bones.

A natural body substance called hyaluronic acid that occurs in the eye and in bone joints has been isolated and is being produced in commercial quantities via biotech fermentation processes. It will be used in renewing lubricating surfaces in worn and arthritic joints, restoring at least some function and reducing discomfort. It already has been used to treat racehorses and seems to have inherent therapeutic qualities against arthritis in addition to lubrication. British doctors have already used it on humans.

The coronary bypass operation for heart disease will be refined in the years ahead but will increasingly be superseded by other less heroic techniques that work as well or better in many cases. Lasers can be used to open closed arteries, and so can a technique employing a catheter and a tiny balloon which is inflated after insertion in a vein or artery to help clear out obstructions.

There also are high hopes for the treatment of acute heart attacks by the use of enzymes to break up clots quickly, limiting the extent of an attack and even undoing some of the damage on the spot. And new classes of drugs may soon replace digitalis for stimulating heart function. Other drugs are being tested for controlling arrhythmic heart disturbances which can bring on sudden cardiac arrest.

Genetic screening of individuals and whole groups to measure susceptibility to carcinogens and other environmental health hazards will be within reach around the year 2000. Just now, researchers aren't sure they can prove susceptibility varies among individuals and groups, but they THINK so. The whole issue raises some tricky legal and ethical questions, most of which boil down to who decides whether the indicated risk is worth taking (on the job, for example) and who bears the cost of taking it.

NEEDS OF THE AGED

Advances like these will be all the more important in an aging society, as ours will be. The rising proportion of elderly in the population will put stress on the entire medical care system to come up with improvements in geriatric therapy. And the elderly as voters as well as consumers of health care will be an increasingly potent lobby against reductions in Medicare in years to come.

The long-term health-care business will expand along with the elderly component of the population. Nursing homes and home health care both will share in this rise, with nursing homes alone expected to nearly double by 2000. Hospitals will get into this end of the business, some converting into extended-care facilities, others opening them as subsidiaries, including hospices where the incurably ill and dying can be given support. Medicare and Medicaid will increase their backing of such alternative-care centers as a further way to reduce dependence on hospitals, where most of the recent increases in cost have been centered.

And as the population ages, more insurance companies will develop long-term policies to pay for extended care of various kinds. Demand for such coverage will grow, and competition in price and benefits will be keen.

LEGAL ANGLES

In the meantime, most if not all the states will have enacted "living will" laws authorizing individuals to specify conditions under which terminal care can be limited or even withdrawn. But future medical discoveries will throw more light on what constitutes "irreversible" brain damage and may open new possibilities for treatment and even cures. And these may create enough uncertainty to keep the issue alive indefinitely—along with many "good-as-dead" patients.

At the low end of the scale, federal and state systems will have to make provision for those who can't afford a private group plan. Medicaid will probably go the same route as Medicare and most private medical service, with a system of per-service cost ceilings combined with negotiated annual-payment contracts between states and HMOs or other group practices. This will put providers on their toes to stay within a budget.

THE HANDICAPPED

Being physically handicapped in America will be less a burden in coming years than it is now. Technology is going to produce a number of advances in the way missing or incapacitated limbs and senses can be substituted for. The results will be uneven, with greater progress in some areas than others, but the overall effect will be to integrate handicapped persons more fully into the society and economy, upgrading their status, quality of life and productivity.

Implants already are providing some relief for hearing-impaired people whose auditory nerves are still intact. An implanted "multi-channel cochlear" device in the inner ear creates a stimulus that can be sensed and, while it hasn't yet reproduced speech, is useful as a supplement to lip reading. With continued refinements, it probably will reach the speech-recognition level well before the year 2000.

For those deaf from birth there is the prospect of a sound-representation system which, through a combination of micro-phone, electrodes and vibrators, will be able to produce recognizable patterns. The device will be installed on the arm or across the stomach and will create stimuli—"feelies," if you will—which the wearer will, with training, be able to decipher as representations of speech. This still has a long way to go and involves intensive training; but it is a ray of hope for the profoundly deaf.

HELP FOR THE BLIND

A paperless Braille system has already been invented. It's a machine that accepts impulses from a text source, either an optical disc or regular printed page "read" by an optical character recognition (OCR) device. The impulses from the text activate a "feeler" panel, on which short, blunt wire points are raised and lowered a fraction of an inch to reproduce Braille symbols that the blind person reads. Costs are high on current prototypes but will come down as the technology is refined and more units are produced. The special disks will be much less bulky than conventional Braille books.

And for blind people who aspire to authorship and editing jobs, there will be computerized word-processing systems with Braille keys and a voice-playback editing system. The writer will be able to hear his work read back by a machine voice which, though it will take some getting used to, will repeat words and even punctuation marks. Editing will be done verbally via a voice-recognition system programmed to understand the blind user's particular way of speaking. Such systems exist now in prototype and are very expensive, but the cost will decline in coming years.

Efforts to replicate vision through skin stimuli have not been successful. Electrodes or microchips implanted in the brain are still just a theory and are unlikely to work until a great deal more research has been done; mark these down for the new century.

But there may be hope for the blind in work being done with nerve regeneration. Experiments already have indicated that severed or damaged nerves can be regrown at least to some extent in other parts of the body. It is probable that sometime in the early part of the 21st century this will be true of optic nerves.

In the meantime, there is a great need for additional computer software programs for the blind to make it easier for them to work at home or in offices on specially prepared computers. These would open new employment opportunities for them—and new business opportunties for software writers.

IMPROVED MOTOR SKILLS

For people with impaired use of limbs, there are two exciting prospects: nerve-tissue regeneration and "robot" augmentation. The latter can take several forms; the term "robot" here is used in its generic sense—meaning an automated device to perform programmed functions.

For the profoundly handicapped with minimal or no control of arms and legs, these robotic devices may operate by means of "functional electrical stimulation." This means systems by which the individual uses whatever communication method he has available—voice, eye motion, breath, biting, shoulder shrugs or fingers, if operable—to activate battery-powered servomechanisms which give motion and strength to braces on limbs or to robotic devices that take the place of missing limbs.

Machines of this type already have helped paraplegics to "walk" in laboratory conditions. By 2000, perhaps sooner, they will be helping the paralyzed or semi-paralyzed to accomplish a broad range of functions.

Technology of this kind has been applied to battery-operated wheelchairs. It's done with microcomputers that can recognize signals—delivered, say, by nods of the head—and translate them into operating instructions. In some experiments it has even been possible for the profoundly handicapped to transmit signals through the skin by use of nerve potential—a technique that requires considerable training and conditioning. In years just ahead, technology developed in other areas—such as space research, computers and communications—may invent a way to guide a wheelchair by means of a light beam projected ahead.

The same goes for the "dynamic braces" and "walking braces" discussed above—prosthetic devices operated by very small motors and microchips and batteries and controlled by voice or other kinds of signals. These would be designed to imitate the normal motion of an arm or leg and to assist the crippled member in functioning. Technology that would make this possible already exists; it has been used in space, for example, to manipulate remotely operated mechanisms. Applying it to the earthbound handicapped should be only a matter of time.

The development of such equipment will be expensive, and so will be the devices themselves, when they are ready for use. Funding won't be easy to find. The private sector tends to pour money only into products for which the eventual demand is so great that a clear pay-off is visible. With some 20 million physically impaired people in American society today, and with the population aging, there *should* be ample financial incentive, but focusing capital on particular problems is often not easy.

One way out of this bind would be government tax incentives to employers to hire handicapped people and loan guarantees to manufacturers to produce equipment that will open jobs to them. These would cost something, of course—but less in the long run than doing nothing to give handicapped individuals a better chance to be productive.

MENTAL HEALTH

Treatment of mental problems is going to develop along radically new lines in the next couple of decades, and so will our attitudes toward them.

It is increasingly being recognized that many if not most severe mental disabilities—such as schizophrenia, manic depression, and susceptibility to drug and alcohol abuse—have their origins in brain chemistry, and that is where fixes will be sought.

"Molecular psychiatry" is the name given to this approach, and it is going to supplement and even supplant much of the conventional analytical treatment of personality and mental disorders that has prevailed since the time of Freud.

The use of chemicals to alter behavior is anything but new, of course; people have been using them at least since the discovery of alcohol. What is new is the growing understanding of ways the brain reacts to and attempts to correct its own malfunctions. And the fast-growing science of biomedicine is playing a central role in this.

Within coming decades more of the links of mind to body will be untangled, and it will become possible to diagnose and anticipate aberrations and to treat them biologically—and even to expand normal abilities and intelligence.

Some of the milestones that will be passed, although not necessarily in this order, include these:

▶ A treatment and possibly a preventive for Alzheimer's disease, as mentioned previously—a growing problem in an aging population.

▶ The cloning and production of natural substances to prevent or control depression, manic-depressive disease, schizophrenia and other disorders that are now subject only to palliatives.

► Monitored treatment programs to alter criminal behavior.

► Ways to anticipate and head off addiction to alcohol and some drugs.

► Methods for counteracting fetal brain damage and for treatment of nerve disorders such as Parkinson's disease by use of brain chemicals and implantation of nerve tissue.

But most impressive of all—and of deepest significance to society and the economy—is the prospect of perfecting a broad range of treatments for mental disorders that currently account for a large share of the 50 million or so Americans now totally or partially disabled by them. This will mean big gains in human productivity and reductions in medical, custodial and social expenditures.

These techniques, growing in part out of advances in brain biology studies employing recombinant DNA, won't be emptying out the mental hospitals any time soon—but progress will be incremental year by year and, as new discoveries come along, probably explosive.

The flip side of brain biology is the new field of pyschoneuroimmunology, in which the psychological stress of one's social environment and trauma has been found to have substantial biological consequences. The physical effects of prolonged grief and fear have been known since prehistoric times. But only recently has it become clear that grief or fear can also cause the weakening of the human immune system, leading to such ailments as rheumatoid arthritis, allergies, diabetes or even cancer. From such revelations will grow new forms of treatment.

The same outlook applies to discoveries that the brain produces its own "uppers" and "downers" called endogenous lygans. They are substances that can mute pain and produce psychological "highs"—that good feeling when everything seems to be going right; these substances can even mask pain.

Scientists believe they can produce a whole new class of drugs replicating these and other endogenous substances capable of enhancing normal states, including creativity and recall. Being of human origin and not simply "chemical," these drugs presumably would not carry the danger of addiction or harmful side effects.

And science is taking seriously the belief that positive attitudes and emotions can help keep the immune system in shape and ward off disease, something folk medicine has always known without knowing why.

Psychological uses of light, for example, are being recognized for a population that lives in urban darkness. "Seasonal Affective Disorder"—or SAD, appropriately enough—is common in northern latitudes, with their long winter nights, and among many elderly people everywhere. Lights are being turned on, literally and figuratively, for treatment of SAD and even for some forms of leukemia, countering jet lag and for boosting worker productivity in offices and factories.

Along with rapid advances in the study of brain chemistry, the development of improved brain-scanning devices is helping to build understanding of what happens in a brainstorm.

Commercial possibilities grow out of all this research. A "neuroscience" industry may develop in several related fields, including pharmaceuticals, chemicals and information technology, over the next couple of decades.

Brain science is essentially the study of how electrical impulses are transmitted through the infinitely complex neural networks that make up the brain. Unraveling these events at the molecular and cellular levels may someday lead to development of a "biochip" patterned after the functioning of the brain and this, as our chapter on computers explains, could have enormous economic importance.

As our understanding of the true nature of mental health and mental disease broadens, much of the stigma attached to aberrational behavior will fall away.

Reliance on short-term therapy and "crisis intervention" will continue to be relied on to help keep troubled people on an even keel. Resort to such techniques may in fact grow, as a feature of employee-assistance programs, while the use of extended therapy declines—both because the latter is so costly and the former so often more effective.

The professions of psychiatry and psychology will move into closer alliances with other fields of medicine and science—especially psychopharmacology. While not abandoning the traditional talk-it-out methods of personality analysis and crisis intervention, specialists will come to rely on a far broader range of tools than is now available.

And life in the new century will be better for it.

DENTAL HEALTH

America's case of dental dread should be fairly well over by the turn of the century. New techniques and medications now under development will have eliminated or greatly reduced most of the mouth problems people take to dentists, and the profession will undergo a massive transformation to accommodate itself to this new state of affairs.

And the 50% of the population that now never sees a dentist may succumb to the bright promise of no-pain dental care—if they need professional care at all. (Some dentists are already using a painless acid wash, with no anesthetic and no drilling, to clean away tooth decay before filling a cavity.)

Fluoridation, the single greatest advance in dental health since the toothbrush, is slowly spreading across the country. About 55% of the population now has access to fluoridated water supplies, and by 2000 this should rise close to 100%.

By 1990 there will be an oral vaccine to kill the bacteria that cause most tooth decay, and it will be given to young children as well as adults. One dose will last six months, and an implant version will also be available. The use of synthetic-resin sealants to prevent cavities is already spreading and within a few more years will be the general practice. The cost, now a few dollars per tooth, will decline rapidly. The treatment will last several years.

By 2000 or so, replacement tooth enamel synthesized from the real thing via biotechnology will be available for the repair of teeth that somehow escape early protective measures. This stuff will be virtually indistinguishable from natural tooth enamel, will replace gold, silver and the plastic materials now in use, and may outlast them too.

And one of these years a vaccine against oral herpes will be found, and cold sores will become obsolete. Research into the natural defenses in human saliva may bring additional anti-infection discoveries.

Since the treatment of tooth decay is the mainstay of the dental professional today, and it's kids who get tooth decay most, an aging population and the conquering of decay will reduce the demand for traditional dental services.

But the aging American population will live longer than ever and keep their teeth longer than before, so dental maintenance for the elderly will be a growing business.

They'll be in the market for preservatives and protections for exposed tooth roots—a common problem among the aging. An antimicrobial mouth rinse already available in Europe and awaiting approval by the U.S. government will help greatly—but first, scientists must find a way to keep it from turning teeth brown.

As for bridgework and dental plates, their use will diminish as improved implant and transplant techniques are developed. The National Institute of Dental Research, part of the government's National Institutes of Health, is making progress toward all the innovations described above.

But while teeth are getting better, the dental profession is not feeling so well. There is a glut of dentists today and real income, adjusted for inflation, is falling for many of them—in part the result of too much federal encouragement of dental studies in recent decades.

Economics will take care of some of the glut. Dental school enrollments will shrink, as student aid becomes less available and the word gets around that dentistry is not as remunerative as it once was.

The dentists who persevere and prosper will specialize: Geriatrics, orthodontics, periodontics, root-canal work, oral surgery and so on. But at the same time, non-dentist practitioners will take over some of the market—independent oral hygienists to do routine cleaning and maintenance and denturists to provide denture care.

And more and more of all dental professionals will be working as salaried employees of health-care corporations of one kind or another.

12

Agricultural Plenty

Coming soon: a vast increase in American agricultural productivity, far more than enough to offset losses of cropland to erosion, development and water salinity or scarcity.

This surge in productivity will be the result of accelerated mechanization of farming and breakthroughs in genetic engineering. American farms—fewer, larger, employing fewer people, and using less water—will continue to produce more food than this country alone can consume. There will be surpluses aplenty for export, but the demand for this surplus will be unpredictable among countries that will also be experiencing productivity gains.

So commodity prices and consumer food prices will stay low, probably lagging the rate of inflation. The variety of foods—including some you may never have heard of—will be almost endless, and the quality will be excellent.

Here are some of the technological gains already achieved or just over the horizon:

Computerized monitoring of crops, livestock and operations, employing remote sensors.

Gene manipulation to produce bigger, healthier and more productive livestock, grains, fruits and vegetables.

Manipulated microbes to neutralize contaminant chemicals, fight crop diseases, fertilize the soil and even prevent plant freezing.

Remote-controlled robots, including tractors and other farm machinery, to till the fields via computer programs.

Computerized control of farm systems, such as ventilation, irrigation, livestock feeding, sanitation and the like.

FEWER BUT LARGER FARMS

We'll get all this abundance from fewer individual farms than today—and from fewer crop acres. These will produce the great bulk of production, while a large number of small family farms will also manage to survive, as they do today, in part because their owners will increasingly be part-timers who have other jobs too. Foreign investment in farm land will continue to grow, as it has since World War II. The federal government won't interfere, but some states will.

Technology is capital-intensive; it can pay off handsomely but it doesn't come cheap. And farmers will be less able than today to count on the federal government for support. Price supports may be cut heavily as Washington digs into its long-term problem of reducing the deficit and controlling budget growth. Farm programs may even be trimmed back to a sort of "safety net" level—some minimum level of intervention.

If this happens, farming will be more on its own than it is now in terms of finding financing and in competing in world markets. There will still be plenty of local-level financing available to farmers, despite the continuing shakeout among rural and small-town banks. Enough will survive to meet local needs.

World population will grow by 20%, at present rates, by 2000. Some forecasters see a similar increase in demand for U.S. food and fiber. This may be as good a guess as any, but foreign demand is difficult to forecast with any precision for a lot of obvious reasons, weather being one of them.

The U.S. doesn't have a monopoly of high technology. The same wave of change that is sweeping America's farms will begin to have significant effects in other parts of the world as well. It already is showing up in France and Australia and might yet in Russia. Other producing countries, such as Argentina, are keeping a close watch on this trend. And as it spreads, overproduction in the U.S. may turn out to be a harder problem to control in 2000 than it is today. Financing of large-scale commodity purchases by Third World countries will require more international cooperation than is possible now. Problems of Third World debt have to be resolved first. In any event, volatility in supply and demand—unforeseen ups and downs—will persist; it may get worse.

AGRICULTURAL BIOTECH

Biotechnology for farming is just approaching its takeoff stage. It holds enormous promise, but turning promise into reality and making it profitable won't happen overnight. The next 15 years or so will see more and more "engineered" products coming into play in agriculture, but it will be 2000 or a bit later before these are in large-scale use. Gene-splicing will play a major role in this future.

Using techniques that are still being developed and improved upon, researchers can use genetic engineering to produce some of the following:

▶ Growth hormones imprinted with specific instructions. The size of cows and their milk production will be increased dramatically, for example.

▶ New strains of corn that will require far less water and make more efficient use of sunlight, thereby helping meet two problems at once, water scarcity and low productivity.

▶ New kinds of bacteria that will devour soil contaminants and render them harmless; fix nitrogen on plant roots and reduce the need for fertilizer; prevent freezing of crops; kill "bad" bugs.

▶ "Bioregulants" imbedded in plants to give chemical signals to plant genes, thereby producing larger yields on healthier plants and reducing the need for fertilizers and insecticides.

▶ Healthier hogs and other livestock, using vaccines that can control or eradicate viral-caused diseases such as pseudorabies in hogs (and perhaps lead to or benefit from discoveries in viral infections of humans, such as AIDS).

▶ Improvements in vegetables to enable them to withstand insects, nematodes, chemical herbicides, competition from weeds and variations in temperature and salinity.

▶ "Designer" fruits and vegetables better suited to mechanical harvesting and artificial maturation processes, speeding them to market.

▶ Improved photosynthesis in plants for faster growth and higher yields, perhaps as much as 50% higher for such crops as wheat and soybeans.

Biotech advances such as these will lead to greater use of confinement techniques for livestock; the risk of spreading animal disease in close quarters will be greatly reduced or even eliminated. The effect will be greater production in smaller quarters—i.e., higher productivity, lower costs.

NEW CASH CROPS?

Other new crops for mostly nonfood uses are probable, although it will be 2000 or later before they are feasible on a large scale. It usually takes decades to develop new crops to the point where quality seed is available and growers are interested in switching from other crops. Soybeans, for example, took over 100 years to reach full development in the U.S., even though they have been domesticated for over a thousand years.

Biotechnology will speed the process. Take, for example, euphorbia, jojoba, meadowfoam, and guayule. Any or all of these unfamiliar plants may one day join the soybean as an important contributor to the daily lives of Americans. Their products might clean floors, wax cars or even lubricate jet engines . . . or provide "synthetic petroleum" and a new source of rubber.

Euphorbia is called "the gasoline plant." It contains a substance with a molecular structure close to that of crude oil. Wild euphorbia can produce the equivalent of up to 10 barrels of crude hydrocarbon a year per acre. Cultivated and gene-altered plants will do far better. In fact, experts foresee yields of 50 barrels an acre. This would be a low-sulfur product that refineries could use with a minimum of contamination. Euphorbia is adaptable to cultivation in the Southwest, but oil prices would have to soar to make it feasible—not a likely prospect any time soon. So put this on hold for the next century.

Jojoba produces a liquid wax similar to sperm-whale oil—a high-quality lubricant—and could become an excellent substitute, if jojoba can be adapted to large-scale commercial production; it does well in semiarid areas. But this calls for further research, and until better methods arrive, costs of obtaining liquid wax from jojoba remain prohibitive. (Jojoba already has established itself as an ingredient in cosmetics and shampoos.)

Meadowfoam is an oilseed planted in late fall. Scientists see it as a promising source of industrial oils. Development work is being carried out in the Pacific Northwest. Crambe shows promise for yielding a high-smoke-point lubricating oil suitable for ultra-hot applications.

Guayule, a flowering shrub growing wild in southwest Texas, produces rubber in amounts of up to 20% of its own dry weight. Guayule rubber is chemically and physically identical to natural Asian rubber, which now accounts for about 97% of the world's natural supply. It could turn out to be a more reasonable source of synthetic rubber than petroleum, as well as a good alternative to the natural product.

Neem trees, now being commercially grown in India, Africa, Latin America and the Caribbean, produce natural insecticides and insect repellants that are biodegradable, meaning they do no damage to the natural environment. A half dozen other plants have similar qualities, though not quite as promising as the neem tree. The U.S. Agriculture Dept. is experimenting with them as potential crops for dry or semiarid areas.

Showy Milkweed contains a number of potentially commercial chemicals, no one of which is economical to produce by itself but which taken all together might make this a viable crop. It has promise as a substitute crop on western land where irrigation may have to be given up, as well as on other marginal lands.

Tobacco leaves, when young, produce a high-quality protein that may yet serve as a nutritional food supplement or for use in jelling or thickening food products. But this has yet to be developed beyond the pilot stage.

WATER WORRIES

Water—rather, the lack of it—will present a problem for agriculture but not an unsolvable one. Adjustments will have to be made, some of them painful but none impossible. The problem is twofold: potential shortages and pollution.

Continued depletion of the water-bearing strata (the Ogallala aquifer) that underlie much of the Great Plains will eventually force a swing back to dryland farming in the Plains states. As it is, farmers are "mining" the aquifer—withdrawing water faster than it can be naturally replaced. This could bring things to a critical point in widespread areas by 2000. It already has begun to affect farming in parts of the Texas Panhandle, parts of the Southwest and Far West.

The first remedial steps are being taken: shifts in irrigation techniques to use less water. Canals and sluiceways are being lined to reduce seepage; control systems are being improved and even computerized; and "drip irrigation"—a very slow, timed release of small amounts of water—is becoming more common. Such systems may reduce consumption by as much as 50%.

Pollution, particularly salt buildup, is a tougher problem and may not be solvable before 2000, if then. Reverse-osmosis purification techniques are coming into use in the Far West to produce potable water from brackish stuff, but this is still too costly for widespread farm use and probably will remain so beyond 2000. The salt buildup occurs for a number of reasons, one being the increasing saltiness of the Colorado River—a prime source of irrigation in much of the West—due in part to dams and diversions over recent decades.

Another cause is the accumulation of salts in irrigated soils where runoff is insufficient to flush them away, as rain would do if it were abundant, and in subsoils impervious to seepage.

Whatever the cause, salt buildup and sinking water tables are forcing western agriculture to look ahead to new techniques and new crops. The Texas Panhandle will probably shift from cotton to cattle in the next several years. By 2000, much of the High Plains will be into cattle ranching and dry farming with minimal or no tillage. As water grows too expensive for farming, parts of the Southwest will shift from irrigated agriculture to industrial and urban development.

Meantime, Congress is reducing subsidies for water projects in the West, forcing the pace of conversion. Whether anything resembling a comprehensive national water policy with programs to match will be developed before 2000 is still questionable. The high cost of any large-scale efforts—say, desalinization or diversion—doesn't fit with the long-term need to reduce government deficits.

SALINE FARMING

Western farmers will have to start thinking soon about substitute crops that need less water. Many of the plants mentioned earlier as having potential for producing substitutes for oils, waxes and chemicals are well suited to dryland cultivation. Grain amaranth, a high producer of protein, could become a crop of choice. And biotechnology, as noted earlier, will help by producing new strains of plants that can get by in semiarid conditions. But between now and 2000, the picture is one of technology in a race with growing water stringency.

Then there are the halophytes. Remember that word; it identifies plants that can grow in salty environments. Science and industry are paying a lot more attention to them.

Something like a dozen out of the thousands known to exist have so far been found to have promise as crops, some of them rich in protein, others suited to profitable nonfood uses:

▶ A strain of corn developed at the University of Arizona.

▶ New strains of tomatoes and barley.

▶ Salicornia, that produces polyunsaturated oil at a better yield than soybeans.

▶ Atriplex, said to yield as much animal feed as alfalfa and capable of several harvests a year.

▶ Mangrove, which has the ability to thrive in seawater and has helped stabilize or create shorelines and islands up and down the coast of Florida and other tropical and subtropical areas.

▶ Chinese tallow tree, which gives nuts, feeds honey bees and makes good firewood.

Salt-tolerant crops might be one answer to the problem of increasing salinization in western and Great Plains areas of the U.S., as well as other parts of the world. The Japanese have known about edible halophytes for a long time. (Check out the seaweed dishes the next time you visit a Japanese restaurant.) Americans will be learning a lot more about them, too.

PREDICTING THE WEATHER

Millions and billions of dollars in values lost or gained through crop failures alone make climatological forecasting a high-stakes affair, to say nothing of the military implications of having better information than anyone else. And yet it is still pretty much a riverboat gambler's shot.

Advances in weather forecasting accuracy are on the way, with improved 30-day outlooks due in another few years. These will depend on a massive computer model of the entire atmospheric envelope, incorporating such elements as solar radiation, ocean temperatures, infrared earth radiation, physical interactions and other data. But the problem IS the data: There's just not enough, not of high enough quality, and this is where a breakthrough is needed.

Our weather travels from west to east on the prevailing winds—and while there is plenty of local variation, the major patterns should be fairly easy to detect. Yet they aren't, because meteorologists still don't know enough about long-range, large-scale variations and how they develop.

Hence the mystification over the weird weather of the early 1980s, the misbehavior of "El Nino," a Pacific Ocean hot spot which became a household word around the world as anchovy fishing fell apart, crops failed and baffling wide swings in high and low temperatures besieged North America and other parts of the globe.

Weather forecasting may become less of a crap shoot as this century ends, if steps are taken to make use of technology available today but still viewed as too costly to employ. One of these methods is "ocean acoustic tomography," a technique for measuring temperature variations at various depths in the oceans. It would involve the planting of sensors in strategic places, reading their output via satellites and analyzing the data on super computers.

Applied to the Pacific, which is our chief "weather engine," it would make it possible to spot and track movements in subsurface hot spots which, as in the case of El Nino, determine the major weather patterns for months or even years ahead. Combined with such conventional measures as surface-temperature monitoring, upper-atmosphere wind tracking and the like, this could give us a much more reliable look ahead at climatological things to come.

We expect the high value of this outcome—in both economic and military terms—will make the investment attractive to future U.S. administrations. We would then know a LOT more about our own crop prospects (and those of the Russians) than we even dream of now.

AUTOMATION IN THE FIELDS

Computers, automation and robots will have an increasing role to play on tomorrow's large farms, as we said earlier. Most of these farms, and a good many smaller ones, already are managed by computers—farmers keeping their accounts, crop records, yields, inventories, etc., on a microcomputer.

Computers will even have a place inside animals. Microchips implanted under the skin of cows and other livestock will be used to monitor and report on vital signs.

Out in the acreage, infrared sensors will monitor field conditions, report on temperature and dryness, and detect abnormal temperature changes in animals, reporting all this information to central computers in the office.

Technology may also produce electrostatic means of spraying insecticides to reduce amounts needed and improve coverage. This, along with some of the biotech prospects mentioned above, will greatly reduce agricultural consumption of fertilizers and insecticides—a point not lost on the major producers of those chemicals. Most such firms have been investing in seed companies to cover their bets; there will be more of this in the years ahead.

Computers armed with new, specialized software will play an increasing decision-support role for farmers and farm managers, helping in choices between various alternatives, helping plan planting and feeding schemes, anticipating various contingencies in price, growing conditions, markets and profit margins. New "expert systems" will help farmers and managers in threading their way through complex situations by applying systematic analysis and seeking out optimum solutions. (For more on expert systems, see our chapter on computers.)

Market information will flood in on computerized networks to supplement what's available today by radio, telephone and teletype. This system will span the world, with fresh information available from all points on computer screens and printers. Farmers will have access to vast data bases for help in making all kinds of decisions and, for the very biggest spreads, to satellite readings on field conditions.

Coming improvements in robotics will make it possible for the bigger farms to employ remote control of machinery and equipment. Sensitive feedback loops will give work-station controls the "feel" of the field itself, and operators watching TV monitors will be able to plow, harvest and perform other field operations as though in the driver's seat. Other systems—feeding, watering, ventilating and the like—will be computer-controlled in ways that respond to changing conditions, including emergencies. Systems will be sensitive enough also to allow for variations—"micro-programs" within programs.

FARM SERVICES

A whole new farm-service industry will grow up to meet special needs of the major farms and many medium-sized ones...financial counseling, management, advisory services and the like. Many larger farms will need compliance services—that is, help in meeting investors' and lenders' demands for information, in tax reporting and in monitoring performance generally. Farm business consultants will help managers select and meet performance objectives and work out marketing plans. Software designers and computer consultants, along with management consultants, will specialize in farm systems. Some of the larger farm co-ops already are beginning to get into this. A new kind of market adviser/crop broker will emerge to help develop marketing strategies.

And, to repeat what we said earlier, abundance will continue. Whatever the problems faced by American agriculture, meeting demand won't be one of them. This will continue to be the best-fed country in the world. We'll still have enough to sell and give away abroad.

13

Transport and Travel

American transportation will look much the same at the beginning of the new century as it does today—despite progress toward computer-guided cars, magnetic levitation trains, hypersonic planes, and other new ways of propelling ourselves around the landscape.

The automobile will still be the chief mode of personal transport; in fact, auto travel will grow by a third—and that means worsening traffic jams. Truck traffic will grow a lot more—80% or so—adding to those jams. Both truck and auto travel growth will be faster than the rate of population increase, reflecting rising prosperity.

Air travel also will rise. Improved planes will make profits for airlines but attract so much additional travel demand that airports and the air-traffic-control system will be under increasing strain.

Rail will hold its own as a bulk carrier, but prospects for major technological improvements in railroads are uncertain until well into the new century.

Urban mass transit will continue to struggle for place in the swarm of auto traffic, doing so without much federal help—meaning limited net growth, since most local and state jurisdictions won't be able on their own to build or expand such systems enough to make a major dent.

ON THE ROAD

Whether traffic congestion problems become severe enough to bring about a large-scale federal response is conjectural. It could happen within the time span we're talking about, but there are no portents of that now and there are some reasons for doubt. If we read the political auguries accurately, the American electorate will not be any more ready to launch vast federal spending programs ten or fifteen years from now than it is at present.

The spreading out of metropolitan areas will, in the meantime, continue to complicate the art of commuting. The traditional in-out pattern of suburb-to-city-and-back-again commuting has ceased to be the dominant one. Most commuters are traveling within the suburbs, seldom venturing into the central city, a pattern that is sure to grow.

To hold down government spending, developers and businesses will routinely be required to provide supplemental road systems and mass transit facilities to serve new areas of population concentration. There will also be more outer beltways— concentric rings of highways around large metropolitan areas.

Interstate highways will need considerable fixing-up, since the system is now nearing 30 years old—to say nothing of lesser roads and bridges. The current federal aid program for such "infrastructure" may have to be extended. Still, simple resurfacing rather than rebuilding may be enough to keep most of the interstate system going. Many older, dangerous bridges could be replaced with cheap mass-engineered structures, or simply shut down and the traffic rerouted in the case of the more lightly traveled ones.

Local and state governments will be shouldering most of the fix-up burden for their own roadways, given probable cuts in federal assistance. This means the quality of local road systems will vary widely—along with the economic health of localities. Older, failing cities in the Northeast and Midwest may have to learn to live with their potholes.

Highways everywhere will need some refitting to take into account the fact that trucks are growing in both size and number, while cars are growing in number but shrinking in size. For improved highway safety, look for more separation of cars and trunks by lane.

The cities, many of which already have fallen far behind in maintenance and modernization of traffic-control systems, will face a worsening problem as the driving population expands and within it, the number of old folks. The over-65s will be a rising proportion of the citizenry beyond the year 2000, and their accident rates are consistently higher than average. More of the elderly will be able to afford cars, while their reliance on them grows—due in large part to the shortcomings of mass transit, particularly in the suburbs where most of them live.

Electronics can play a large part in meeting problems of this kind and probably will, limited by cost. Autos will be smaller and hence more vulnerable to impact; yet they will contain an increasing number of early-warning systems to alert drivers to danger. Highway controls over speed and density of traffic can be built into the pavement; several countries, most notably West Germany, are experimenting with such systems. But the high cost of installation in this country's many thousands of miles of roadway probably means it will be put off for decades.

IN THE AIR

Airline travel will grow some 5% a year in the U.S. and a bit more than that internationally. Capacity will be up more than 50% worldwide by the mid-'90s; over a third of that growth will be American, with only a small part going into long-range travel, the rest into medium and short-range.

The propeller will make a comeback in high-speed aircraft by the '90s, technology having cured its two worst drawbacks (noise and vibration), and this will lead to a rebirth of propjet technology at near-supersonic speeds and at fuel economies of 40% to 50%—which will mean a revitalization of the market for business planes and other short-haul aircraft.

Greatly improved versions of short-takeoff and vertical-takeoff planes are in the works. Major U.S. and British manufacturers are close to producing both military and commercial models. The vertical takeoff planes will be employed chiefly as commuter and corporate aircraft and will be capable of landing and taking off in close quarters, such as the tops of office buildings, unused city piers and special pads. They'll behave a lot like helicopters but at less cost and improved stability. Hybrid, tilt-rotor, vertical-takeoff craft will be developed for special high-altitude, thin-air fields like those at Denver and Mexico City.

New designs and new engines incorporating ceramic technology may even make the supersonic transport (SST) a profitable plane. New versions may have vastly improved distance capabilities and might be able to fly nonstop from the U.S. to Australia at a profit, which the Concorde cannot do. There probably will be enough wealthy people in a hurry to support a small fleet of such super-SSTs.

The hypersonic space plane is still one for the sci-fi types, although it is coming closer. Research funding has been proposed for a rocket-like plane (Reagan's "Orient Express") that will be shot into the stratosphere from, say, New York and arrive two hours later in Tokyo. Look for commercially viable projects like this no sooner than early in the new century.

Which countries and which companies will build coming generations of commercial air transports is still up for grabs. The dominant plane in world fleets in the '90s is likely to be a 150-passenger jet. The multinational European Airbus project aims to fill this gap before U.S. manufacturers can get moving.

Japan may have an entry of its own as well. U.S. manufacturers want our government to lend them a hand via relaxation of antitrust laws to promote more cooperation on research and development and to explore with other countries the possibilities of joint production programs. But if European governments carry out their seeming intention to "target" heavy resources on development of the Airbus, including subsidies and market protections, it may already be too late, although the improved propjet planes mentioned above could mean intense competition for the Airbus.

U.S. firms are likely to retain their lead in the larger widebody transports, especially as super computers become available for rapid modeling and analysis of aircraft and component design, along with expected major improvements in engine technology. Developmental work already is underway on a proposed 600-seat jumbo airliner.

Commuter airlines will more than double their growth in the next decade or so, continuing to take over local routes given up by the bigs, becoming local-service carriers and expanding the number of cities they serve. They will be heavy users of upgraded propjets.

Business flying also will grow, and more of it will be done in expensive, sophisticated turbine-powered planes, the number of which is likely to double before 2000. Turbine-powered helicopters in business use will grow some 7% a year, although the steep-and-vertical takeoff planes mentioned above may begin to cut into this before long. Plastic planes are likely to take over much of the general-aviation market within a decade or less . ... fiber-reinforced plastic bodies lighter and stronger than anything now on the market. Highly fuel efficient, especially when fitted with new, computer-designed configurations, wings and tail assemblies.

Few if any new major airports will be built in the rest of this century. Enlargement of existing ones or addition of smaller, satellite airports is the more likely development. To try to keep ahead of the rise in congestion, local governments will turn increasingly to higher landing fees and tighter scheduling. These will be aimed mostly at general and business aviation, with the objective of spacing their landings and takeoffs to avoid peak hours and keep them out of the way of commercial airliners.

Airport authorities will be under pressure to improve their internal traffic circulation on the ground—to find ways to move passengers and freight in and out with less delay. But this is going to be expensive, and federal assistance on any massive scale is unlikely until at least the early '90s.

Technology will help meet the problem of air congestion but won't solve it. The federal government will develop and install improved traffic-control equipment around the country and require airlines to use collision-avoidance equipment now becoming available. Super computers will also take over more of traffic control and scheduling, smoothing out glitches and overloads. Measures of this kind will probably enable the system to just barely keep up with the increase in air traffic until late this century, when vastly improved technology may come along.

RAIL TRAVEL

High-speed intercity rail travel won't make great progress in this country until the cost comes down dramatically, and there isn't much sign that it will in the next couple of decades.

"Bullet trains" of the kind operating in Japan and France are under study for use in such routes as Washington-New York-Boston or San Fransisco-Los Angeles. But governments that can't provide a smooth roadbed for conventional slow-pokey trains aren't about to indulge in the multibillion-dollar investments such projects entail—and neither is private industry.

But railroads will install new electronic devices to improve their safety, communications and reliability. Microprocessors will cut energy use in locomotives and replace manpower in monitoring brakes and other systems during freight hauls. Ceramic engine technology may make turbines cost effective for high-speed power plants before the turn of the century.

"Maglev" (for "magnetic levitation") trains are over the horizon. Based on the repulsion between the same poles of two powerful magnets, these run not on wheels, but glide on a micro-thin layer of air, kept just above a steel-and-concrete guideway by magnetic repulsion. Potential top speeds range from 250 miles an hour to 350. A test train in Germany already has hit 180, faster than any other existing conventional train. The maglev isn't just fast—it's quiet and won't jump the track.

Serious study projects of this technology are underway in several countries and in several areas of the U.S. The closest to realization is a 250-mile route that would run from Los Angeles to Las Vegas along the median strip of Interstate 15. Florida is looking into a maglev line connecting Miami, Tampa and Orlando.

Just one problem, and it's a familiar one: Cost. A maglev rail system could be built in five to ten years if a well-financed start were made right now—meaning it would be ready to go just about the time improved engine technology is expected to lower the cost of air travel. So put maglev and similar technologies down for the 21st century—barring a jump in energy prices to the crisis level. In the meantime, conventional and affordable means of transportation will win out over the exotic and expensive.

HOME AWAY FROM HOME

Travel of all sorts, for business and pleasure, will increase, and every field related to travel will benefit.

But there will be a surplus of hotel rooms the rest of this decade and into the next, due to overeager speculative building brought on by favorable tax laws and foreign investment.

Foreigners are buying up or building hotels all over the country in prime locations, figuring this to be one of the safest ways to park capital for the long haul. They are right, up to a point; but the point may be reached sooner than anticipated. Competition also is intensified by the increasing participation of conglomerates in the hotel business.

That's not bad news for the traveler, of course. Rates will have to be competitive wherever overbuilding has become a problem.

The bright spot for the future of the lodging business is the increasing demand for rooms by both business travelers and pleasure travelers. The increasing affluence of an increasingly old population will lead to specially designed lodging, such as "elder hostels."

Many older motels are going to disappear, some because the profits just aren't there anymore (less vacationing along the interstates), others because they stand on suburban land that has become more valuable for redevelopment than as a motel site.

But the suburbs are where most of the hotel action will be in years to come; as the older places are taken out for other development, new ones will take their place in easy-access locations along major routes.

Hotel chains are planning new high-tech, high-quality units in major cities, to cater to the upscale crowd. If your expense account is more modest, you will still find ample space available; chains also are planning to continue replacing old "commercial" hotels with modern suburban units of middle price.

There will be a continuing trend to shorter but more frequent vacations—three-day weekends and the like—in addition to the conventional two or three-week annual vacation. This will benefit the close-in resort spots, places within an easy drive or short air hop of major population centers.

BUSINESS TRAVEL

Travelers who do business on the road will find hotels eager to make life easier for them in years to come. There will be plug-in connections for your portable lap computer so you can dump the day's correspondence and reports (perhaps written on the plane) into your office's computer via phone lines in a few seconds' time. Some hotels will offer computer rooms for your convenience in case you're not carrying your own hardware.

Check-in will be computerized, a matter of inserting a credit or debit card and receiving a "key" in the form of an electronically encoded card (assuming you remembered to make a reservation). Check-out will be a reverse procedure, probably carried out in your room's own terminal.

Hotels will provide business-oriented services such as electronic banking, language translation and the like, and will also make pitches to different market segments, particularly women, more of whom will be out on the road as they move up corporate ladders. Improved security arrangements, 24-hour room and valet service, built-in hair dryers, irons and the like—all these and more will become standard for hotels catering to business women.

Conventions and conferences will continue to grow in importance to hotels. Trade associations are proliferating, and they are finding more excuses for conferences—sometimes on finely subdivided aspects of their principal interest. Hotels are offering all the inducements they can think of for attracting such affairs, including building new units in the two dozen or so locations around the country that seem to be the favorites of convention planners (places like Los Angeles, Atlanta, New York, New Orleans and Washington).

Airport hotels will cash in on this trend by setting aside special facilities for teleconferencing and inviting firms to fly in their regional people, offering them quicker turnaround time compared to hotels in town.

Teleconferencing doesn't faze hotel planners. They feel certain it will grow, but not in a way that will cut into their trade. In fact, it may even stimulate trade, since most such electronic get-togethers involve satellite meetings around the country, where those who can't attend the conference can sit in on the proceedings via two-way TV. So most better hotels are being equipped to handle such conferences, and new ones are getting all the needed built-ins as a matter of course.

14

Cars of the Future

By 2000, autos will be so electronically wise, so excruci-
atingly attentive and protective, that you'll feel either pampered
or persecuted. But you won't be bored.

Would you feel comfortable in a car that, when you open the
door and sit down, wraps you in a seat belt, adjusts itself to your
contours—lowering or raising the seat, tilting the back, moving
the steering column—and refuses to budge, or even to start its
engine, until you pronounce the magic word "Shazam!"? A car
that will navigate your trip by satellite and computerized maps? A
car in which voice commands will replace button pushing?

If not, better hang on to whatever you're driving now. But by
2000, assuming the old crate or a reasonable facsimile is still
running, you'll feel like a World War I pilot.

You probably wouldn't complain about getting about 50 miles
per gallon in city traffic. Such a car will not be cheap, of course,
but then, cars aren't cheap today. Still, the year 2000 car may
actually be somewhat less expensive than today's in relation to
rising incomes, inflation and quality improvements.

THE NEW LOOK

Cars on average will be about two feet shorter than today's—
subcompacts just under 12 feet, biggest cars 16 feet or so.
Sleeker, more aerodynamic. Aerodynamics will be the driving
force in design from now on, carmakers intent on reducing drag to
save fuel. The smallest cars will be essentially teardrop shaped,
with the hood and windshield on the same rakish plane...flush

doors, wraparound windows with few if any posts, hoods sealed for a single front-end molding behind a bullet-shaped nose.

Rather than fixed size groupings, there will be a continuum of sizes—the bigger, the less rounded. Upscale models will be wedge-shaped (high rumps, low noses) with a more boxy, formal-looking cockpit (get used to this term; it means the driver's seat) and trunk.

A typical family of four might have three cars: A tiny electric/gasoline hybrid for errands, a two-seater for the teenagers and a six-passenger sedan for family trips and the like. Outdooring families might also have a van/wagon utility vehicle as well.

THE GADGETS

High-tech computer-based electronics will bring revolutionary changes. Control systems will monitor operations and provide instant diagnostics, extending the capabilities and universe of the driver. The engine compartment will be lined with black boxes ...computer modules.

One module will adjust the suspension struts (which replace today's springs and shocks) by instant changes in hydraulic pump pressures, feeding air or bleeding it from the struts as needed to maintain stability. No dip, no sway, no list; all happening so fast that you're not really aware of it.

As the driver glances at his steering wheel he will see at its hub an opaque screen displaying symbols for headlights, parking lights, left and right turn, windshield wipers, and the like. The symbols will be touch controls, replacing the knobs, buttons and switches now in use. The steering wheel will also have at its center a tiny two-way speaker; that's for voice commands and for telephone calls. Yes, car phones will be standard equipment on many models, optional on others.

All these controls will be linked to computer modules by a single, thin optical-fiber wire making the circuit of the car, replacing the thick, complicated (and sometimes mixed-up) bundle of coated copper wires now in standard use.

The steering column will probably be skinny, a shocking contrast to today's sturdy column; but since it no longer will play a mechanical role in steering—which will be done electronically—sturdiness won't matter. Many models will have all-wheel steering, so you can maneuver more nimbly in traffic and sideslip easily into tight parking spaces.

Troubleshooting will consist of messages flashed on a screen to warn the driver of trouble anywhere in the car. The screen will flash urgent emergency instructions if needed: "Compression loss in third cylinder...Faulty valve lifter...Slow down...Replace Module V3, front left wall, engine compartment."

Most cars will have satellite-guided navigation by 2000 or soon after. Maps projected on an eye-level screen will guide motorists on extended trips. The maps will come from cassettes or optical disks programmed for the places where you're driving.

A built-in transponder in the car's roof will keep in touch with a cellular ground station (that is, one within your immediate range; they'll be everywhere) which in turn will determine the car's position and display it on the screen, on top of the map.

When you indicate your destination on the screen by touch control or via a cursor lever, the navigation system will show the optimum route for speed and economy; it will tell you how long the trip will take and can display names and locations of places to eat and places to stay on the way.

Navigation systems will also give warning when your car is too close to the one ahead—given your speed and road conditions—and warn also of approaching emergency vehicles.

We mentioned voice controls. These probably will be an option before they become standard equipment; not everyone will cotton to them. The system will allow a car owner to voice-activate the car—tell it to start, to turn on its headlights or to perform a number of other pre-programmed functions. The system will make use of computers that can be programmed to distinguish one voice from other noise, to prevent theft.

In the dark, windshields will turn into night scopes via technology already developed for the military, enhancing available light and bringing up details to nearly daytime clarity; perhaps this could be applied to rear vision as well. During the day, windshield glass will darken to fit the glare, much as light-sensitive eyeglasses already do, returning to clear glass as the day wanes. This will help save your eyes and your air conditioning as well.

Transmissions will be computer-controlled, and instead of gears will rely on a complicated twin-shaft arrangement interconnected by belts. Movement from one speed to another will be smooth through a wide range of engine speeds. Electronics will eliminate the need for any kind of clutch or other coupling. This is called "continuously variable" transmission. An intermediate step, now under development in Japan, will be a five-speed automatic, electronic system that allows a manual shift at the two lowest speeds. This promises higher fuel economy. All-manual transmissions will still be available for those who really want them.

Electronically controlled antilock braking, the kind airplanes have had for years and which is just now appearing on a few cars, will become standard. This system applies and releases the brakes many times per second to prevent lock-up and skidding in panic stops.

Tires will have a lower profile and wider tread, which will greatly improve stability and road-holding qualities. But some scientists are betting on the opposite—a high-profile, narrow tread. The theory is that such tires will blend better with aerodynamic fender fairings and reduce air drag.

All tires will be made of better synthetics, combined with fibers of some sort into ultra-tough compounds. An inventor in Indiana claims he has a compound employing epoxies that will make a nearly indestructible synthetic rubber, but it's not yet proven.

TOUGH MATERIALS

Cars will contain a lot less steel, replaced with aluminum and other lightweight, corrosion-resistant stuff. Car bodies built of composites will be hard to dent. Panels—doors, hood, trunk, etc.—will be virtual throwaways, replaced rather than repaired if badly smashed. Body repair and paint shops won't have much to do and probably will fade out. Replacement panels will come factory-dyed to match the originals. They won't need waxing.

New composites will take over inside the engine as well... high-temperature-and-corrosion-resistant materials coating cylinder walls, combustion chambers, piston bearings, turbocharger rotors and the like; some of these already have begun to show up. Radiator fans, drive shafts, parts of the transmission and clutch, casings for electronic systems—all will be made of plastic-like composites.

Ceramic parts already are appearing in engines and will be common by 2000, in rotor blades, cylinder parts, valve faces and ports, heat sensors and other applications where extreme hardness and heat tolerance are needed. All-ceramic engines are a longer shot. Glass will be replaced in some cars by new kinds of stronger, reinforced plastic.

FUELS OF TOMORROW

Given our forecast of abundant petroleum through the end of this century, there's no reason to expect engines to change from present-day fuels. So the internal combustion engine will continue to prevail in both its gasoline and diesel modes. But use of propane will grow, chiefly if not entirely in fleets—trucks, buses, utility vehicles, etc.

Electrical specialty vehicles, current versions of which already are in use by the Postal Service, electric utilities and others for limited applications, will have made their entrance in a big way, probably first in the form of hybrids: Gasoline or diesel engines coupled with a battery. The battery would do the easy work, such as running along flat roads, and the engine would take over on hills, propelling the vehicle and recharging the battery at the same time. This mode is likely to appear first in small runabouts for personal use and in fleets of small delivery vans. Present-day batteries aren't up to this kind of performance, but those of 2000 will be, and may be up to a lot more than that, including a truly competitive all-electric car.

Year-2000 engines will be much smaller—perhaps only half the displacement of present ones. But they will rev up much faster—two or three times faster than present engines, which will more than make up for the smaller size. This will generate tremendous heat, which is where the reinforced composites and ceramic components come into play.

The diesel, pretty much a flop in passenger-car use these days, may make a dramatic comeback before 2000 in the form of a new "adiabatic" engine. It will turn up first in industrial and commercial applications and in large diesel trucks, then in passenger autos. This will be an all-ceramic, ultra-high-heat machine much more efficient than any car engine produced previously. It will retain and recycle all the heat generated in combustion, thereby eliminating the need for a cooling system or radiator and achieving very high efficiency ratios. It will be able to use cheaper fuels than other engines and will have far fewer moving parts, thus being more reliable and longer-lasting.

What about gas-turbine engines? Well, they're under development for the military, with the objective of beating conventional internal-combustion engines in acceleration, efficiency, fuel consumption, reliability. These will use many ceramic parts and operate at very high temperatures. They probably won't turn up in civilian use until the early decades of the new century.

FIXING THEM UP

Auto parts will be largely modular—designed to be yanked out and replaced. You may not even be able to poke around under the hood of some cars without messing up your warranty; hoods may be sealed to all but authorized repair persons, who will have to put the car up on a hoist to lower the engine from its housing.

Sophisticated car owners will save themselves a bunch by learning to replace modules and other prepackaged gadgetry themselves. The stuff will be available in chain stores, where picking up a module will be no more complicated than buying a couple of shirts. Auto parts stores will continue to thrive and will be doing a good business in obsolete parts for early 1990s models when 2000 rolls around.

Say goodbye to the old-fashioned gas station with the repair shop in back. The service station of the 2000s will be neat, even antiseptic, looking something like a credit bureau with gas pumps out front. It will still dispense gasoline, oil, diesel fuel, antifreeze and the like. But instead of a grease-pit backshop full of mechanical equipment, expect to see a bank of gadgets that look a lot like computers, which in fact many will be.

There won't be as many gas stations as today; they will be more widely dispersed in urban areas but bigger. Most of the bigger ones will be highly automated 24-hour operations, equipped with pumps that accept credit or debit cards and print out a receipt.

Automation will make it easier to install gas-dispensing pumps on private property to serve businesses, apartment complexes, or even a neighborhood—depending on how local fire ordinances are worded. The advantage of automation lies in the fact that pumps will be activated by credit or debit cards, and an accurate account can be kept of how much each driver uses over various periods. Such systems can be hooked up with data entry for mileage readings to calculate fuel economy and other fleet information.

NEW-STYLE SHOPPING

Buying a car will be a different kind of experience. Oh, there'll still be high-pressure sales tactics and haggling over price, but note these trends:

There will be fewer but larger dealerships, most of them handling several makes. Some dealers will be chain operations, with mini-showrooms scattered around in shopping centers and downtown malls. Buyers can do their preliminary homework in such places via computer printouts and video terminals. Computer graphics will make it possible to "rotate" the images on the screen, so that cars can be looked at from every angle, including the insides.

More than that, such hookups will make it possible for buyers to put together their own cars out of body, color and component options. They'll be able to sit in a simulator that will look like and feel like the driver's seat, with all gadgetry in view.

About price: Today's $12,000 car—which is roughly average—will cost about twice as much in 2004, figuring inflation averaging about 4% or so. But then so will everything else go up that much, including average incomes. So taking into account the improvements in cars, this may be something of a bargain.

Autos will not only be more fuel-efficient in 2000, thus less costly to operate, but also longer-lived, with fewer model changeovers, less planned obsolescence. Big cars will probably average 35 mpg, with rates of up to 60 for smaller models. A car bought in 2000 ought to last about 15 years. First owners will probably hang on to cars for about six years.

This lengthening of service life is one reason the auto market won't expand much. We figure annual sales of about 12 million in

2000, compared to about 10.5 million in 1985. The vast majority of these cars will be finally assembled in the United States by American workers, but the auto industry will look a lot different from today's. Over the next 15 years, many of today's auto plants will close down. Most of the new assembly plants will be in non-union Sunbelt states, and many of them will be either foreign-owned or joint ventures between American and foreign companies. In a culmination of trends now underway, cars sold in the U.S. will be such complex bundles of both domestic and foreign-made parts that it will be difficult to even classify them as American or imported.

ELECTRIC CARS

Picture—and this won't be easy—a small, boxy electric car that weighs about 1000 pounds and can run about a thousand miles or so at top speeds of 100 mph without refueling, with efficiency equivalent to about 200 miles per gallon of gasoline. Its basic power plant is about the size of a large breadbox, and there won't be any thousand-mile-long extension cord.

This of course is the dream (and nightmare) that has been haunting the auto industry for decades; it may sound ridiculous, in view of all the past failures and currently slim hopes. But perhaps it isn't. Such a vehicle may turn up within the next decade or so, and that would change all bets about the future of the world auto industry overnight.

That breadbox will contain a super-battery of a kind the world has yet to see. First it must prove itself in the military-space applications for which it is being designed. This is expected to happen before 1990, in the shape of a battery designed to be lofted into space and powerful enough to knock down enemy missiles with laser weapons.

Next would come a scaling-up program and then civilian applications of the battery. An electric vehicle would be one of the first. The car could be built of composite materials such as graphite-fiber-epoxy mixes that are lighter but stronger than steel. A small electric motor at each wheel would be self-braking (and in the act of braking, would recharge the battery), and the entire rig could run years and years with only nominal servicing.

What we are talking about is described by its inventor as an entirely new kind of storage battery employing a novel principle that promises high energy density and high discharge capabilities, although it would run at relatively low voltages, without environmental or other hazards to worry about. It would operate at ambient pressures and temperatures—meaning with no special compression or heating/cooling requirements.

Such a battery is now in the research and development stage for the Department of Defense. It is classified; Pentagon officials won't talk about it. If it doesn't work, you may never hear another word about it. But if it does, you'll hear plenty.

15

The Money Business

Explosive changes in personal and corporate finance over the past decade are just a taste of what's to come between now and the year 2000.

We're already seeing electronic movement of money, instant crediting and debiting, worldwide capital markets, the ubiquity of credit cards, and the ascendance of mutual funds as the dominant investment vehicle for most individuals.

We're already in the throes of massive deregulation in personal financial services, blurring old distinctions between banks, insurance companies, savings and loans, brokerage houses, and even giant retailers.

What's in store is a lot more of the same, but at a quickening pace.

The big change coming in banking and finance is this: There won't be any such thing as idle money—not even for an instant. Every dollar you earn will begin making more money for you virtually from the moment you earn it. Conversely, most dollars you spend will leave your account almost instantly, getting credited to someone else's account. Goodbye "float."

That's what market competition, aided by new computer and communications technology, is doing to the American financial system. Only the ignorant and careless will fail to benefit from it; in fact, it would almost take a conscious effort not to.

Most of the old restrictive rules in financial services are breaking down. New technology is overleaping them so rapidly that government cannot keep up. The power of federal regulatory agencies to restrict the entry of new players and new services is slipping away. It is unlikely that Congress will be able to restore it in any substantial part, although it may try in the next few years.

We are seeing de facto deregulation of finance on a larger scale than almost anyone could have foreseen only 10 years ago—de facto meaning willy-nilly, without central direction. Within another several years, certainly by the turn of the century, personal and business finance will have changed almost beyond recognition. Here are some of the major developments to be expected:

Full-service banks will become fewer but larger through continued mergers and consolidations. They will operate branches across state lines—first on a regional basis, later nationwide.

But many other forms of "banks" will pop up under different names...institutions where people can make deposits and withdrawals and borrow money. Retailers will become a major provider of financial services to individuals and companies.

A blizzard of plastic—credit and debit cards offering an amazing variety of services—will mount and mount, but then will die down again, to be replaced by a few combination cards doing the same things.

Financial advisory services will become widely available via computers and in other forms, and many of them will offer complete investment management for even small individual and business accounts.

Obtaining cash or credit will become almost totally automated via machines that will be widely available in bank lobbies, retail establishments and on the street.

Both securities trading and high-speed movement of financial deposits will be available on a worldwide basis around the clock, with open access for brokers, financial executives and individual investors.

Banks will press automation as fast as they can, turning to computerized "expert systems" to do much of the front-end work on loan applications, opening of new accounts and so on.

The "cashless, checkless society" you have heard so much about will be close at hand by the year 2000. Pocket money will probably consist of credit/debit cards plus a few coins and bills for the sake of habit, street vendors and small children. Paper checks will be available for personal use, but many or most businesses will not accept them—even from people with the best of credentials—or will charge a fee for accepting them.

Electronic funds transfer will be the predominant mode within 10 or 15 years—and there goes the float and the bank's annoying habit of holding checks for a week or more before crediting your account. Individuals and firms will be able to specify precisely when they want payments made, thus ending the need to play games with the delay. And any idle cash left lying around will be in an interest-bearing account anyway.

FAST MONEY

This business of channeling cash automatically into an earnings mode can be carried to some interesting extremes. Employers might even begin paying wages and salaries each day, by depositing them electronically in some special employee account or money-market fund, commingled or individual. This sort of thing could become an important fringe benefit in the years ahead. And direct deposit of paychecks and government checks will become common.

Corporate treasurers who already are concerned with placing short-term balances wherever they can earn the most will have vastly greater vistas open to them. Shifting balances among domestic and worldwide accounts will be relatively easy with the use of communications networks and computerized expert systems to spot and take advantage of opportunities.

Individuals will have much the same opportunities—if they are ready to invest in the necessary computer hardware and software, as many will be. A small but speedy personal computer plugged into a communications network and drawing on carefully structured investment programs and expert systems will be a powerful tool for savvy savers. More individuals will be able to make a full-time career out of investing and speculating—in stocks, bonds, currencies, commodities, whatever.

They will have ready access to enormous data banks, including the ability to tap directly into Securities and Exchange Commission files to get a company's latest 10-K submission and other nonconfidential reports, all of which the SEC will soon insist be submitted in computerized form.

Within a decade or so we will see the rise of continuous data base accounting which will keep investors and investment advisers up to date on current corporate performance, rather than having to wait for quarterly or other periodic reports. All this open access may revolutionize the investment advisory business, wiping out some services but creating possibilities for others.

PERSONAL INVESTING

Most Americans will continue to want face-to-face investment advice despite the proliferation of computerized services, and investment professionals will find plenty to do. Most will no longer be order takers, but instead will be in the business of producing a complete financial blueprint telling you how much of your assets should be in stocks and which ones, how much in bonds, in real estate, tax-sheltered limited partnerships and so on.

They'll even tell you how much and what kind of insurance to carry, whether to lease or buy a car, and how to finance your children's college education. Stockbrokers, insurance agents, mutual fund salesmen—investment consultants with a narrow specialty—will become rarer or will team up with broad-gauged financial planners.

The number of financial products will continue to grow, including options and futures trading. All of which will give investors many more ways to hedge against volatile price movements.

But small investors will probably not be heavily involved in direct market speculations. In fact, the trend in recent years has been the other way, and we expect it to continue. Mutual funds, of which there will be an increasing variety, will be the preferred investment mode for most smalls; diversification will provide more insulation from market volatility induced by in-out movements by big institutions, including pension funds. And more mutual funds will specialize in market segments where the rise (and occasional fall) of new technology and new industries will continue to spark excitement.

Mutual funds will be the principal products on the shelves of financial supermarkets—the staple, if you will. The supermarkets will sell financial guidance plans too, but they'll be standardized. Punch in data on your income, family situation, assets and debts, and the computer will feed out a "plan" to follow in doing your shopping among the supermarket's products.

And then there will be financial-service boutiques to cater to the affluent tier of investors who will get a more sophisticated and, of course, more personalized plan with continuous attention from a broker. Fees will be higher too.

CAPITAL MARKETS

The New York Stock Exchange will continue to be the market for the bigs, the elite of the American economy, but the NASDAQ over-the-counter market will overtake it in volume and will become the true national stock market. The American Exchange will play a minor role in stock trading, confining itself almost entirely to options.

More and more new companies will, as they grow, choose to stay with the OTC market rather than switch to the NYSE. This will expand the practical effect of a national computerized market—with great enough liquidity to withstand heavy in-and-out trading without causing radical price movements. That, in turn, will lure pension funds seeking stability into buying a much broader array of stocks, making more companies into "blue chips."

Worldwide securities trading has opened our markets increasingly not only to foreign investors and speculators but also to possible abuse by Americans and others looking for ways to circumvent protections against insider trading and fraud. U.S. insiders, in other words, could use access via foreign countries to slip in and out of U.S. stocks undetected. Our government is working on the idea of forcing a waiver of secrecy as a condition for participating in U.S. market transactions. But this may take some years to work out, either through negotiations with other governments, most of which are leery, or by legislation, or both.

A parallel development is the rise of what amounts to merchant banking in the U.S. on the European model—more large financial institutions, including brokerages, acting as venture capitalists by channeling seed money into new start-up firms. These are longer-term commitments than many so-called venture capitalists have been willing to make in such speculative ventures, and they may prove to be a key ingredient in the rise of new firms and new industries in this country. Foreign capital also is being attracted into biotech, computers, space commercialization, communications technology and other fresh fields where the prospects for huge paybacks are especially attractive.

The rise of electronic banking and investing isn't unalloyed good news. Its flip side is this: The ease with which funds can and will be zipped around the country and the world for maximum return may well put some regions of the U.S. on shorter credit rations. Investment capital may in effect be sucked out of the already lagging states or regions by the more prosperous ones. This threat hasn't yet developed on any large scale and it may never, given the prospects for eventually reviving such areas as the industrial upper Midwest with flexible manufacturing and the like. But it bears watching.

WHERE WE'LL BANK

Dividing lines will be fuzzed among banks and the savings and loans, thrifts and credit unions. S&Ls will become more like banks, offering much the same range of services, while the thrifts will suffer competition from mortgage pools, pension funds and quasi-governmental mortgage packagers, although the latter may find their scope narrowed by congressional restrictions on their credit activities, confining them more rigorously to special market segments. Already major stock brokerage houses are acting a lot like banks, offering central asset management accounts that combine checking privileges with ease of investment.

Banks and thrifts will experiment with ways to safeguard their profits. One, already well underway, is the trend to charging fees on every kind of service provided to customers—including eventually a fee for going to a teller window instead of an automatic teller machine. (ATMs will be the preferred mode of operation in most banks within a few more years, and there may even be a small transaction fee for using *them*.) And banks may eventually be required to provide "lifeline" services free to low-incomers.

There also is a growing trend to specialization, with some banks and thrifts focusing on consumer banking or commercial accounts or catering to upper-income customers. Markets will become highly segmented, but consumers will have more choices every year.

There will be fewer rural banks in the new century, and people in rural areas will be resorting to other bank-like institutions that will be turning up in increasing numbers. The "nonbank banks" that began to appear widely in the early '80s will be reined in by Congress via legislation putting limits on their growth...probably a ceiling of a hundred or so. These are financial companies that get around federal regulation by deliberately refusing to perform certain services that would qualify them as "banks"—such as not offering ordinary, non-interest-bearing checking accounts or not making commercial loans.

Large retail chains—Sears, Penney's and others—have jumped into this act, opening their own "nonbank" operations as just another department in their department stores, and this has caught the attention of the old-line banking industry like a whack across the forehead. Now some larger banks are beginning to move in the same direction as a way of branching out across state lines (nonbanks being unregulated) and even across the country. And others are getting interested—insurance companies, conglomerates, mutual funds, even labor unions. By 2000 or so, the distinction among various kinds of "banks" and "nonbanks" will have blurred practically out of sight.

A crosscurrent to this movement is the way in which the insurance industry itself is changing under the stresses and opportunities this sort of unregulated growth is bringing to bear. As the old barriers to competition in financial services crumble away, insurers are broadening out to offer their own smorgasbord of investment instruments, including mutual funds and a variety of variable-return insurance policies, along with financial counseling services, commercial loans, home mortgages and brokerage.

This churning is riling the waters for smaller insurers, and many will be swallowed up by bigs as the alternative to going under. The larger companies are expected to increase their market share some 20% by 1990, according to industry estimates. At the same time, regulated, old-line banks are going to be allowed into the insurance business themselves, taking over perhaps 8% of the life insurance market in a span of five years or so.

CREDIT AND DEBIT CARDS

As for credit cards and debit cards and combinations of the two, it may be difficult to tell the players without a program for the next several years. Experts in banking and in bank regulation are bemused (and some are alarmed) at the extreme proliferation of options. Banks increasingly are offering their own combinations, ditto for retailers; charge cards also are spreading.

A credit card allows purchases on the cuff. The retailer is guaranteed his payment, and the consumer pays a high interest rate on his or her continuing balance. The debit card is the opposite—it transfers cash electronically from the purchaser's bank account to the retailer's bank account via "point-of-sale" (POS) machines, making the necessary entries in each as it goes.

The combination now beginning to turn up is a card that allows the holder to use either credit or debit to finance his purchases but which automatically extends a line of credit when and if the customer's bank account runs dry...depending on his eligibility and on what turns up in the instant credit check performed by the POS machine.

These combination machines will be versatile: Automated gas pumps, for example, that will be activated by a plastic card and will issue a printed receipt. Ditto for computer terminals that will make hotel, airline and rental-car reservations for you, and which will be found in shopping centers and offices.

The overriding issue is who pays for the services these cards provide. In most cases, of course, it is the consumer, through interest charges on outstanding debt plus membership fees.

But in the case of debit cards, retailers are rebelling against the idea of allowing issuing companies to skim their percentage off the top of the cash before it gets back to the seller. This is, in effect, a fee for service. And that is why more and more retailers are moving to issue their own debit cards or are installing ATM machines on their premises to provide ready access to cash.

What's in the debit card for the consumer? Just now, not much, except convenience; people who like to pay cash or by check have been taking to debit cards in droves. Gas stations and other retailers like debit cards—especially retailers who have stopped accepting personal checks or would like to because of the cost of handling the paperwork, not to mention bum checks.

In the future, debit cards will hold more appeal. Perhaps retailers will begin to offer discounts for their use or for cash, as gas stations already are doing—that is, if Congress doesn't step in and forbid it. Most retailers hope Congress leaves the issue alone. They think the marketplace should and will decide; consumers will vote with their own cash for the system they prefer.

After all, the chief driving force behind promotion of debit cards is the need to hold down paper-handling costs; if they can manage this, say retailers, they can hold down prices...which will be good for inflation.

We said earlier that, after a blizzard of plastic, the consumer will begin to see daylight in the form of combined or "universal" cards. This transition may take 10 years or so, but the first signs are on the horizon, with the new Sears Discover card and the expansion of features on the major bank cards and travel-and-entertainment cards. We'll see the combining of functions of credit and debit with a range of other services—such as access to certain clubs, to cash via ATMs, to financial counseling, travel scheduling, auto rentals, varying lines of credit and anything else the issuers can dream up.

Whether these cards will be the product of today's credit and charge card leaders or of new companies remains to be seen. The old-line credit card firms aren't sure themselves but are looking for ways to maintain their markets in the face of what may become almost frantic competition.

And many people may find it comforting to know that they have only one card to report if a wallet is lost or stolen; today or next year, they may have more than they can remember.

Major banks expect to be issuing more credit/debit cards as the point-of-sale machines spread. By 2000, there will be POS terminals at probably 90% of the retail counters in the entire nation. POS credit verification will make it easier for banks and for retailers to keep a continuous check on bad-credit losses. Upcoming generations probably will be more credit-than-cash minded, and banks would like to accommodate them within the bounds of prudent management. So far, banks have held their losses to about 1% on sales, but only through standards that limit credit-card ownership to about 40% of adult Americans.

THE SMART CARD

If you're comfortable with all of the above, get ready for the "smart card." This is a French invention; it has been around several years but has not yet caught on in this country, chiefly because it would upset too many established patterns without guarantee of an early payback. But interest is picking up, and at least one major national card company is planning to test it.

The smart card contains an embedded microchip smaller than the nail on your pinky. The chip, which takes the place of the magnetic strip on the back of today's cards, can store an amazing amount of information. Enough to indicate your current bank balance, for example; or your total credit load at any moment; or, as the capacity of tiny chips expands, an entire medical history and a great deal of other useful information you might like to carry around with you.

Part of that micro capacity—which is going to grow by leaps and bounds—can be devoted to anti-theft and anti-fraud measures. There may never be such a thing as perfect security for any kind of plastic, but there are ways to reduce the likelihood of misuse by encryption and code numbers of various kinds. These will be brought to a high level of reliability in the next 10 years or so—which is about when we expect the smart card or some version of it to take over.

Such cards will be launched on a test basis by one or two major American banks in the next year or so, chiefly among their upscale customers. The cards will be compatible with present credit/debit card technology; that is, they will have the same "mag stripe" on the back in addition to the embedded chip, so that they can be used with present electronic equipment. Machines that read "smart cards" won't be in general use until the mid-'90s.

THE BOTTOM LINE

It's clear that this country's financial-services industry is in the early stages of a rolling readjustment to new ideas and new technologies that may produce some surprising effects on the economy.

It will mean, for one thing, that the response of markets to day-to-day developments will be far more sensitive; virtually instantaneous, as communications technology ripens. This could lead to short-term volatility but also to longer-term stability, in that investors would have a wealth of information to guide them, hence be able to make sounder judgments than now.

Individual savers who prefer not to take too many chances will have increasing access to ways of making their money grow with relatively small risk. And that is bound to be healthy all around.

Business firms will, by the same token, have much broader access to capital markets and to instruments and methods for both maximizing and stabilizing their own financial health. And that too will be good for the economy.

Still, there are concerns about how such a lightly regulated, profit-and-competition-driven financial system will perform under pressure. And as deregulation progresses, more problems are sure to turn up.

The Federal Reserve is bound to lose some of its power to control money and credit unless Congress intervenes, and we don't see that as likely. The Fed will automate its own check-clearing procedures in due course. But the growth of unregulated "nonbanks" and the progressive speeding-up of financial transactions will reduce the Fed's sway over such basic financial controls as reserve requirements and the federal funds rate, which it uses to influence money and credit.

And the more closely our financial markets become interwoven with those abroad, the more vulnerable we may be to shocks and aftershocks that erupt in foreign economies.

There is another side to all this: The velocity of money—that is, the rate at which it turns over in transactions going on in any given time period—is going to rise dramatically in the next decade or so. Thus there will be the effect of a larger amount of money in circulation without an actual corresponding increase in the money supply. We think that will be anti-inflationary, and we think that is good news.

16

Lifestyles and Leisure

The way Americans live over the next 15 years will be heavily influenced by rising median age, rising affluence, more leisure time, better health among the elderly, more choices of leisure activities and an increasing tolerance of divergent lifestyles.

All of this spells boom times for travel and leisure industries, the arts, and many spectator sports (if not too youth-oriented).

The variety of marital lifestyles and household composition established in recent years is in some ways bewildering—at least to statisticians and forecasters—and this diversity will continue indefinitely.

LOVE AND MARRIAGE

Although marriage will continue to be the norm, the average age of marriage is rising, and a divorce rate of around 50% seems likely to continue, with minor ups and downs. (The trend to later marriage and later childbearing increases the chance that marriages will last, perhaps helping to moderate that 50% divorce rate.)

A high proportion of the divorced will remarry, but it's probable that three out of five children will spend at least part of their childhood in one-parent households, the number of which will rise somewhat the rest of this century. How will the children of divorce behave when they reach marrying age? Probably not much differently from their parents.

And the POSSLQs are here to stay. Pronounced "posselcues," they are Partners of Opposite Sex Sharing Living Quarters, a term invented in the '70s to describe the phenomenal (300%) increase in the number of such households.

While their numbers are not going to jump THAT much again, neither will they diminish. Despite the generally conservative trend of the electorate, attitudes toward lifestyles have become more tolerant, and the generation that grew up promoting pre-marital cohabitation doesn't seem likely to turn against it in the near future. Most but not all POSSLQ couples wind up marrying, but at ages somewhat later than other first-timers.

A small but rising proportion of the population is turning to permanent singlehood, either by choice or by chance. In the case of women, this may be because of rising educational levels. A more highly educated woman has spent more years studying and working before getting serious about marriage—by which time her choice of suitable partners among older, equally educated men has diminished, while her need for the financial support of a husband has diminished too.

This, along with the falling birthrate, contributes to the continued slow shrinkage in average household size.

The lower birthrate increases the labor force participation of women and leaves a larger share of rising incomes for spending on adult needs and preferences.

There will be continued growth in the number of households headed by single minority women, mostly blacks. No turnaround is in sight for this phenomenon, which is putting growing burdens on social-service budgets in cities that can ill afford them.

Improved techniques for birth control (and its opposite, fertility enhancement) will come from biotech research into the process of hormonal production and release within the body.

WHERE WE'LL LIVE

The suburban lifestyle of the '60s and '70s is changing; children of the suburbs don't necessarily want to raise THEIR kids in the suburbs, and more of them will be looking to farther-out, semi-rural and small-town environments, which can have upsetting effects on the future of many now well-established suburban shopping malls and centers.

Job mobility will help loosen things up, making for more decentralization. Twenty-first century communications modes and computer networking are already heaving into sight. A growing number of computer-connected workers, including professionals, software specialists and housewives working part time on information-processing of one kind or another, will be able to locate pretty much where they want.

Ditto for companies, more of which will be opening branch and departmental offices outside crowded metro areas for the convenience of the kinds of skilled workers they need. Commuting time, the bane of most big-city workers today, will probably be even a bigger headache by century's end—but not for those lucky folks whose office is either in the home or just a short distance away. We don't see "telecommuting" becoming a big deal, but it IS going to spread. Business planners ought to crank this into their forward assumptions.

Computers will bring enormous gains in productivity and expanded leisure, opening opportunities in entertainment and the arts for careers devoted to helping a more affluent population enjoy its spare time.

WHAT AND HOW WE EAT

Emphasis on wellness, fitness and health foods to go with them is sure to continue. The younger generation that created the health craze will carry it along into middle age, and their parents—the expanding over-65 group—will apply it to their own self-interest in staying healthy and independent in an era of weakened family ties.

The market for low-calorie, low-caffeine, high-fiber food and drink will grow by a third or more between now and 2000 by industry estimates. Producers are planning to cash in with all sorts of new items catering to various age groups and tastes. These will include special items for the elderly in small-serving plastic containers that can be heated in a microwave, easily opened, used as a serving disk and easily resealed.

More and more meals will be eaten away from home in restaurants, employer-owned cafeterias, schools, etc. In part, a direct result of more working spouses and more single-person households.

Fast-food outlets also will continue to spread, except in areas already saturated or nearly so. The variety of items they offer will keep on expanding, a continuation of the trend developing in recent years...hamburger joints putting in salad bars, offering baked spuds, chicken and other dishes.

Regular full-service restaurants will keep on growing in numbers to accommodate the increasing numbers of affluent eaters who like to see cloth napkins and tablecloths. These too will offer greater menu variety. More health foods, salad bars, whole grain breads. Better variety of "light" entrees. All this is part of the continuing emphasis on eating not just well but better. Americans in general will keep up their interest in quality of diet, better health and nutrition.

Of meals eaten at home, an increasing share will be of the carry-out type, bought at a local fast-food place or perhaps at the supermarket. The latter will be going after this growth trend in an aggressive way, selling more salads (made up or at do-it-yourself counters), fried chicken, roast beef, individual desserts and so on. This is high-profit stuff and a good way for chains to reclaim some of the consumers' food dollar they've been losing to the fast-food sellers.

A rising share of at-home meals will be fabricated somewhere else and will need only to be dropped into boiling water for a few minutes or popped into the microwave for less than that. Retort packaging of food products will become more widespread. Retorts are flexible cans made of multiple layers of foil and plastic, the contents sterilized. They have long shelf life and are cheaper to ship and store. These days they'll keep up to a year and a half at room temperature, perhaps longer as improvements come along, including nuclear sterilization, which is effective and practical but still unpopular because of lingering radiation fears.

On the horizon is a whole new line of plastic containers which will probably take over from the retort package before 2000—versatile containers which can be heated in a microwave and then used for table service. (A leader in developing this technology calls it a "food system.")

Some food industry planners foresee a trend to "grazing," meaning less emphasis on three squares a day, more snacking. And the industry wants to be ready for this trend—if not help bring it about—by providing a variety of enticing and healthful foods in small, ultra-convenient packages that can be heated in microwave ovens.

Basically, Americans will eat much the same foods as they do now. No big shift is likely toward exotic items or synthetics. Beef will take a lesser share of the food budget than other "lighter" meats. And meats, eggs, dairy products, fruits and vegetables will remain the mainstays. Commercial fish and shellfish farming has a big potential as new techniques and markets are developed and as biotechnology brings genetic improvements. Fish has dual appeal—to farmers as efficient food converters and to consumers as low-calorie, low-fat food.

Hard booze will continue to lose ground, due both to these trends and to the spreading crackdown on alcohol abuse, drunk driving in particular. More and more states are repealing below-21 drinking age laws and boosting sales taxes on alcoholic beverages. This backlash will continue to be hard on liquor advertising, which is growing more circumspect and restrained.

Beer sales won't increase much if at all; it's popular with youngsters, and there will be fewer of them. Wine sales will climb perhaps 2% or 3% a year. Among distilled spirits, the trend to what the trade calls "white goods" (gin and vodka, versus bourbon and other whiskeys) is likely to continue. Best sales of all may be among the new "light" concoctions like wine coolers and reduced-alcohol liquors.

RELIGIONS

Church attendance will grow in absolute numbers through the end of the century, but hit a new low as a percentage of the population. Most church authorities don't see too much hope of a turnaround in the coming century.

Overall church membership in 2000 is expected to be something like 156 million, compared to about 140 million in 1982; but given population growth, that means churchgoing is barely holding its own.

Church attendance, adjusted for population, reached a high point in the late '50s when some 49% of adults claimed to be churchgoers, compared with about 40% today.

A trend to "secularization," the name churchmen give to this phenomenon, is at work in most of the Western world. It is especially apparent in the Scandinavian countries where new trends in Western social mores often seem to pop up first; only about 10% of the population there is churchgoing. The usual pattern seems to be holding: The trend is spreading to Canada, and signs of it already are showing up here.

Except for the Episcopalian and Lutheran churches, most "liberal" (non-fundamentalist) Protestant religions in this country are losing members by the thousands. "It's the temper of the times," says one Protestant church official who follows these things, "competition between the country club and church on Sunday morning." Growing affluence, in other words, seems to have that effect on religious adherence, and, he points out, the children of non-churchgoers tend to follow their parents' patterns.

Two groups will buck the trend: the Catholic church and evangelistic/fundamentalist sects. In each case, the growth will be among low-income groups and is expected to continue indefinitely. Such churches will hold a special appeal for more conservative people who seek the structure, ongoing support and emphasis on traditional values in times of turbulent change.

Catholicism has, along with other religions, been a major loser in the years since World War II. But Catholicism is now stabilizing and may begin to gain members in the years just ahead. The bulk of these will be recent arrivals—principally Hispanic immigrants but also many from Catholic countries in Asia, including Filipinos.

This trend, likely to pick up volume the rest of this century, may change the color mix of the Catholic church, but not its basic nature. It has always been an "immigrant church." Its losses of communicants have been heaviest among the middle and upper-middle classes, while its gains have been at the lower-income end.

Catholicism in this country faces a labor squeeze: Too few men in training for the priesthood, too few nuns as well—certainly not enough to offset the continued loss of clergy to retirement.

More parish-level duties will be taken over by laymen and by lay deacons. As the shortage of priests worsens, the church will get around to ordaining women, but this may not be in the cards until well into the next century.

Parochial schools, despite continuing difficulties with staff and finance, are becoming "magnet schools" in many major cities, managing to stay open and teaching mostly black, non-Catholic children whose parents send them there for the discipline and calmer environment than found in public schools.

Jewish congregations as a whole also face shrinkage, due not only to a birthrate below the replacement level but also to intermarriage and dropouts. The American Jewish community numbers about 6 million today, only a third of whom are synagogue members. Despite a continuing trend to religious awareness among many younger Jewish families, overall numbers could fall to near the vanishing point sometime in the next century, if these trends persist.

THE ARTS

All kinds of performing and visual arts will benefit from increasing affluence and leisure time. Federal support for the arts won't grow and may even decline for some years ahead. But corporate funding, state and local government aid, and individual giving will increase.

Opera, ballet and symphonic performances are increasingly available in home video formats, which leads some people to fear the loss of live audiences. But the opposite seem to be happening; broader exposure is helping build the live audience. The social effect of being part of a live audience will retain its appeal as a change of pace from stay-at-home viewing.

Pay-by-view cable television offers the biggest potential for growth in the arts field, providing an important new source of revenue, as it will in movies and sports. Nationwide live telecasts of major arts events, via satellite and high-resolution and stereo TV, will pull in large audiences in places too small to attract big-league orchestras, opera, ballet, and solo artists.

Small and medium-sized firms will become as active in local arts funding as the corporate bigs. Some of this backing will take the form of tie-in deals that give customers credits toward the purchase of arts tickets. There will be more business support, too, for the construction and renovation of local and regional arts centers, using old auditoriums, movie palaces and the like.

There will be major growth in public participation in the arts—amateurism, if you will. The upcoming generations, children of the Baby Boomers, have had plenty of exposure to the arts as audience and students. There will be no shortage of either audience or volunteers to join and manage local arts organizations.

LEISURE TRAVEL

Americans love to travel, and they'll be doing more of it in the years to come. The Baby Boom population bulge points this way, and resort and travel planners are smacking their lips over the prospect. This population group, notes one travel trade association, has "been known to consider travel as a necessity, not a luxury."

Its members already are better traveled and better educated than their parents, and their disposable income will on average be higher—and easily stretched via the coming explosion in plastic cash, the debit-&-credit cards with which practically everyone will be armed.

The retirement-age-and-up crowd not only is going to expand but also will be considerably better-heeled than today or yesterday. Resort owners and investors have plans for them. They'll be heavy users of the new wave of low-rise, garden-style, timeshare condos in the Sunbelt, many of which will have golf courses at hand or within easy reach.

As resort prices rise around the country, timesharing will be an increasingly popular way for middle-income people to buy rights to use a vacation retreat at predictable future prices, and fitness and "wellness" centers will be an integral part of many of them.

But there are limits here too...boredom being one of them. After a few visits, the timeshare may lose its appeal. There is an electronic answer to that, and some hotel chains and others are planning to provide it: Computerized vacation "exchanges" that will make it easy to trade time in your spot for time at someone else's. Payment will be calculated with due credit for tradeoffs between properties and instantly "cleared" by credit or debit card. This sort of operation probably will broaden in coming years as bright promoters come up with new ideas. Boats, for example.

Because the proportion of youngsters will be declining, you'll see less emphasis on kiddy-oriented theme parks with hair-raising adventure rides; these have already peaked. In years to come, developers will be looking for ways to lure an older and more upscale crowd.

There will be indoor theme malls in urban areas, packed with entertainment features, good food-and-drink places and attractive retail outlets. Some of these, planned now in several major cities, will be below ground in sprawling spaces connected by tunnels and walkways and accessible from apartments and office buildings, as well as subways.

Many cities also will be looking for ways to entice private developers into joint deals for entertainment centers of various kinds on city-owned land or on land the city might acquire, along a waterfront or in some other attractive area.

"Destination resorts"—places people travel to for a stay of a week or more—will be competing harder than ever for attention. Those within fairly easy driving distance of large metro areas will continue to do well, but others in more remote spots will be increasingly dependent on air travel to keep their attendance up. The reason: Long-distance driving won't be so popular in tomorrow's smaller cars. Average length of trips will diminish, but airlines will offer more kinds of package deals, including special off-peak fares and car rentals. So will some resorts.

Theme parks probably have had it for some years to come, with the notable exception of the Disney parks in California and Florida. Few others have done well, and plans for new ones have been canceled right and left.

Ski resorts, facing an older population, must diversify, go year-round with all sorts of warm-weather attractions, such things as Alpine slides, water slides, chair-lift rides, golf courses, classical music and jazz festivals.

Cruises will diversify to push their market *down* in age, luring the young traveler with a variety of adventures—cruises to nowhere, learning cruises, party cruises, whatever they can think of. And more experimentation with combination cruise-and-fly packages.

The recreational vehicle business is in for better times. Older Americans, the principal buyers of self-propelled motor homes and trailers, will be not only more numerous but also better heeled than now, which the industry regards as a good omen. Producers plan to offer new models that are both more luxurious and economical to operate, with streamlining and high-efficiency engines and special gear ratios.

Auto companies will offer models with features aimed at the trailer crowd—four-wheel drive and stronger towing capacity combined with fuel efficiencies of up to 25 miles a gallon, perhaps even better as improved engines come along.

Motor-home travelers will need a lot more campgrounds than exist now and they will want quality. Traditional campgrounds will not enjoy growth in business; the trend is to motor-home parks called "preserves," in which quality and scenic values will be stressed, along with services and recreational facilities. Some will be condos or timeshare resorts.

Shopping around for a camp spot will become a matter of checking in with the nearest computer terminal—perhaps in a travel agent's office, a shopping mall or in your own living room via a home computer and a telephone modem.

Timesharing probably will extend to the motor homes themselves. Some owners will elect to leave them parked in camps, where others can rent their use for specified time periods, with the camp proprietors charging a fee as intermediaries.

BOATS AND PLANES

The boating boom likewise shows no signs of slowing in the years ahead. In fact, its continued growth may begin to create problems for boat owners and sellers alike: Overcrowding on lakes and waterways.

Boat-storage and service space will be at a premium, and many owners will have to travel some distance to find an affordable slot. As space for full-fledged marinas grows scarce, more will turn to "boatels" sandwiched into whatever is left over along shorelines—no-frills places where boats can be hung or stacked under cover for a fee.

Sailboats may grow some new kinds of sails: Stiff, lightweight panels resembling vertical airplane wings. They'll take the place of jibs and spinnakers and, via fine-tuning of their attitude and surfaces, impart greater speed and maneuverability.

With increasing affluence and leisure time will come an increase in private airplane ownership, and new models will be smaller, less expensive and more fuel efficient. Super-light aircraft will continue to grow in popularity for fun, not travel, and improvements will be made in their now-questionable safety.

PETS

Pets will be a rising part of the American population indefinitely, in part because so many people will be living alone, especially the expanding elderly group. With a majority of them living in apartments where dog ownership is either banned or difficult, cats are likely to be the pet of choice. "Kitten wanted" signs will replace "free kittens" notices on community bulletin boards.

The doggie scene will be divided even more than now between minis and compacts for apartment dwellers and the conventional full-sized models for home guard duty.

The veterinary business will expand in step with all this, and health insurance for pets will become widely available, along with improved vaccines and other remedies for common pet ailments. Vets will be able to plug into computerized diagnostic services via telephone lines to check out x-rays and cardiograms of ailing pets. One such service, called Cardiopet, is already in operation.

The health-food trend applies to pets, too: new varieties of geriatric foods for elderly animals, others for pregnant pets; low-calorie diets; and a kind of birth-control additive that can be put into dog food at the factory.

SPORTS

Consider the demographics of sports over the next 14 years. An aging population will go for the less-strenuous outdoor sports. This will be good for golf, not so good for downhill skiing (better for cross-country skiing), okay for tennis.

Sporting goods manufacturers will be doing their best to make sports easier and less embarrassing for novices—young or old. Oversize tennis balls and racquets, hollowback golf clubs that allow even duffers to hit the ball straighter, Cayman golf balls for scaled-down courses, smaller basketballs for women players—all are symbolic of this trend.

Golf, the perfect low-stress sport for an aging population with lots of time on its hands, will be limited only by the availability of real estate. Courses will have to move farther out into the countryside as developers buy up closer-in acreage. The big growth will be in short-yardage "stadium" courses, for faster play and easier spectator viewing. In the Sunbelt, golf courses will be the obligatory centerpiece of most new retirement developments.

On the spectator side, the TV audience for all sports will grow, due to improvements in reception and vast expansion in availability of channels. But paid attendance at games will shrink, both because ticket prices are likely to rise faster than incomes and because of TV overexposure. Legalized betting via home computer may come along before 2000.

Spectator sports are simply one form of entertainment. How the entertainment dollar will be spent a decade or two from now is up for grabs. There will be a lot of competition for it.

College sports will continue to grapple with recruiting abuses under the pressure of public criticism and state legislation, but probably without much major change from today's conditions. Achieving a wholesome balance between college academics and athletics will be just as difficult in 2000 as today.

In addition to the traditional college sports, keep an eye on lacrosse, which is beginning to spread as a high school and college sport and which may make the Big Ten in the next decade or two.

In international sports, the single most important development is likely to be the emergence of China as the dominant entry. The People's Republic has made a commitment to athletic excellence that began to show at the 1984 Olympics. With its massive population and the discipline built into its system, China can be expected to challenge and even surpass the U.S. and Soviet Bloc countries in many sports.

International stresses are probably going to force the Olympics to settle on either a permanent site or a series of sites that are politically acceptable to enough countries to avoid boycotts.

A breakdown in East-West relations could of course result in a dual Olympics—one for the communist world, one for the rest.

But it is equally possible and perhaps more likely that several fully successful international gatherings of athletes will be held between now and the turn of the century.

On the spectator sports scene of the year 2000, professional football, baseball and soccer will be winners, basketball a loser. It will shrink, undergoing considerable modification in the process, while the others will grow in size, audience and profits.

Here are some highly speculative forecasts:

Baseball: The major leagues will go through another round of expansion over the next several years...new franchises turning up in cities like Denver, Washington, D.C., Tampa-St. Petersburg, New Orleans, Indianapolis and Vancouver, B.C. Perhaps further afield toward the end of the century—say, to Mexico City, San Juan, even Tokyo—if travel-cost problems can be licked and valuable domestic TV markets protected.

Eventually, multiple divisions will be contested in the season and the play-off format will have to be altered to fit. The World Series will be played at some warm-weather site to assure smooth staging and vigorous promotion. Artificial turf and indoor fields will make for further changes in the way the game is played.

Women will move into bigger roles on the field as umpires at first and, later on, perhaps as coaches, announcers and team executives, even as managers—which should help widen the audience to include more of them.

And by 2000 or thereabouts, it may be the only spectator sport still within reach of the "common man," with a low enough ticket price to lure him away from his TV set and bring him to the park.

Football: The pro game will stay popular for the appeal of its violence—which some reformers would like to tame down via rules modifications, larger fields, improved protective equipment and the like. This sort of "reform" hasn't much chance of success at the pro level, but perhaps some in college football.

Soccer: It's on its way to becoming a major indoor sport. Soccer promoters will abandon all pretense that the outdoor game can succeed in the U.S. the way it has elsewhere and move the game indoors, where the big bucks are.

Interest in the game—both indoor and outdoor—will be bolstered by the large number of kids playing today who will be tomorrow's adults bringing their own kids to games.

And if promoters and players can lend more nuance to the game to lift it from its present status as pinball on a carpet, indoor soccer will grow in respect, paid attendance and TV exposure.

Basketball: The pro game has probably reached its limits under current conditions and will have to be altered to keep the public interested instead of turning to college play, which already draws bigger crowds and TV ratings for major games. Pro players have outgrown the structure of the game: too big and too talented. The backboard and basket may have to be raised and the court lengthened. Otherwise, it may be a fading TV attraction by 2000.

Hockey: Increased international competition may be the only way for this sport to attract growing interest. As it is, too many teams make the play-offs to generate much excitement. Entry of more players from abroad, especially from the East Bloc, and perhaps of entire clubs, is likely. European teams may join the National Hockey League to compete for the Stanley Cup. Besides recruiting foreign players, pro teams will rely heavily on U.S. college teams as their "farm" system.

17

Building for Tomorrow

New residential construction is heading into a modest slowdown in the '90s, as the percentage of young adults in the population shrinks.

But as in so many other fields, an aging population and changes in office work and manufacturing will make enormous opportunities for builders who see them coming. In construction, there will be tremendous demand for remodeling, second-home construction, and rehabilitation of houses and office buildings that were new in 1960—a quarter-century ago in years, but even longer ago in terms of energy efficiency and high-tech features tomorrow's owners will want.

The decline in population growth will be concentrated in the adult age group where first-time home purchases are traditionally the heaviest—the under-35-year-olds. Their drop will be about 22% through the year 2010, and with this goes a decline in new family formations. Demand for new housing will slide along with it.

From a current annual rate of about 1.7 million, starts will bottom out around 1.5 million in the mid-'90s until the young house buyers become more numerous in the second or third decade of the new century.

Certainly not a disaster—but not much to crow about either, compared to the 1.8 million average of the '70s. But the '70s were something of an aberration. Starts had averaged under 1.5 million during the previous two decades, and what lies ahead for building is just a return to the old pattern. But that's cold comfort to the builders, some seven percent of whom will go out of business in the next 10 years, while many of the rest will have to tread water pretty hard.

Construction-materials suppliers will do better than the housing industry as a whole. Demand for rehab and fix-up supplies in general is expected to grow throughout the rest of this century.

Construction of speculative office buildings is going to taper off and go into a lull while demand catches up with oversupply in many metro areas of the country. That could take a while, given the current vacancy rate of 16%, the highest it has ever been. Overbuilding has in large part been a response to tax incentives, but the depressing effect on rents may well offset the tax advantages.

Still, there will continue to be plenty of activity among developers of less ambitious, low-rise, high-amenity suburban office buildings and office parks in growth areas—particularly where local programs to attract high-tech firms provide incentives.

Another trend to watch: renovation of relatively new office buildings to update their heating, air conditioning and elevator systems with computerized, energy-saving technology and to install facilities for the handicapped. Some of this may include new exteriors to get away from the manufactured, prefab look.

Commercial-industrial builders will find attractive pickings in the market for new, smaller factories as the concept of "flexible manufacturing" catches on. High-tech won't need large factories, certainly not on the old, conventional scale of basic manufacturing. Five thousand to 50,000 square feet may be the practical range.

The construction industry, no less than the economy at large, is heading into a time when a lot of taken-for-granted features will undergo substantial and occasionally wrenching change.

HOMES FOR ALMOST ALL

An increasing proportion of the housing industry will turn to rehabilitation, renewal and conversion. Older housing will be upgraded and redesigned into multiple units to accommodate the needs of a large segment of the population that can't afford a new house.

Affordability is a large part of the problem. It's not just house price tags but also the availability of mortgage financing at bearable rates. The cost of owning a house already takes up to half the average family's income, counting the whole works—mortgage payments, insurance, taxes, utilities and so on. Mortgage payments alone run between 30% and 40% of family income, but were only 20% in the '70s. With interest rates trending lower than in the '70s and early '80s and personal incomes rising, we expect overall affordability to improve in the years ahead—but not back to what it was for the parents of tomorrow's young home buyers.

But what depresses one segment of the housing market may boost another, and the affordability issue is an illustration. It will divert more housing into the rehab and conversion end of the market, and old houses will be turned into two and three-family units, not just in the cities but also in the older, close-in surburbs—and later on, to some of the farther-out ones in large metro areas.

The 35-to-44 age group will expand by about a fourth in the next 15 years, and by 2000 the vanguard of the Baby Boom will be entering retirement age, which will bolster the market for older homes in the next decade or two. This is going to be a well-off generation, and many of its members will be moving on and up to larger houses—although not necessarily new ones...more likely, older ones. Another boost for the rehab market, and a healthy outlook for trading-up and house resales in general.

Old folks will be more numerous toward the end of the century, which will create strong demand for specialized housing. The parents of the Baby Boom are now in their 50s and 60s, and by 2000 the ranks of the really old—85 and up—will double...close to five million of them.

This is a new phenomenon and will put extra demands on the housing industry—and provide opportunities as well. Many builders and developers will specialize in modes of housing tailored to the needs of the elderly, ranging from backyard "granny flats" and small apartments tucked into existing houses on up to new "congregate" group-living accommodations with varying degrees of built-in health, medical and recreational facilities.

HIGH-TECH HOUSES

Technology will be an important factor in all new housing. For the affluent elderly, builders will offer built-in security systems, emergency communications and alarms, electronic monitoring equipment for medical conditions plus video and teletex shopping arrangements. For the less affluent, much of this may be affordable on a shared basis in retirement villages, apartment complexes and the like.

Most new homes in the '90s and beyond will be wired for communications and central electronic controls, incorporating fiber-optic cable as it becomes available. Central systems will monitor energy use, programmable for the operation of appliances around the clock. Upcoming designs will provide appliances that require far less complicated electro-mechanical features and controls. Fast-response fire sprinkler systems for residences, already available at ever-declining prices, will be common in new construction in a few years, spurred by municipal fire marshals and the easing of building codes to offset the developers' cost of installing sprinklers.

All these high-tech systems call for the writing of industrywide standards, along with modernized local wiring codes to go with them. Builders and manufacturers will lobby hard for them everywhere.

SMALL HOUSES

Driven by cost restraints, builders will continue downsizing and leaving more interior areas unfinished for buyers to tackle on their own time. Smaller lot sizes too, where local zoning authorities are willing to accommodate the trend and to permit "infilling" of available space in built-up areas.

As an offset to smaller and fewer rooms, house builders will offer as much open interior space as they can get away with: Cathedral ceilings, half-partitions in living room, dining and recreation areas to create a roomy feel.

To make better use of available sites, builders will turn increasingly to "clustered" development, houses gathered closely on cul-de-sacs and the like with patches of green between the clusters, instead of the more conventional spread-out, block-by-block patterns of the older suburbs.

There will be even more concentration on townhouse developments for singles and childless couples, including "stacked" townhouses—clustered vertically as well as horizontally. And more "zero-lot-line" houses where zoning permits—houses built right on one boundary line, with no setback, to give more usable yard.

Manufactured housing will expand by close to half by 2000, including all sorts of modular and precut types. But mobile homes, the kind that are factory assembled and then trucked to a site, probably won't do so well. Builders anticipate a modest decline in their shipments, but only in line with the overall drop in housing starts.

Japanese imports will take over a rising share of the American rehab and manufactured-housing markets. Builders in Japan already are producing more manufactured units for their own market than are being built in ours and have developed some good-looking designs using a variety of new materials. One is a precast ceramic-and-aggregate concrete wall which incorporates air bubbles for lightness and strength. This will be turning up here at competitive prices.

HOUSING FOR THE POOR

The outlook for public and other low-cost housing is bleak. Government subsidies are being trimmed or withdrawn and aren't likely to be restored in much volume for some time to come, given the spending restraints in Washington. So there will be a great deal of unsatisfied demand in coming years, and states and localities will be more on their own in meeting it. The impact will be worst in the older, industrial states where mass-employment industries are shrinking and so are local revenue bases.

One result will be the deterioration of many older suburbs into outright slums. These will be the only affordable housing for families at or near the poverty line. The middle class will move farther out into distant suburbs and, in more crowded parts of the country, these will begin to blend together into more and more metropolitan sprawl.

By the early-to-mid-'90s, the problem may have grown severe enough to force reconsideration of federal low-cost housing. With the deficit under better control and tax revenues rising as the high-tech boom gathers force, the time then may be ripe for a revival of such programs.

OFFICES OF TOMORROW

The restoration trend in office and commercial buildings will continue, with particular concentration in older cities where architecturally interesting structures are available and eligible for historic preservation tax credits. Facades of many of these will be fixed up with the use of new, lightweight substitute materials to reproduce the original features of old, weather-scarred exteriors.

The steel-and-glass box will continue to dominate the suburban skylines of most growing metro areas, chiefly because it's cheaper than most other styles and Americans have at least grown used to it. But many architects believe, or at least hope, that movement toward more imaginative and eye-pleasing design is developing, impelled in no small part by growing nostalgia for earlier tastes and by boredom with the plain box. Affordability and investor preference will have the final word on that.

Office buildings, like homes, will incorporate communications technology—prewired with fiber-optic cable and the like. Flat broad-band cable to carry digital communications of all kinds and suitable for laying under carpet will be used as quickly as local codes catch up.

But the recent trend to installing common computer and switching facilities will fade out. Many developers find these to be white elephants when incoming tenants choose to install their own equipment or are branch offices of companies with individualized networks.

There will be fewer sealed buildings. Most new ones will have openable windows, and some older ones will be refitted with them to combat the interior pollution that can build up from chemical fumes given off by furnishings, heating systems and office equipment...not to mention smokers.

There will be experiments with "holographic" windows that focus daylight deep into interiors, and with heat pumps to use warmth generated by building occupants and their electronic gadgetry.

In some larger cities that continue to attract investors, office buildings will soar ever higher to cram more income production onto increasingly valuable land. Technologically, at least, there is no longer any reason why Frank Lloyd Wright's dream of a mile-high tower could not be realized.

Builders will find location progressively less critical to industrial clients and to many kinds of office development. Ease of communications via computer and high-speed networks will encourage dispersal of facilities to lower-cost areas, and a growing number of employees will become rural commuters or even telecommuters, working at home and transmitting their product to the office. These trends are worth watching for their potential impact on land values on the edge of metropolitan areas and beyond.

WHERE WE'LL BUILD

Builders expect to follow the population trend to the Sunbelt; they foresee high rates of growth there in all construction modes. But this won't be a smooth pattern. Activity will concentrate in metro areas where it already is intense—the Los Angeles-San Diego corridor, for example; in and around Phoenix; the Miami-Ft. Lauderdale area; and so on. In between, large stretches of Sunbelt states will remain sparsely inhabited with continued patchy development of retirement communities but also with growing worries about water supply.

The "new town" wave has probably had its day, at least for this century. It is unlikely that there will be many more launchings of self-contained communities on empty land outside population centers. Most of those built in recent decades have had trouble attracting and holding enough industry to support local employment and have been taken over by other developers, turning into commuter communities like any other.

PAYING FOR HOUSING

The adjustable-rate mortgage will have its ups and downs but won't go away. However, many in housing finance doubt it will become the dominant mode. The conventional fixed-term, fixed-payment mortgage will be preferred in an era of stable and generally lower interest rates.

We'll probably see a reduction in the kinds of mortgages offered, with conventionals available for terms of 15 to 30 years and the ARM itself becoming more standardized in its traits—frequency of rate adjustments, interest rate caps, the kinds of indexes it is tied to, and so on.

More builders will get involved in the front end of mortgage finance, working with lenders to tap capital markets and obtain advance commitments to encourage buyers. Secondary markets will grow and diversify, especially if future administrations continue to push the "privatization" of the Federal National Mortgage Association and the Federal Home Loan Mortgage Corporation. Creation of the Home Mortgage Access Corporation is an example of a builder-related conduit for issuance of mortgage pass-through securities and builder bonds backed by mortgages to finance house sales.

Within a few years a kind of "one-stop shopping" may be the common thing in finding both a new home and the financing for it, all done in the real estate office. Customers will be able to "drive" through a neighborhood via video presentations to single out houses in their price and size range before going out to poke around in person, which should eliminate a lot of aimless cruising. Computerized classifieds will be available at home via phone; they will be displayed on home computers or TV sets.

Brokers' computers are already able to search through financial markets around the region or the country for the best available mortgage deals and serve up summaries for comparison purposes, choosing one to fit the needs and abilities of the individual buyer. Computerized mortgage search firms will grow, making the residential housing finance market a truly national shopping mart.

It should even be possible to process loan applications on the spot via computer networks, the convenience of which will shave both the time it takes for such deals and their cost. Origination fees might even come down a point or so.

18

New Home Appliances

The home appliances and tools of tomorrow will be characterized by lightness, portability, longer life, more choice of sizes, and technological sophistication paired with simplicity of operation. They will use tiny computers to save energy and water and to adjust the machine's effort to the particular task at hand.

Many appliances will be programmable to operate when you're out, and soon you'll be able to turn them on and off by telephone when you're away.

Upcoming generations of clothes washers and dryers will incorporate fundamental changes that should double their life span: automatic load-leveling devices to prevent undue vibration and noise, and most important, new variable-speed electric motors which, via microchip controls, speed up when confronted with extra strain and slow down under easier conditions—the opposite of the way most motors work today. This is what will eliminate mechanical drive connections, including clutches, and contribute most to appliance durability.

The same kind of variable-speed technology will be featured in a wide range of small kitchen appliances, such as mixers that won't spatter when lifted from the bowl.

Manufacturers plan to introduce soon a new intermediate "compact" line of appliances to fit between the standard large sizes and the minis made for apartments and motor homes. These will be downsized to fit the modest dimensions of most new houses and the needs of singles and working women.

The old "suds-saver" feature that used to recycle wash water has all but disappeared but will probably turn up again eventually, as an option to comply with local ordinances in water-starved areas.

Refrigerators will have greater capacity without getting bigger; their outer walls will be thinned down to a half inch or so, employing new thermos-type insulation panels developed in Japan and soon to show up in this country. Houses will be getting smaller but not kitchens, so producers plan to continue their line of full-sized refrigerators and freezers along with the compact and mini sizes.

Thanks to improved motors and compressors, the reliability of all home appliances should improve by at least 25% in the next few years, and their warranties will reflect this.

Most large appliances will have radically different control panels featuring diagnostics: screens that will display messages when something goes wrong, giving instructions on how to test for malfunctions. You'll be able to phone this information to a service person who will advise on what's needed—probably saving a great many house calls, since many components will be simple pull-out, push-in packages that can be picked up at an appliance shop. The farthest-out version of this kind of service is the wired-up appliance that will report its problems direct to a service center, but don't expect this to be cheap or widespread before 2000.

Central control systems for all appliances in a house are becoming available so that you can set on-off times for each of them before traipsing off to work. These can also be set and reset over the phone and will deliver emergency messages if something goes on the blink. Home sound and security systems can be plugged in as well.

New kinds of microchips to control the flow of current to such appliances as air conditioners, furnace blowers and fluorescent light fixtures will reduce electrical consumption in homes, offices and factories by adjusting to variations in demand and eliminating costly speedups and cutoffs.

The biggest new trend in small tools for home use will come in cordless technology. Improved batteries will greatly increase the power and durability of a wide range of portables, which will run at steady power under variable loads, using variable-speed motors controlled by microprocessors.

For example, saws won't choke up or kick back in tough stock; microsensors will adjust the power instantly. New heavy-duty portables will show up earliest in construction equipment—saws, impact hammers, drills and the like—and then will be adapted to home-size tools. The chains on chain saws will be redesigned to widen the cut and reduce the chances of a blade binding in wood.

The new engine technology that is taking over in autos will also help improve the power-to-weight ratio in yard and garden power equipment. Most mowers will continue to use gasoline engines, but they will run more smoothly and quietly, and replacement parts will be combined and simplified.

Electric mowers will be in demand by new homeowners in the small yards that developers and builders will be offering in the suburbs as well as by old folks. And if good enough batteries come along, they'll go cordless.

Another trend to watch: more yard stuff for rent. Producers plan special lines of equipment to sell to rental stores, which are expected to expand all over the country. These will be scaled-down versions of commercial items that most homeowners need only occasionally, perhaps just once a year. Things like tillers, garden tractors, chain saws, mixers and others.

19

Home Entertainment

Thanks to dramatic improvements and cost-cutting in electronics, the home will soon offer virtually everything in entertainment the stage and movie theater have, except the "reality" of live performers or a screen 20 feet tall.

And in terms of technical fidelity and choice of content and timing, the home will have many advantages over the theater.

In another few years, today's technology of video cassette tapes or disks rented at a local store and brought home for replay will seem quaint. The new marketing of home entertainment will more closely resemble the pay TV systems of yesteryear or today's emerging pay-by-view cable systems.

By the year 2000, recorded home entertainment will come directly into a satellite dish on your roof or over phone lines. This will offer the full range of movies, sports events, rock video, classical and pop music or anything else that can be transmitted digitally, from one computer to another.

Satellite reception will not be free, however. Cable networks are already beginning to use sophisticated signal scramblers to make sure that dish owners have paid a subscription fee for device to decode the signal.

Use of phone lines to receive conventional video programming won't come overnight. That would require a total conversion of the nation's phone system to fiber-optic transmission, and the expense will be a major deterrent for years to come. And there will be regulatory hurdles to clear, too, not to mention the opposition of a growing cable industry. But in the meantime, transmission of digitally coded TV and sound will be taking off.

THE NEW DISKS

Your record collection will shrink drastically in physical volume, while growing enormously in capacity. That's the prospect for the '90s, and by the year 2000 almost all recordings will probably be delivered digitally, which simply means translating information (sight, sound, whatever) into the language that computers use. The result is delivery of sound and scene with a fidelity that far exceeds the best now available via conventional tapes, records and TV sets.

Record stores and movie rental shops will gradually metamorphose into electronic data bases. To buy a record—whether of a song, a symphony, a music-TV performance or, for that matter, a movie—you will call the store, place your order, pay for it with your credit/debit card or charge it to your phone bill, and push a couple of buttons. The store will feed your order directly to your home recorder in a flash. Record stores will probably keep some kind of retail outlet available for browsers, but their biggest business will be done by phone and, most likely, by "intelligent" computers that can take and fill voice orders.

The new record players will in effect be computers programmed to play music and video. They will use either floppy disks similar to the 5-1/4-inch disks now used in computers but of a higher, more dense quality, or some improved version of the laser-read "compact disks" now growing in favor on the hi-fi scene. Both will come down in price, but the floppy-disk variety is likely to be the cheaper, selling for only a few dollars plus the recording charge, and may even become cheap enough to be regarded as disposable.

The player will have connections for plugging in your TV—a digital, wall-hung thin screen—or your computer monitor. At the same time, TV fidelity will be improving via new "high resolution" technology now in the works.

Either way, you will get picture quality far above anything now available and sound fidelity to match or exceed today's best compact optical-disk players, which already have begun to supplant tape players for the cognoscenti. And conventional 33-1/3 rpm records will be found mostly in museums and on the shelves of diehard traditionalists.

Laser-optical-disk storage is now the leading edge of digital recording, whether of sound, visuals or numerical data, but the floppy-disk technology described above will increasingly compete with it.

The advantages of the optical disk over conventional technologies are simplicity and durability (hardly any moving parts), improved fidelity and, most of all, enormous capacity. Whole libraries can be stored on one or two of them. Rooms full of data shrunk to a few small disks which are inscribed upon and read by laser beams. Today they work only as prerecorded disks for playback; tomorrow's will be as versatile as tape, capable of being edited, added to or wiped clean for rerecording.

GOODBYE DISKS?

And in coming years even this capacity may be dwarfed by advanced physics, so-called bubble memory, which provides infinitely greater space on a microchip and is permanent—that is, not subject to any kind of loss or degradation except by outright physical damage. And still only in the conceptual stage but sure to be tested before 2000 is a further improvement on this which, if successful, will provide almost infinite expansion in data-storage capacity: Literally millions of pages on a single microchip.

Chip storage of this kind may well replace disks of ALL kinds by 2000 or soon after. A bit of plastic the size of today's credit cards could carry enormous amounts of information, to be played back as sound or as a display on a video screen. This kind of gadget would be almost indestructible under ordinary conditions and of course highly portable, which opens up all kinds of commercial and military applications.

THE DEVICES

Tape recorders will shrink to vest-pocket size with improved fidelity over today's best professional kinds and with many times their capacity. Radio and TV broadcasters will shift away from tape equipment, which is delicate and expensive to maintain, to the new digital kinds of storage-and-playback systems—a potentially huge market in itself. TV cameras and broadcast equipment will all be digital within less than a decade.

The more compact such equipment becomes, the easier it will be to adapt it to other home uses, including video cameras and playback systems. Do-it-yourself home movies already are heavily trending into video, and within, say, five years or so, they will have gone completely that way, simple and foolproof enough for a child to use. Professional-level video editing—including freeze frames, superimposing of images, and all the rest—will become routine for amateurs.

The television screen itself will go in two directions—flatter and bigger in area. In just a couple of years, the long-predicted and long-delayed skinny screens will hit the market, large screens just a few inches deep that you can hang on the wall; they'll have a liquid-crystal display rather than cathode ray tubes. The new high-resolution sets will deliver unprecedented picture clarity.

The video cassette tape may not have a long-term future, but it will enjoy spreading popularity and improvements over the next few years. The recording and playback unit will eventually be incorporated into the TV itself, and it will play in stereo, as some TV programming now does on suitably equipped TV sets. TV stations and networks will probably broadcast around the clock, perhaps on multiple channels, for the benefit of people who want to record what they don't care to stay up for.

Direct access to satellite channels will grow cheaper and easier via home dish antennas which will be no more expensive than a good conventional rooftop antenna is today. The Japanese already are moving into the market with one version.

But some time in the next decade or so the VCR will come under fire from the floppy-disk technology already described. The two systems will probably go head to head for a while before one or the other wins out. Our guess is that the floppies will emerge on top in the long run; they're more versatile, incorporating the VCR's capabilities along with other tricks.

The movie industry will be watching all this closely—and perhaps buying into it. The young crowd that the industry now caters to will be shrinking, while much of the older crowd may prefer to do its watching at home. The producing end of the business will do all right; there'll be a huge demand for films. But distributors may be squeezed by direct electronic merchandising, and theater owners may have to think about reviving double features and free dinnerware.

The spread of home computers and digitalized recording equipment will bring on the growth of new kinds of over-the-wire services—"TV clipping services," for example, outfits that will watch for whatever the client wants from TV around the country and provide a recorded collection of its findings. There will be home and business instruction materials of all kinds, software distribution, and tax consultation. "Videotext"—whole newspapers on the video screen—will come of age in the '90s, after a lot of trial-and-error floundering.

The new equipment will allow home viewers to do their own TV editing, recording and superimposing of programs so that two can be watched at once on a split screen, plus selecting freeze frames to be zipped out on high-speed printers (an expensive extra) or simply stored for future reference. Radio programs can be recorded at the same time; and all radio shows, even on AM, will be in stereo by the mid-'90s.

Still photography won't stand still, either. Electronic cameras using magnetic disks instead of film will produce stills that can be displayed on your TV, where, via digital techniques, you'll be able to edit them—heighten or soften contrasts, adjust color, crop or enlarge—and then print them out. The cameras themselves will make all picture-taking decisions for you—although some pros and advanced amateurs will insist on models with control-overrides for special situations. Film (and later, the magnetic disks) will become so sensitive that flash will hardly ever be needed.

Digital gadgetry will take over more and more of the music business in the same period, for professionals and amateurs alike. Electronic keyboards plugged into digital recording and playback equipment will produce all the sounds of individual instruments in the orchestra. These home synthesizers will be far more versatile than today's best professional models.

HOME AS ENTERTAINMENT CENTER

In sum, the next two decades will see an acceleration of the 60-year-old trend towards the home as the place where we enjoy top-quality professional entertainment.

Until the 1920s, professional music, dance and comedy were available only to the relatively few people who had the means to see them live in local concert halls and cabarets.

Radio changed all that, bringing both great culture and low-brow entertainment into the homes of millions of people at low cost.

Developing in parallel with radio entertainment was the movie industry, which took people out of their homes in droves. The development of television in the late '40s brought predictions of the demise of both radio and motion pictures. The sentence was premature. The movie industry was once again declared terminally ill a few years ago, and this time the slayer was supposed to be cable television and, later, video cassettes.

Well, traditional in-theater movie viewing is not dead, having proved remarkably durable as a great escape—literally—from cares at home.

Nor are the live performing arts suffering from the ready availability of canned performances. An increasingly well-educated and affluent population will provide a growing audience for both pop and classical performances. If anything, recorded performances, especially video versions, will make superstars of more and more serious performing artists, whetting the public's appetite to see them in person.

Live performance will remain a vital part of the American scene, but make no mistake about this: Electronic renditions of the arts, played in the home, will be the entertainment boom field of the next several decades.

20

News and Information

Just about all the news and information Americans will receive in the years ahead will be produced electronically and, more and more, delivered the same way. Even your home newspaper will be made up and printed entirely by electronics (many already are).

Television and radio will continue to be the primary sources of news for the majority of the population, ahead of newspapers and magazines, but print will still be the dominant source for in-depth, specialized information of all kinds, including political, business, and leisure information.

Traditional network television, supported solely by advertising revenue, is heading into rough waters. People will continue to turn away from mediocre network programming in favor of rented VCR movies and specialized programming on pay-per-view cable systems.

Already many viewers are taping their favorite network shows for later viewing, at which time they skip over the commercials with the fast-forward button on the VCR. Even bigger threats to commercial revenue—and ultimately, the survival of traditional network television—are new devices that "zap" (blank out) commercials during viewing and taping.

So far, advertising rates for network television don't reflect the increasing market share of cable and non-broadcast video viewing (i.e, rental tapes). And they certainly don't take into account the growing disregard of commercials by "time-shifters" and "zappers." If someone comes up with a way of estimating what

189

portion of the audience never saw the commercial, network ad rates will suffer.

Radio has seen most of its great leaps forward already, in the '70s, with the explosion of FM stereo and the trend towards market segmentation—all news, talk, classical music, country, rock, religious, etc. Not much room for dramatic changes here; aside from improvements in AM with clearer signals and stereophonic sound, but radio will remain a major news source, entertainer and companion for people in every age group.

THE PRINTED WORD

The world of print publishing will depend upon electronics and computerization, with enormous labor savings, to remain competitive with the broadcast world and with new forms of electronic communication, such as newspapers that will come into the home on personal computers.

Publishing and printing of news and leisure reading will be healthy and a growing industry for a long time to come. But there will be evolutionary changes brought about by demographics and technology.

The habit of reading the printed word is so ingrained in educated people that it has survived every assault against it for more than 60 years: radio, the movies, television, and now "videotext" versions of daily newspapers and magazines.

With a computer database service received over a home computer, the user can merely print out the news, feature articles, ads, and photos he wishes to keep. But it seems improbable that these will cut deeply into newspaper or magazine circulation for a long time. The big drawback will be cost; even though it will come down, it will still be substantially higher than receiving printed material in the mail or by home delivery.

People still seem to want "hard copy" they can hold in their hands, take from room to room, save, clip, pass along to a friend. And the more visually attractive the printed medium is—such as full-color photography in magazines—the harder it will be for electronics to dethrone. High-definition TV may pose a competitive problem for some magazines that rely heavily on high-quality photography, but no time soon. Home print-out equipment, for making permanent color photos off a high-resolution TV, will be very expensive for a long time.

Utilitarian reading with lower production quality, such as newspapers and trade publications, will be more vulnerable to the competition of electronic delivery.

The printed word will survive, but the days of easily won mass-media growth may be over. Periodicals will increasingly aim for segments of a many-segmented market, leaving the rest to television.

Demographic trends are favorable to the printed word. It is preferred by older, better-educated people, and there will be a lot more of these in the population over the next few decades.

The youngers, those still in grade school today, will be more open to innovations, but there will be proportionately fewer of them in the population. The middle aged, the biggest group of all, are today's young up-&-coming generation... on the leading edge of technological change but still raised on print as well as electronic media.

MAGAZINES

The circulation (and possibly advertising) growth of large, general-interest magazines is probably over. Meanwhile the number of specialized magazines is still growing—something like 200 new ones appear every year—and so is their overall readership. The mortality rate is high, of course, but for each failure another venture is launched.

Fierce competition among media today is demoting advertising space and time to the lowly status of a commodity, and all broadcasters and publishers will have an increasingly hard time raising, or in some cases even maintaining, current ad rates. Media owners of the future will need to shift more of their costs to the reader and viewer. For very large magazines, higher subscriptions prices will result in lower circulation levels, but the savings in direct-mail solicitation expense may make them more profitable.

Using satellite transmission to regional printing plants, large national magazines will intensify their use of regional and local ad pages, offering advertisers far more flexibility in targeting specific audiences. Editorial and ad lead times will be greatly shortened by technology.

NEWSPAPERS

For most newspapers, the chief competition will be TV—especially 24-hour news shows—and other newspapers, not computer-served text services.

Newspapers will invest heavily in new technology, including processes that make it easy to put together whole pages electronically, eliminating the paste-up process that itself eliminated hot type. (Full-page make-up is already here, and getting easier all the time.) Regional editions will spread until some dailies are attempting to cover large areas of the country. And more of the largest will probably experiment with national editions to compete with *USA Today*, the *Wall Street Journal*, the *Christian Science Monitor* and the national editions of the *Washington Post* and *New York Times*.

Satellite-transmission techniques will make regional printing of national editions easy. The *Wall Street Journal* has already shown the way, sending whole pages by satellite and reconstituting them onto printing plates using a facsimile process. And newspapers are even experimenting with new inks that don't rub off on your hands.

Weeklies will proliferate as suburbs spread farther out, nibbling at the edges of metropolitan-daily circulation. Interest in local news will force the big dailies to do more zoning and regional editions, requiring additional printing plants and a lot of electronics. Local and regional sections will go daily in the larger metro areas. And papers will spruce themselves up with improved typography and color to attract and hold readers.

Even the foreign-language press is likely to thrive; most of its members will be small weeklies, plus a few dailies. The bulk of them today are in Spanish, which will continue to be the dominant second language, but others are springing up in Asian languages as well. For a model of what may become of most of these foreign-language papers in a few decades, consider the Jewish press: It used to be printed exclusively in Yiddish; now, most of its papers are in English.

NEWSLETTERS AND BOOKS

Newsletters will continue to flourish on every conceivable and marketable subject, finding new special niches, but more of them will be on-line, meaning available via computer networks. These will appeal chiefly to business clients and others who need the information in a hurry and are able to print it out on their own inexpensive dot-matrix or daisy wheel printers.

Book publishing, too, must adapt to changing times, and it will. Many authors of fiction and nonfiction works are writing and editing their manuscripts exclusively on computers today. The book you're reading now was created entirely on word processors, including editing and transmission over telephone lines to a typesetter.

Book publishing will eventually move toward a hybrid state: More books issued with a TV or computer disk in a back pocket. This probably won't spread much beyond educational and how-to-do-it stuff, but those markets will be substantial.

Consider the possibility of books printed on demand: Entire books or parts of them could be zipped out on a printer leased by the publisher to booksellers and libraries. For owners of the right kind of computer laser-printer, such service might be available in the home, offered by book clubs or even magazine and newspaper publishers. But most of this instant-print technique is more likely to be used for specialized, out-of-print and other marginal titles; best sellers will still be a bookstore item.

Library and publisher storage of books will probably be revolutionized, however. Books will be stored electronically via optical scanners on small cards, on floppy disks or recorded by lasers on optical disks, each of which can hold several hundred at a time. These can be called up for display or printout as needed. And of course publishers' and library catalogs will go on-line, available via computer as well as in print. The capacity of electronic storage is likely to grow to the point where thousands of pages can be crammed into an area the size of a dime.

Some visionaries even foresee a computerized book, about the size of a hardback, which would have a page-sized screen inside the cover. You will display any book you want by inserting a tiny disk or cassette that you have bought or rented. You won't turn pages, but press a button to display the next page or advance to another part of the book. The "book" might even have a tiny keyboard for taking notes.

"For summer reading," says Raymond Smock, official historian of the House of Representatives and a student of such things, "you could take the Great Books of the Western World to the beach and stick them in your back pocket."

21

Courting the Customer

Two related trends will become dominant on the marketing and advertising scene in the next decade or so. One is pinpoint targeting of markets. The other is direct selling to the targeted market.

More and more producers of goods and services will be going straight to the consumer with merchandising appeals intended to bypass the middleman. Hardly a new concept, but one that will soon be implemented with far more effective tools and methods—in direct mail and computerized "teleshopping," for example—than have previously been available. This trend is going to shake up the entire world of retailing.

Competition for the attention of the American consumer is already intense, and it's going to get ferocious: more commercial messages, briefer in duration, in more varied forms.

There will be no shortage of outlets for commercial messages. TV channels will continue to proliferate via networks, cable and satellites, not to mention local-area low-power stations. Cable alone may reach 90% of all households by the turn of the century. Radio already is everywhere but still growing, with another 100 or so AM outlets alone likely to go on the air in the next several years. The advent of stereo on AM outlets will expand their audience, while quad sound will do the same for stereo. Newspapers and magazines will grow and prosper.

The total number of advertising messages being poured out every day is likely to double during the '90s. That means the average American will be within sight or sound of twice as much advertising as today. That will be a repetition of what happened in the past 15 years.

At the same time, advertising messages on TV and radio have been getting shorter; they almost HAVE to, simply to make room for growth and still leave time for program content. Along with this goes a progressive loss of effectiveness.

The over-50 market will be an especially active one, and marketers will have to change some of their attitudes toward it. These people will be increasingly well-off, having discharged most of their large, fixed obligations, and their income will rise steadily into the new century.

They won't want to be treated as "oldsters" whose brand loyalties are fixed. Contrary to misconceptions on Madison Avenue, middle-aged people are just as interested in new products and willing to try them as younger consumers.

They have preferences and propensities to spend that change as they move up in years. They will buy many kinds of services to replace those that used to be provided by family structure— including not just health care but all kinds of personal-support systems. But they will also buy recreation, travel, financial services, and goods of many kinds.

RETAILING

Retailers will have to play their game more skillfully in an increasingly competitive market from here on well into the 21st century.

There will be plenty of profits to be made. Personal income and especially family incomes will rise, and upscale consumers will be numerous. But catching and holding their attention will grow more difficult, and so will the art of bringing them to the point of buying. Fierce competition for the consumer's dollar will make discounting a permanent part of the retailing landscape, squeezing profit margins.

The demographics of the next couple of decades tell the story. Population growth will be slow, and an aging, better educated population will be less swayed by "youthquake" trendiness, more sophisticated and conservative in its tastes, harder to sell.

Some retail planners foresee a lessening emphasis on high style, high fashion. These will still have their place, of course, but a smaller one in the overall scheme; the thinking is that working women—and 60% or more of women will probably be in the labor force by 2000—will give less weight to trendy styles and go for appealing but less expensive lines. This also reflects theories about what the aging of the population means in terms of taste.

To meet the competition of direct marketing and specialty stores, the big retail chains are gearing up to make their stores more distinctive, not simply as stores but as collections of lines, each of which will be a specialty store in itself. Chains and even independent department stores will increasingly go in for house brands...their own designer labels on clothing and other goods, as a way of building store loyalty among consumers.

But chains will be cautious about opening new stores and will site them with great care. There will in fact be far fewer openings in the coming 10 to 15 years than in the past couple of decades, when population growth and suburban sprawl were the dominant trends. Retail outlets will probably move to two extremes: Very large stores, including warehouse stores, to lure buyers with the convenience of finding everything in one location; and small, in-filling outlets in smaller communities and rural shopping areas.

There also will be considerable retrofitting—the rehabilitation of old stores. This turns out to be less expensive in many cases than new construction.

Retailers will go to increasing lengths in years ahead to give their outlets some kind of distinction from the rest of the pack—paying greater attention to decor, "themes," even entertainment for shoppers. And there'll be a proliferation of smaller chain outlets patterned after successful retailing operations in Western Europe, where operators get higher sales productivity out of less floor space than is the norm in the U.S.

The two largest retail-volume states are California and Texas, in that order, but further growth within the Sunbelt as a whole may not outpace retailing in older parts of the country. The critical factors are population density, which will remain far greater in older areas for a long time to come, and return on investment.

Within Sunbelt states, metropolitan areas like Los Angeles-San Diego, Dallas-Ft. Worth, Houston, Miami-Ft. Lauderdale, etc., will continue to draw heavy retail interest.

Independents and specialty stores will have to scramble to find and maintain their place on the retail scene. We expect more cooperative buying and advertising groups to spring up among them, and manufacturers will continue to offer co-op advertising deals to help them along.

Competition for the low end of the market will be concentrated in the markdown warehouse outlets. Discounting, especially for cash rebates (say, in the form of debit cards), will continue and spread indefinitely.

There are likely to be relatively few large regional malls built in the next couple of decades, but many existing ones are going to be refurbished and given a new look, complete with electronics of all kinds. Smaller shopping centers and strip malls will continue to be wedged in wherever there is room in the spreading suburbs that ring every city.

The store mix will change in malls as time goes on. The typical large generalized department stores will become rarer, and a growth in specialty shops will fill in for them—some operated by the department stores themselves. These will be aimed at relatively narrow markets, such as teenagers, working women, the "stylish stout," and so on.

SELLING FOOD

In food retailing, supermarkets will probably look much the same 10 or 15 years from now, but there will be a lot more flash—electronic gadgetry of various kinds—and many will turn into super-supermarkets. The chains are convinced that economies of scale will be in their favor and the next 10 to 15 years will see a sorting-out of superstore formats: the big and the bigger.

There will also be a struggle between these and the super-warehouse markets, which will be somewhat rougher, highly discounted operations, catering to the low end of the market in major metro areas, offering fewer services and less variety within categories.

All these outlets will be combinations of food and other household merchandise seeking to meet as many of the retail needs of shoppers as they can. They will build on today's already visible trends, including more prepared, ready-to-take-out meals, in addition to salad bars and deli counters.

The upscale supermarkets will offer machine-scannable coupons via electronic dispensers, and displays and shelf pricing will increasingly be done with digital readouts, making it easier to change prices when needed.

Checkout counters will be more highly automated than today, equipped to register prices instantly by means of improved scanners, and credit and debit cards will be accepted in more places. There will be automatic teller machines (ATMs) handy for obtaining shopping cash. Some stores will include do-it-yourself checkout counters where customers can dump their purchases on a moving belt and watch as the the items are priced (on a screen) and automatically bagged.

Superstores will streamline their operations with more computerized coordination among themselves and suppliers. Restocking will be more automatic, suppliers anticipating needs and making prompt deliveries. Shipping containers will be more standardized, and shelf items will be undergoing constant redesign to take up less space while presenting a better face to the shopper. Stores will go in for computerized sales analysis, keeping closer tabs on what merchandise moves and what doesn't.

There will still be plenty of room among the bigs of retailing for the smaller convenience stores, and they will thrive if well placed and carefully run. Fast-food and neighborhood food stores will proliferate through the suburbs for people in too big a rush to wait in line at the superstores.

Convenience stores will be smartening up their act by adding services such as cash machines and even gas pumps out front if there's room for them. More of them will offer take-out fast food and build up their range of shelf items, offering a wider choice and even getting into gourmet items.

SHOPPING BY COMPUTER

Direct marketing—both by mail and with computerized "teleshopping"—is going to be the fastest growing segment of retailing, and will upset a lot of retailers in the process. It's a trend we expect to be in full bloom by the early '90s, continuing into the new century. Several major corporations in foods, communications, data processing, travel and other consumer lines already are using the technique.

It's all part of the targeting process in which marketers shift from costly and often wasteful mass techniques to singling out groups most likely to be responsive to the given product or service. And it's working—a bandwagon that will collect riders as the century ages.

Catalog shopping will begin to blend with computerized teleshopping within the next five to 10 years. Large retail chains in collaboration with TV networks, stations and cable companies will be offering electronic catalogs via home computer at a small subscription charge. Shoppers will be able to order up visual-and-sound displays of whatever merchandise they're looking for—or even to indulge in a sort of random walk through whatever goods are being featured by sellers at any given time.

Computer-generated graphics will give an almost three-dimensional view of items for sale; in fact, developments in holography may bring a hyper-realistic kind of three-D to home screens eventually, although just how soon is still uncertain.

Clothing will be displayed by live models on the TV. Appliances, gadgets, goods of all kinds will be offered with appropriate sales pitches. Orders will be placed via the computer keyboard and payment arranged through use of credit or debit cards and codes supplied in advance. Delivery will probably be the same or next day in most instances, provided orders are placed before early afternoon and depending on how well suppliers are able to position local-area warehouses.

This mode of teleshopping will replace recent experiments with so-called dumb terminals placed in subscribers' homes. Such terminals are able to respond in only limited ways and don't permit much interaction between buyer and seller. By plugging into personal computers, merchandisers will be able to offer a wide range of services in addition to their goods: software programs, access to databases, magazine subscriptions, travel arrangements, investments, etc. Only imagination limits the possibilities.

Catalogs won't disappear; they may in fact become even more ubiquitous and highly targeted to specific audiences. But in many cases they will be an adjunct to teleshopping—offered to viewers as a way of carrying the sales message along, say, on business flights, when they will have more time to study them.

Teleshopping has obvious limitations. It is an elite merchandising medium; only people with home computers will go for it at first. But there will be a lot of them and they will be money-makers with plenty to spend: Working couples, and especially working women, who lack the time and patience to cope with the hassle of mall and store shopping; many shut-ins and older well-off people; and everyone who is simply too impatient to go out and stalk the merchandise.

For the rest of the population, a majority by far, in-store shopping will still be the dominant mode. It's a social experience for many people; they welcome the adventure. Housewives, the lonely elderly, lower-income families, youngsters and others will continue to flock to the malls.

DIRECT MAIL

The most effective consumer lists for a direct-mail campaign are composed of identifiable people who have bought something similar to what you're selling, whatever their demographic traits and wherever they may live.

But if a direct merchandiser wants to target all the affluent residents of certain cities, he can mail to "occupant" in high-income Zip codes. With broadening use of nine-digit Zips, the Postal Service will help marketers target affluent markets even more precisely.

The ultimate mail targeting will combine nine-digit Zip codes with detailed demographic information from the annual census, broken down not just to neighborhood or even city blocks, but just one side of the street on a given block. Of course, census records don't give the identity of the household and its individuals, but mailers can still reach those unnamed households.

Zeroing in on consumer groups will become easier as the Census Bureau refines its polling and reporting techniques. The 1990 census will employ new technology to speed the gathering and analysis of data. The big change is concurrent processing, in which the editing of incoming data will be done by machine. This will greatly compress the time between initial interviews, follow-up (when data are incomplete) and computerization of results for quick access. Interrogators will carry hand-held gadgets to enter data directly in machine-readable form.

Maps of census areas will be computer-generated, both for planning and directing the census itself and for later provision of results to the public.

Data will be made available through microfiche, computer floppy disks, tapes and even laser disks containing an enormous amount of information. All these will be offered for sale within several months after completion of the census.

Before the 2000 census rolls around these techniques will be even further advanced, probably including optical-reading devices to speed delivery of data. Direct merchandisers will have a greater wealth of information available than ever before to use in planning campaigns.

ADVERTISING

As the number of advertising messages proliferates, surveys indicate that viewers and listeners remember less about ads than they used to. And they respond more to the hard-&-fast sell than to the soft pitch.

The typical TV commercial, today's 60 or 30-second pitch, may become the 15-second shot, or even five seconds. Advertisers will have to get their messages across immediately—no fooling around; there won't be time for buildup.

Tomorrow's TV viewers will be better educated, more sophisticated than today's, which poses another problem for advertisers: Bluff and oversimplification won't sell well to people who think for themselves. In the main, these are adults who read a lot and will want information.

Advertisers polled recently by the Newspaper Advertising Bureau said they think this will bring a trend to building brand image through information about the product rather than emotional or other subjective appeals. In part, the coming decline of the youth end of mass markets points that way. Ads aimed at younger people may still be big on charisma and rock music, but there will be fewer of them—youngsters AND ads aimed at them as a proportion of the general mix.

Comparison advertising that identifies and sometimes criticizes the competition is also likely to become more common, ad planners tell us.

The growth of VCRs is expected to boom along until a majority of all households have them, and this presents advertisers with a special problem—how to sneak ads onto home video cassettes. They're working on it: "zap-proof" commercials built into rental-shop cassettes, even commercials so attractive that viewers won't WANT to zap them.

In parallel with the trend to brevity in TV ad spots is its opposite: "info-specials," 15-minute or even longer programs intended to be a subtle blend of entertainment or information with advertising. The ad industry will experiment with these in various forms and if they work—that is, if they sell—you'll be seeing a lot more of them.

The major TV networks will shrink as competitive channels spread. Network ratings—which the ad industry watches like hungry hawks—will fall behind in the scramble for viewers' attention. Advertisers will move to more widely diversified combinations of TV outlets to gain wider exposure and higher ratings.

Magazines will continue to be an effective way to target specific audiences. Publishers, reeling from the solicitation expense of maintaining artificially high circulations at low subscription prices, will intentionally shrink their circulation and charge readers more. Advertisers will get fewer total readers from a given magazine, but they'll have the confidence that their message is actually being seen by more highly motivated readers.

Some tried-and-true advertising techniques won't change much over the coming years: newspaper ad supplements and inserts, for examples, and fliers and shopping papers dropped in your driveway. These are relatively low-cost ways of blanketing large areas with ad messages and will be around indefinitely.

So evidently will be the somewhat newer idea of "marriage mail," the term advertisers give to the mailing of free samples along with an ad pitch. This has proven to be an often effective way of introducing new products or widening the appeal of established ones.

And coupons: They will continue to show up in the mail, but stores also will begin offering them direct to shoppers via electronic displays and printouts.

But billboard advertising may be one of the biggest surprises of all. Japan already has come up with billboard-sized TV, on which movies and announcements can be run continuously—say, weather and traffic advisories interspersed with commercial messages and other graphics. And U.S. firms are developing billboards with movable parts, bright-day lighting via fiber-optic technology, and other gimmicks to grab motorists' attention.

AD MAKING

The creation of advertisements is undergoing a technological revolution that will come to full flowering in the next several years. Computer graphics—computer-generated images that can be manipulated, turned around, merged and blended with other graphics, including still and moving film—are taking over as the chief tool of the creative people. These techniques will produce ever more arresting images and make TV commercials harder to ignore. They will in fact become more entertaining.

Computers will become dominant in the entire planning and executing of advertising. No more hashing things out around a conference table with charts and presentations on an easel. Ad creators—artists, copywriters, market analysts—will combine their talents on the agency network, and each work station will display the coming-together of an ad concept. Computers already can store and display still photos and soon will be able to do the same with movie clips.

Turnaround time from concept to completion will shorten drastically, making it far easier for agencies to move with short-term developments, fit themselves more tightly to trends in public taste, and, for that matter, help speed up the trends themselves as advertising intensifies its efforts to mold public wants to the products being offered.

For clients of advertising agencies, this kind of development offers the prospect of more sensitive tuning to markets. Retailers, producers and others with anything to sell will find a much broader range of choices available to them in the visuals and the sounds involved in TV-radio ads and in the print media.

It will be possible to rush new ad campaigns to outlets in hours rather than days or weeks. Electronic transmission—whether by satellite, fiber-optic cable or whatever—will distribute new ads to the media in a flash. Arranging for air time or print schedules will be the slow part, but even this will be speeded by new communications techniques. Computers will find the slots wherever they are available.

22

Managing Business

The challenge to business management over the next two decades will be coping with change more rapid and deep than ever encountered before.

The forces of change sweeping through the economy won't allow much time for contemplation or foot-dragging. There will be intense competition, both domestic and foreign; more deregulation of markets; high-tech revolutions in goods and services; change in what consumers expect of business; speeding-up of product cycles; churning in the labor market; the spread of computers.

The swiftness of change will put an extra premium on agility and quickness of response. Companies both enormous and tiny will retune their command structures to fit new ways of doing business and of stimulating innovation, while keeping step with the needs and demands of new generations of employees.

Management structures will be less heirarchal, more decentralized, to give firing-line managers a bigger say in formulating strategies.

The process will be neither easy nor simple for many firms whose traditional management systems are going to be challenged and even threatened by new, upstart companies.

ENTREPRENEURSHIP

A wave of entrepreneurship is sweeping through the economy. Deans of graduate schools of business see it in the sudden upwelling of interest shown in classes on how to be a start-up boss instead of a corporate climber. Executives of big corporations see it in the number of younger executives and technical personnel splitting off to set up their own companies. And venture capitalists see it as a great opportunity for bankrolling promising new outfits.

Employment is steadily falling among the Fortune 500 companies, but it's booming among the new smalls, which turn up annually by the hundreds of thousands and account for most of the net growth in jobs. Some 90% of all American companies have fewer than 500 employees but together account for over half the working population outside government. That's today; tomorrow will see an even stronger tilt toward small business.

Individuals are finding it easier all the time to go into business for themselves as professionals, consultants and providers of other kinds of services. The home computer is a home office staff; for many start-up firms, it makes a secretary and clerk unnecessary. Communications via computer networks can reach everywhere in the world; and mobile communications will soon tie everything together no matter where the demands of the business take its owners.

Trends like these have a common tie: ingenuity, which, along with financing, seems to be the only limiting factor in the future of small business. Getting a new idea—finding a new niche and filling it—will be the key ingredient in becoming an all-American success story.

Flexible manufacturing makes it possible for a small factory to go head to head with the bigs in the production of batch jobs—limited quantities of specialized stuff, whether made out of metal, ceramics, plastics, composite materials, cloth or, for that matter, wood. Computer-controlled machines can be reprogrammed in a flash, compared to conventional methods.

This kind of plant is going to turn up all over the country with the help of limited partnerships and other venture-capital financing arrangements. Some will be financed by bigs, who will be among their chief customers. Dozens of these incubator centers are springing up around the country, most of them the result of two- or three-way cooperation among universities, private investors and government agencies. Hundreds will be at work by the '90s.

Computers are narrowing the differences between big and small, creating a more level playing field on which the small firm can maneuver with increasing nimbleness, often outrunning the more cumbersome and tradition-bound giants. As computers double and double again in capacity, while software designers continue to come up with new and more versatile programs, small firms will be able to plot analyses of business prospects with the best of the bigs.

It's the goal of most small businesses to become big businesses, and it's a special goal of many of today's entrepreneurs to guide their creations to sufficient size to attract purchase offers from giant corporations. Some entrepreneurs cash in their chips from one business start-up and go right out and start another firm, sometimes in an unrelated line.

But relatively few new firms become great successes, of course; the mortality rate has always been high in small-business start-ups, and this will be even more the case in a high-tech world. There is an enormous amount of churning going on in the newest sectors of small business, and for every success story there probably are a dozen-odd flops. But there also are a lot of comeback stories—the second and third tries that finally make it.

To foreign observers, this is a striking feature of the American business scene—the fact that failure is a temporary condition, like a bruised knee, compared to the common situation abroad, where the social and financial liabilities associated with failure can be permanently crippling.

SMALL-BUSINESS NICHES

The outlook for small business is brighter than it has been in many years—maybe ever. The next couple of decades will see the creation of thousands and thousands of new small companies. These are going to change the face of American business, while creating a lot of new wealth for their owners.

The growing complexity of business and society creates demand for a host of new services. Companies increasingly will turn to outsiders to help choose and install computer networks, new kinds of office equipment, communications and the like, as well as to provide temporary personnel. (Many small firms in the future may operate with only a minimal permanent staff.) Working couples, working singles and older folks will be customers for a variety of personal services—house-sitting, grocery and clothes shopping, financial services, fixing the home computer, grooming and boarding pets, installing phone wires within the home, and countless other services.

An unusually high proportion of new firms will be in manufacturing and services, as opposed to retailing, which has always been the mainstay of small-business activity. Retailing will still account for the largest share of total small businesses, but to a diminishing extent.

Some of the new companies will be decidedly low tech, providing traditional products to ongoing industrial and consumer markets, but many of them will be high-tech firms creating brand-new things in many fields.

Most of the growth will come in business and professional services, such as computer programming, communications, law, advertising, printing and accounting, and in personal services, including health care and financial services.

The ultimate small business is computer software design, where one brilliant programmer working at home on a personal computer can devise a new system that could sell hundreds of thousands of copies. The development expense is minimal, but marketing that program will require the same kind of clever advertising and promotion—not to mention capital—that every new product has always required.

In the field of biotechnology, small firms are going to form a much-needed bridge between the academics and the corporate bigs. Some already are doing this, via limited partnership arrangements with corporations. The latter furnish start-up capital, while a university furnishes research and development expertise. The entrepreneur in the middle identifies markets, seeks them out and brings new products developed in the laboratories into the competitive stream. Some already have made fortunes for their participants.

FRANCHISING

Franchising will continue to account for a big portion of small-business growth in coming decades, but like retailing, it will account for a decreasing share. American franchisors will look for growth overseas, with good effects on the U.S. balance of payments (as an export of services) and on the economies of other countries.

The fast-food field is already jammed but will grow even so, failures making room for more new twists. Upscale restaurant franchises will probably expand. Computer and software franchises will be around forever, but there are too many right now and a shakeout is underway. There will be substantial growth in non-food personal-service franchises—everything from lawn care to emergency medical centers, package-wrapping to house-cleaning services.

There are good profits to be made in franchising, either as originator of the franchise or owner of an affiliate. But the risks can be substantial, and more and more states are enacting licensing regulations to protect buyers and investors from poorly financed and organized franchisors.

Despite this growth in regulation, overall franchising is expected to flourish for the indefinite future, although at somewhat slower rates than in recent decades. One reason for slower growth is that costs of buying into many kinds of popular franchises have gone up faster than the rate of inflation. But in the broad field of services, where most of the action will be, there will still be plenty of entry-level opportunities, and this will be especially important to would-be entrepreneurs who are women and minorities.

THE VIEW FROM 2000

Looking back from the year 2000, tomorrow's executives will probably conclude that the hardest-driving factor of all was the spread of computer technology, its penetration into all facets of business. But this was the factor that made it possible for management to cope with all the other changes, including competition.

Back in 1986 it seemed as though computers were everywhere; but now (here in the year 2000), it is clear that their full impact was only beginning to be realized. And management was just beginning to get into its hands what had been promised much earlier but not delivered: total "management information systems" that linked all elements of a business together in a coherent network.

And with this development, the rule that "information is knowledge and knowledge is power" took on new meaning. Now everyone had access to information, and power became diffused. Top managers, from the CEO on down, discovered that they could no longer simply rely on technicians somewhere on a lower floor to churn out the data they needed. Now they learned about "decision-support systems," through which they could watch company business the way controllers keep track of air traffic.

These systems were designed for them and run by special staffs reporting directly to top managers. Their purpose was not simply to track operations but to anticipate and analyze problems and opportunities, using "expert systems" and other routines that emulated human thinking processes with a high level of sophistication.

Some top executives who could not or would not use a keyboard terminal turned instead to voice-activated computer equipment. And turnaround time on corporate decisions began to shorten.

"Issues management" became a recognized specialty and a central part of corporate governance: an informal system to provide early warning on developments of importance to the business on all levels...market trends, community issues, government moves, impending shortages, international crises and so on—anything that might constitute a problem to be avoided or opportunity to be seized.

It was informal, in that it steered clear of paperwork, reports, committees and conferences in favor of a day-to-day awareness of change, delivering its alerts in ways that could quickly be plugged into policy-making mechanisms. In this way, issues management acted as a forward scout for the strategic planners whose concern was the company's long-range place in the market.

Issues managers helped corporations cope with the transition in the '80s from federal to state involvement in corporate affairs. As federal programs levelled off or shrank, authority spread, both by default and initiative, to other levels of government. Anticipating problems became all the more complex for multi-state companies.

LATERAL MANAGEMENT

Coming back to the present, we see that the trend to decentralization in government is having its parallel in corporate management, with the pace being set by the new entrepreneurial firms that have sprung up like weeds across the high-tech scene. Many or most of these have grown out of someone's brainchild— an invention or some new application of technology—and they have made it or failed on the strength of their adaptability and agility.

Technology-oriented rather than management-attuned, these new proprietors have surrounded themselves with like-minded people whose concern with racing the competition to market is stronger than any predisposition to hierarchy and routine. Some have been spectacular failures; others have had to be rescued by more conventional managerial types. But there have been equally spectacular successes, and these have had their echoes in a number of large, old-line companies that have adopted the new style of commando management.

The years ahead will see a continuing shift from top-down to lateral authority and communication in many companies. Top management won't surrender its authority but will share more of it. Growth in employee-consultation systems is certain. More and more firms will draw on the expertise of people on the production floor or in the delivery mainstream. Less attention will be paid to young corporate-finance wizards with their MBA degrees; too many corporations have gotten burned in recent years by following the advice of green "strategic planners" far removed from the reality of daily operations.

Borrowing from the Japanese, as they already have in such things as inventory management and quality control, more firms will experiment with the team approach to specific challenges and production issues. Project groups will be ad hoc, set up to deal with a problem, perhaps several problems, then dissolved and reconstituted to deal with others. Their responsibilities may often overlap.

And managers will increasingly be assigned a field of expertise and a staff to go with it, providing services across many other lines. For example, companies producing electronic appliances will set up product development teams drawing on expertise from staffs in charge of engineering, design, circuitry, market research and so on. Defense contractors have worked this way for many years.

Such systems are not inherently or necessarily more efficient than all others; they may in fact turn out to be cumbersome in certain settings. Hierarchal systems often respond faster than employee democracies, which is why the military uses them. But even that analogy breaks down in combat, where there may not be time for going through channels, and the competition American companies face looks more like combat every day.

The management information systems mentioned earlier take on added importance in decentralized decision-making; they are how top management monitors operations, inserts fixes as needed, and makes sure people aren't just wandering off on their own.

Boards of directors of publicly held corporations are likely to change as well. There will be less cronyism, less rubber-stamping of management, as they grow more oriented to shareholder and public interests. Shareholders will insist on more outside directors, truly independent from the salaried management of the company. Many of them will be experts in the company's field, with competent staff assigned to them to provide research and other support. There will be more sensitivity to conflicts of interest and to community concerns. All of these reforms in corporate boards will be designed to anticipate and head off criticisms from stockholders, community activists and pressure groups.

Generational changes going on across all lines in society and the economy won't bypass management ranks. Young new executives will be moving up and will bring to bear a new generation's ideas about relations with the public, stockholders, consumers, government and employees.

EMPLOYEE RELATIONS

Corporate human-resources policies will take on a different coloration, oriented more strongly toward bringing employees into management's confidence and vice versa. Lucrative reward and incentive systems will spread among high-tech knowledge workers, particularly as the supply of them grows even more stretched in the '90s and beyond.

Creative woolgathering will be encouraged by many firms where innovation is valued. Engineers, designers, technicians and others will be given occasional paid sabbaticals to pursue ideas that may or may not pay off. And creative people will be given more opportunity to work out ideas in informal groupings. (This is one reason why decentralization of workplaces and dispersal of employees via remote work stations will have its limits.)

Management will take a tough, pragmatic attitude toward unions, doing what can legally be done to keep them out or to disarm them if they're already in. They'll use such measures as employee complaint systems to provide open channels for dealing with problems fairly before they can become disruptive. The best preventive against union organizing will be, as ever, treating employees squarely in both compensation and participation in key decisions.

The compelling drive for productivity and cost control means that line management will be assuming greater authority over personnel practices, including pay and benefits, promotions, transfers, opportunities for training and so on. Human-resource executives at the top may still be in charge of setting broad policy, but the scope of their authority over the troops in the trenches will lessen.

The supply of middle-management talent should increase in the '90s for two reasons: The Baby Boomers will be moving up into those ranks and that age range, and computers will be taking over some portion of the work done by the lower strata of those ranks—chiefly in number crunching and operations monitoring and control. Whether this will lead to an actual surplus of people in that broad category is debatable. Many forecasts indicate that it will, and that the shortage of openings for this surplus will lead to plateauing salaries and considerable dissatisfaction.

Perhaps, but we don't see it that way. It is just as likely that broad business expansion, after all growth elements are plugged in, will tend to sop up most of this group. The rate of formation of new businesses will rise steadily—many of them set up by

Baby Boomers themselves—and rising profits and incomes will nourish the growth of even more firms and create more jobs.

That has been the record in the current expansion, and we see it continuing as the convergence of new technologies boots the economy to new heights.

23

Office Automation

Two main lines of development will change the way offices operate in the next several years: electronic information processing and computer networking.

In the transition, business will get over its paper mania and learn to pass most of its information around electronically. This will be done via transparent interconnections that will remove time and distance as critical factors in the sharing of information between and within businesses.

Call it electronic mail or anything you want, the prospect is that whatever cannot be communicated by voice on a forward-and-store basis will go by digitalized print. Often the tradeoffs between voice and print will be equal and the two will become indistinguishable; either can be stored for replay if the party sought isn't available at the moment of transmission.

Goodbye stamps and postage meters, goodbye courier envelopes for intra-office messages, goodbye mail sacks. Farewell to waiting for the mail.

It won't be easy to break the craving for paper that has typified business offices since they stopped using mud tablets and pointed sticks. But competitive pressure and the lure of enormous gains in productivity will help. The "paperless office" you have been hearing about for so long is on the way, at last. But "paperless" is a relative term, as we shall see.

Electronic data delivery and storage in its various forms will be more reliable than paper for the routine transmission and storage of information, and will require much less space. The era of reliance on rooms full of filing cabinets is coming to an end. Ditto for the era of moving computer data around in great stacks of folded paper, which is about as efficient as using a wheelbarrow to deliver airmail.

Networking of computers via integrated office-communications systems (combining digitalized voice, graphics, data, etc.) will allow instant transfer of work from office to office, computer to computer. It will permit the combining of several computers to share work on complicated problems for quicker processing. And it will simplify the job of keeping tabs on distributed operations in "real time," meaning as they take place.

Management will at last have the "total information system" it has yearned for ever since computer salesmen invented the term. The victim of overselling in the early days of office automation before it was really ready, TIS or MIS (for "management information system") is finally coming of age.

Putting together an up-to-the-moment status report, complete with large-screen graphics, will be simple. It can be called up by an executive at his own computer console and for his eyes only or made available on a teleconference basis to an entire organization, from top to the tips of branches.

A few things will happen to the work habits of executives. For one, they will learn to type, well enough to handle a computer keyboard. A few years from now, this won't be a problem. Most of tomorrow's executives are today's youngsters experimenting with computers at home or school; keyboards will be old stuff to them. And keyboards will be simpler, computer programs "friendlier." There will be no clerical stigma attached to typing; it will go with the territory.

Improvements in voice recognition systems may come along fast enough even to bypass the keyboard. They exist today in primitive form; in a few years they may be sensitive enough to accept large vocabularies. Executives will be able to dictate their correspondence directly into printed or electronically transmitted form.

The last several years have seen a revolution in the localizing and personalizing of corporate analysis, brought on by personal computers and easy-to-use spreadsheet software for making financial projections. With their own computer capability at hand, execs have vast analytical powers in their own grasp. Decentralizing of computing skills is changing the whole balance of power and authority in many offices, and this democratizing effect will grow as virtually every rising young executive becomes computer literate.

THE PAPERLESS OFFICE

Paper companies tell us their sales actually are up nicely, thanks to computers, which turn out to be great consumers of the product. They look forward to more computers and more paper consumption, especially as people order up "hard copy" print-outs.

But papermakers MAY just be in the situation of the fellow who said crystal radio sets would never hurt vaudeville. A revolution is getting underway in the paper-shuffling trade, and by the turn of the century it will have eliminated tons of paper every year—literally. The elements to watch are these: Laser-disk data storage. Fiber optics. Computer software. Government regulation. Here is how they will interact:

Laser disks, smooth plastic disks encoded with information that is read out by a laser beam, can store incredible amounts of information, the equivalent of a library on what looks like a 45-rpm record. In a few years, this method of storage will be as versatile as magnetic floppy disks are today; users will be able to edit disks, enter new or changed information, find and display or print it out in an instant. The disks will be permanent; duplicate copies can be easily made and separately stored for backup purposes. Thus entire vast files will be shrunk from room-size to disk-size.

Fiber optics will provide enormous wide-band communications capacity for movement of data, voice and graphics in digital form. Cables thinner than lamp wire will link office machines into coordinated nets for interchange of data and concerted data processing on command.

Computer software will be devised to manage these nets and to provide verification of signatures and time of entry. These will be as foolproof as advanced technology can make them and will become admissible as legal documentation. Programs already exist with built-in redundancy to confirm that data have been received as sent without error; these will be improved as time goes on.

Government regulation will adapt to these developments and make digitalized electronic submissions the standard for all sorts of documentation and reporting—SEC filings, most kinds of corporate and partnership tax forms, census reports and so on— as well as record retention. Much of the "paperwork burden" will disappear; an electronic burden, considerably lighter in clerical preparation time, will take its place.

The dividing line between "hard" (printed) and "soft" (electronic) copy may become blurred. Deciding when and how to make a record of message transmissions within an organization or between it and the rest of the world will be a matter of company protocol, spelled out in advance.

THE PHYSICAL SETTING

Technology will redesign the environment of the office. Desks will be "work stations," which will begin to resemble airplane cockpits. Computers and other free-standing equipment will be integrated into the work station, with the computer represented by a thin flat screen projecting a brighter, clearer image, thus easier on the eyes; voice and other communications equipment will also be built in. Desk and chair will behave like the seats in your new auto: They will adjust to fit your comfort at the touch of electronic controls.

With noisy typewriters and copiers redesigned into word processors and fantastically high-speed laser printers, the loudest sound in most offices will be the human voice. As computer terminals become more talkative, a prospect for widespread use within 10 years, office designers will have to come up with new acoustical shielding ideas. The "open office" design will be the first to go; most office workers will have at least some small private space to themselves with surrounding sound barriers. (Good for morale.)

Portable computers will be part of the executive's standard traveling equipment to a much greater extent than now. These will be smaller, thinner than the thinnest sold today, their size reduction limited only by the need for an accessible keyboard and display screen. These will serve as work stations for the road, with easy access via the nearest telephone (or built-in modem in the hotel room) with the home office and the rest of the world. Notes, data, progress reports and the like will be moved along as easily as they are when working at one's own home or office work station.

REALLY PAPERLESS?

And finally, about the "paperless office": There WILL still be paper around, although much less of it; people will use it when they have to, and some government and other reports will still be filed on paper. The biggest change is that once paper has served its fleeting purpose it will be dumped, not stored. Offices will store information, not paper. Acres of space and tons of load-bearing capacity now devoted to file storage will be freed up for other purposes.

And then what used to be the file room may become the exercise room, where employees will loosen up after a few hours at their adjustable work station.

24

Government Regulation

The role of government as regulator is continuing to diminish, with a good chance that there will be further shrinkage over the decades just ahead. Unexpected events and shifts in the political winds could change that, of course, but present trends clearly point that way.

The currents of deregulation will be uneven in strength—and even in direction. For example, there will be less regulation of general business activities, but probably more environmental regulation; less antitrust regulation, but new laws dealing with computer security.

The reason we see generally less regulation has a lot to do with political demographics. Younger voters, those in their twenties and early thirties, are more conservative than younger voters used to be—they voted heavily for Reagan—and will be moving up into their middle years by 2000. The Baby Boom generation, now pushing 40 and also pro-Reagan in the last election, will be the dominant one through the turn of the century. Neither group is likely to change its basic politics enough to turn the government around in that time span.

Strong economic growth of the kind we foresee will further decrease government's appetite for business regulation, on the principle that "if it ain't broke, don't fix it." The resilience and strength of the American economy stand in strong contrast to the stagnation in centrally planned ones, with their deadening layers of regulation.

SLOWING OF REGULATION

The direction we're heading now may not necessarily be toward further wholesale deregulation, although that cannot be ruled out. What's likely is restraint on issuance of *new* rules or the elaboration of old ones.

Future presidents will probably follow Reagan's precedent and impose their own direct control over the regulators—requiring top-level review of all new agency rules. Even in the hands of a less conservative administration, this tool would at least expose to scrutiny the proliferation of rules that used to be a way of life among Washington's regulatory agencies.

Congress is another matter, but it too is going to tread more warily in enacting laws that create new bodies of federal regulation and intervention in the private economy. Certain dire circumstances could bring on more such laws—say, environmental calamities of one kind or another or serious abuses of the financial system—but the threshold for fresh regulation is getting higher year by year.

Increasingly sophisticated computer systems will help slim down the regulatory overhead for American business and the government itself. File-by-wire will become the standard for much of the routine reporting that now goes on in taxation, corporate regulation and the like. We'll see computer-to-computer input, which should eliminate not only paper but the need for staff sprawl to hand the paper around.

Computerized "expert systems" that virtually run themselves can, if properly written and administered, help hold down on staffing in many federal agencies. These and other measures to put the clamp on agency budgets will be popular for years to come as Washington struggles with the deficit.

SOME KEY SECTORS

Here are our judgments on regulatory trends in several sectors:

Antitrust: Federal antitrust policies are changing. A new sympathy for joint research and development ventures among several corporations in the same field, for example. Our forecast is that Congress will soften antitrust strictures even further in that direction, to help American firms keep a jump ahead of the foreign firms which—especially in Japan and most of Western Europe—get substantial government assistance for "targeted" joint ventures in areas of keen world competition.

Accountancy: A contrary trend may set in, however, concerning relations between accounting firms and corporate and financial clients. Government is likely to get tougher about potential conflicts of interest between the audit function and counseling services provided by auditors—especially as the fast-moving world of high-tech venture capitalism produces further examples of audits that failed to warn of impending failure or fraud.

Financial services: Federal financial regulation is eroding rapidly, and interstate banking, previously forbidden, is on the way. It's too early to say whether this trend may be interrupted. The scope and complexity of today's financial systems far exceed the ability of federal and state agencies to truly monitor them, and many observers feel that this short-handedness constitutes a kind of *de facto* deregulation.

The outlook for financial regulation depends entirely on how safely things operate in the coming few years. A wave of major bank failures, which would pose a threat to the integrity of federal deposit insurance plans, would bring a new degree of government control.

Civil rights: Civil rights are an area where regulation already has declined and probably will shrink further. Enforcement of traditional civil rights—voting rights, equal access to education, fair housing laws, credit rights, etc.—will continue, varying in strength from one administration to another. But the most controversial aspect of civil rights enforcement—affirmative-action "goals" for employment and school desegregation—will meet with increasing opposition from voters, Congress and the courts. The result will amount to a de-emphasis more than a basic shift of direction; but new experiments with old employment-regulating and school-integration schemes are unlikely.

Compensation: In areas of payroll control—minimum wage and hour laws, statutes setting wages on federally financed construction and contracting, regulation of collective bargaining, etc.—it has been years since Congress showed much interest, and while there haven't been any repeals or substantial downgradings of current laws, they may begin to show up before long.

Public health and environment: Regulation of public-health issues will probably persist and may even expand. New problems arising from biotechnology, for example, could lead to broader powers for federal agencies. Otherwise, Congress will content itself simply with surveillance and nagging.

There will probably be a similar story with general environmental laws on air and water and waste-disposal policies. Despite major improvements in these areas over the past 20 years, our growing awareness of the health risks of a dirty environment will bring more rules affecting manufacturing, auto exhaust and disposal of trash.

Computer crime: Frauds and thefts committed using intricate computer procedures will be one of the biggest elements in the growing case load for all courts, and out-of-court settlements and arbitration may not be much help.

Federal legislation probably will grow in this field, along with state laws, and the courts will be immersed in trying to unravel complex electronic scams.

For relief, the courts may have to look to the computer industry itself, for new systems built into computers for verifying transactions, preventing unauthorized entry and establishing proof of authority to transfer funds and securities via computers. But the real key will be control over information, which, in an information-oriented society, may be better than money.

SETTLING DISPUTES

The American judicial system will see some changes that could be called deregulation—chiefly in the direction of moves to encourage more out-of-court settlements in civil cases. Federal and state judges will get tougher on this score, pushing litigants toward alternative dispute-settlement modes, including arbitration with right of appeal. Discretionary authority to do this already is on the books.

Many large corporations are moving the same way, resorting to special private panels of arbitrators and retired judges to settle disputes among themselves—thereby saving a lot not only in legal fees but also in management time.

State courts are cooperating by restricting resort to federal courts where litigants are from out of state.

Congress may step in with curbs on undue litigation and on the common practice of shopping around among the federal circuits for a more favorable appeals court. And exasperated judges will begin slapping on fines and fees for pointless appeals—perhaps assessing costs to the losing party.

Still, America has more lawyers than it needs and they will be busy finding things to do, which is bound to mean even more litigation, heightening the pressure on the courts to find alternative means of controlling the case load, including arbitration and other out-of-court techniques. Whether Congress will agree to creation of a new federal court to sift cases appealed to the Supreme Court is doubtful, however. The profession itself can't agree on the need for it, despite Chief Justice Burger's contention that the High Court is accepting too many appeals and needs protection against itself.

Further down the road, computer systems will take on more of the litigation load. Expert systems, programmed with a total knowledge of specialized areas of law and court precedents, will act as automated dispute-settlement devices. Law offices and judges are already using computerized files to search the law and help prepare research papers and briefs. So why not appeal to a robot? What could be more impartial?

25

The Labor Market

Unemployment will fall in the decades ahead, and job growth will in some cases outrun labor supply, creating skill shortages in various lines. But there will be a surplus of underskilled and unskilled labor, and people in this fix will be a problem for society, a worse one than now.

While this is happening, labor unions will continue to lose membership, bargaining power with employers, and political clout in Washington.

Most of the labor outlook to the year 2000 is good for society and the economy. These are the broad trends to watch:

▶ A substantial decline in the number of people looking for their first jobs: fewer youngsters, due to declining birthrates, and fewer adult women, because such a high percentage of them will already be in the work force.

▶ A slow but steady decline in unemployment, with a good possibility of rates around 5% or less by the turn of the century.

▶ A low enough rate of job displacement by automation and imports to allow for retraining or relocation of many workers; most of those hit by the heavy layoffs of the early '80s will be in retirement by 2000.

▶ A modest buyer's market for middle-management talent. Employers will have excellent pickings among the most skilled and productive groups—Baby Boomers moving into their prime years with skills, education and experience.

The net of all this will be a hefty boost for productivity which, along with the spread of high-tech and automation, will set new records for long-term growth. Skill shortages will be spotty, occurring mostly in new kinds of specialties spawned by new industries, and some employers will have to scramble to fill important slots.

But no shortage of computer-oriented workers. Training and experience in computers will be taken for granted in the 2000s, and college-educated people will be in plentiful supply. Colleges will try to stay ahead of the curve by offering a lot of skill-sharpening and updating courses; so will employers.

Older workers will be available to fill in where needed, if firms try hard enough to recruit them or induce them to stay on the job. But every indication is that early retirement options will continue to be taken up by a majority of eligible people, most of whom will be better fixed for retirement than their parents were.

Firms that need youngsters for low-paid entry-level jobs will have to beat the bushes harder than now. They'll recruit retirees in many cases for at least part-time work and turn also to new immigrants, of which there will be a growing supply.

Low-income blacks and especially black youth will not benefit much from this situation without fairly heavy government investment in special job-training programs for them; employers probably will shy from such commitments themselves, as long as they can make it with others who are more easily trainable. Which points to a continuing dilemma: Voter attitudes may be hardened against such government social-welfare expenditures at a time when the consequences of letting bad enough alone may be painful, even explosive.

"Affirmative action" programs to promote employment of women and minorities already are on the wane, and any return toward quotas—or even strongly enforced "goals" and "timetables"—is improbable. But growing stringencies in the labor market, especially among skilled workers, will continue to expand the breadth of employment opportunity.

Employers will fit a lot more flexibility into their work schedules and their personnel policies—split shifts, part-time jobs, job-sharing, variable hours, work at home and so on—to make it easier to recruit and hold skilled workers but also to hold down payroll costs.

PAY AND FRINGES

There will be growing diversity among compensation and benefit systems throughout the economy, with increasing innovation and risk-taking among companies in newer high-tech lines. (See our chapter on Managing Business.)

For most other old-line firms, the era of booming employee benefits is ending and well before 2000 will have turned into something different. Employees will bear more of the cost of their own fringe benefits, but also will be given a wider range of choices among options that suit their personal circumstances. Which in turn will help employers weed out or at least trim back on those benefits that are the most redundant—as in the case, say, of working couples.

Traditional pension plans will fade in the next decade, in favor of employer payouts tied to profits and productivity: so-called defined-contribution plans. These are easier to manage, subject to less detailed federal regulation and, like the future work force itself, easier to trim in lean years.

Wages and salaries are likely to be tied more closely to performance, as unions lose power to negotiate uniform rates across an entire industry.

By the mid-'90s, however, the pendulum may begin to swing back the other way in employee benefits...from the current trend to cost-sharing and cost-cutting back toward fatter benefit packages. This view, which we have heard in our discussions with benefit managers and employers, is based on the potential development of labor shortages about that time.

If so, it will probably be a spotty revival and will turn up chiefly among firms locked in fierce competition for the kinds of high-tech specialists that will be in demand in tomorrow's growth economy. Companies of this sort already are offering better benefit and incentive packages on average, compared to firms in more conventional lines.

For workers in the latter, rewards will come principally in the form of wage hikes and productivity sharing, which will help soften the impact of cost sharing on the benefit side.

WORKING WOMEN

Women will account for about two-thirds of the net growth in the labor force in the years ahead, even though their rate of entry into the job market will slow. By 2000 it probably will have leveled out a bit below the male job rate. The proportion of adult women at work will rise faster than their total numbers, reaching three out of five well before the turn of the century. Most working women today are under 45, but as they age, most will stay at work, while younger women will flood into the job market.

The number of working-wife families will rise by well over a third before 2000, which is one of the reasons that disposable income is expected to grow so smartly.

The disparity between male and female earnings will narrow, for legal reasons and, more significantly, because of the growing work experience and educational levels of women in the work force. Automation will open up more kinds of jobs to women by lessening or eliminating physical requirements that favored men. Women's numbers will grow in managerial ranks and among the new entrepreneurial class.

The controversy over "comparable worth"—the concept which holds that pay should be set on the basis of job content and skill requirement, not market worth of the job—will have died away by the mid-'90s, with both sides claiming victory. Although it is currently perceived as a feminist issue, women being the principal advocates of comparable worth, it actually applies beyond sex dividing lines.

What will settle it will be a few more court decisions upholding the plaintiffs' claims in certain egregious cases of pay discrimination via assignment by sex to "traditional" jobs, in both public and private employment. These will touch off a general revamping by employers of their job-classification systems to make sure that the weights applied to various jobs are uniform throughout the system—AND to make sure they can attract competent women employees; there will be growing competition for them. All of this will take Congress off the hook, and there won't be any need for federal legislation.

For women who can't or don't want to work full time there will be steady growth in part-time opportunities. Remote work stations—computers and other business machines in the home, tied to a company network via phone lines—will be a major factor in this.

But one way or another, the great majority of women in the Baby Boom generation, plus their daughters as well, will probably be deeply into the work ethic from now on. They'll drop out long enough to have a child or two but most will be back on the job, especially as day care becomes more generally available.

This will continue to work changes in American lifestyles in general. Working women will account for much of the explosive growth in services and shopping modes designed to save their time—the appliances and catalogs and computerized teleshopping that will be a force in retailing in the years ahead.

UNIONS

Unions by the year 2000 will for the most part be vestigial remnants of their present selves, more closely resembling their earliest status as representatives of crafts and as social-welfare organizations than as high-powered collective bargaining centers.

The shrinkage that already is taking place among unions will accelerate in coming years, and this means loss not just of membership but also of economic and political clout.

The industrial unions will scale down along with their industries, having no independent life of their own. The companies that survive in manufacturing will be smaller, highly automated and much less labor intensive.

The former blue-collar worker will wear a white collar and do his or her work at a console in a control room or patrol the shop floor to tend to the needs of robots and automated assembly lines. He or she will be well paid, well trained and highly valued—but also dispensable.

The unions' ultimate weapon—the strike—will lose most of its teeth. For a model, look to oil refining, where unions have existed for years and strikes come and go with little impact on operations or on the public. This doesn't mean that unions will be totally powerless. If a strike goes on long enough, some services and functions may be disrupted—maintenance, repair, installation of new equipment and so on. But the more automated an operation becomes, the easier it is for supervisory personnel to step in and run things...as newspaper pressmen and telephone operators found out some years ago.

Unions face a generational change along with the rest of us. People coming of age in the years ahead will be less comfortable with unions than their parents and grandparents were. They're not necessarily anti-union, just less familiar with union successes than with failures: their inability to stem layoffs caused by lower-wage import competition and by recessions, inability to win major political goals, and a somewhat reactionary stance among many of them on issues like the hiring of women and blacks. And the younger working-age people, who already have helped elect and reelect Reagan, will be carrying those attitudes along with them as they move into middle and old age.

Unions also will have to scramble to catch up with the growth in the number of women in the work force—a trend they so far have failed to do much about. With few exceptions, unions are male-dominated, male-oriented and, in the case of many, even hostile to the rise of working women. Overcoming these self-inflicted disadvantages in time to recruit successfully among the growing wave of working women is probably more than most unions can manage.

The generational shift described above applies to union leadership as well. Most of today's chiefs will be long gone in 2000, presumably replaced by men and women grown up in a far different atmosphere from the days of blood, sweat and politics that created our modern labor movement. Most will be college-trained specialists able to talk the professional lingo of the educated people they hope to represent.

They will concentrate on service industries for the same reason that Willy Sutton robbed banks: That's where the money is. Service employment is where most of the future employment growth will be. If unions are to reestablish themselves as a major force in the U.S. economy, it will have to happen there. They already have something of a foothold. Health-care unionism is growing. Teachers and roughly half of all government workers are unionized. Large groups of retail and miscellaneous service employees are also.

But building on this foothold will not be easy. Two factors will work against them, in addition to the attitudinal changes mentioned above:

Employers will increasingly anticipate union appeals to employees by providing the kinds of wages, benefits and grievance systems that unions promise, but at less cost to themselves. And they will hold in reserve the ability to find cheaper ways to get work done through automation and offshore sourcing via foreign suppliers and subsidiaries.

Technology is and will increasingly be international. Service lines are going to be no less innoculated against foreign competition than are today's manufacturing lines. Already, for example, giant American magazine subscription centers send renewal notices and other files of subscriber information to low-cost places like Ireland for key-punching onto computer tape, then ship them back to the U.S. to run on their circulation computers. Credit-card companies ship paperwork to places like Haiti.

The pattern of employment is undergoing basic shifts. More and more firms will pare down their permanent staffs to "cadres" of managerial and other key people and contract out the rest or hire temporaries. Defense contractors have been doing this for years; it creates an accordion effect in work forces—the ability to expand and contract as the times and the order books dictate.

This kind of flexibility will be a key ingredient of the competitive battles to come, and it will be hard on unions. They have yet to find any practical way of organizing such employees—unless unions change their stripes, as we indicated at the outset.

Unions could transform themselves into social-service organizations providing help for members and would-be members off the job as well as on. Such services as day and night child care, counseling, debt management, even health care—in effect, providing the benefits that employers either cannot or will not lay out. This was a major guiding principle of unions in the garment trades and other lines early in this century, and it could become so again. The AFL-CIO already is groping in that direction, talking of ways in which unions could become "associations" for the nonunion worker.

In a way this will reflect the changes in society as well as in business—the dismantling of family structure that used to provide many such kinds of care and attention, especially to the elderly. There will be rising needs for people to take care of each other through organizations of a kind that don't really exist today, along with helping to meet the special problems of a rising immigrant population in low-paying occupations. Unions may help fill that vacuum.

WANING POWER

But they will be a long way from the muscular power-wielders they used to be back in mid-century. No more wage "patterns." No more industrywide strikes. Few company or even plant strikes. And far less political heft. Labor is still the country's single largest organized group, but its ability to bring this power to bear in politics is dwindling and will continue to do so as membership falls.

Unions rose in good part thanks to New Deal legislation which, though still on the books, will be under increasing attack: The minimum wage, federal construction wage standards, collective bargaining rules, a host of related laws and regulations that become more and more vulnerable as voter attitudes shift and as unions lose their ability to marshal defensive votes in Congress and state legislatures.

Federal regulation of collective bargaining is likely to shrink. Congress in years to come may give greater weight to voluntary dispute-settlement procedures and cut back on its support for the National Labor Relations Board, which has become a focus for wrangling and delay more than expediting peaceful settlements.

The decline in union political power will also mean an easing of pressure for protectionism. Unions in manufacturing have been in the front lines along with their industries in demanding tariffs, quotas and other anti-import measures.

But this drive will ultimately collapse of its own weight. Voters will eventually rebel against the higher consumer prices protectionism causes and the shield it builds around inflated wages for a relative few, and automation will proceed to wipe out the jobs the unions sought to save.

In most basic lines where unions are entrenched, collective bargaining will continue indefinitely, but on a new basis of mutual recognition that labor costs must and will be held down or jobs will disappear via automation, imports, "outsourcing" to non-union suppliers, or all three.

In manufacturing, but even more so in the knowledge industries, employers will give increasing weight to employee-consultation systems, "quality circles" and the like, drawing on worker insights on operations and policy while at the same time dealing with employee discontents before they fester. "Ombudsman" systems will become common, taking over one of the unions' most cherished, traditional roles—that of processing grievances.

Large financial and service companies with their hordes of computer-bound rank-and-file workers will become an inviting target for unions, although a trend to decentralization with the use of part-timers and at-home workers will make the target harder to hit.

Professional associations will probably follow the example of the National Education Association and start acting more like unions. Lawyers, physicians and other professionals and managers might become more militant as job competition grows and their societal status declines.

The movement toward labor-management cooperation in productivity-building efforts will continue into the '90s, when it may become a victim of its own successes. The more concessions unions make in exchange for short-term job security, the more they may be signing their own eviction papers.

When the work force becomes small enough, union ability to bring pressure on management evaporates—and so, most likely, does the union. Productivity bargaining pays off for both sides as long as it makes possible improvements that boost profits AND wages, or at least protects jobs. But when productivity has been lofted into a new, higher orbit by automation, as it will be in one line after another before 2000, there isn't much left to bargain about.

That's why unions will be far different in the new century, surviving by the skin of their teeth in manufacturing and growing only in the largest, most centralized service lines that haven't yet found ways to automate themselves.

26

Computers in Class

Education is the only major American industry that has yet to be thoroughly computerized, but its turn is coming. Computer hardware and software makers are eyeing education as their next big bonanza.

By the turn of the century computer-aided education (CAE) will have swept the educational establishment from top to bottom, with revolutionary results. This will turn education around—away from the downhill path of mediocrity so repeatedly condemned in myriad studies issued in the early '80s.

Is this a pipe dream? By no means; it's already beginning.

Computers will be in every classroom, part of the general order of things. This means the lowest grades through the highest, with complexity of equipment and software rising with the grade. Developmental work now well advanced will produce new generations of computer work stations simple and inexpensive enough to be put in front of just about every schoolchild. These keyboards, each with its own display screen, will be tied into a small computer under the teacher's control. The central unit will have its own large-screen display so that work going on at individual work stations can be shown to the entire class. And the teacher can use the large screen as a blackboard for the entire room. With a smaller burden of rote and routine, teachers will have more time for individual tutoring and attention to problem learners.

None of this involves new or complicated technology; the hardware and the techniques already exist and have been in use in classroom-like situations for some time. What will take time is the development of scaled-down and inexpensive designs and of the instructional software to go with them. The need is for systems that will convince penny-pinching school boards that they are more cost-effective than today's methods.

The coming increases in computer capacity that we already have described will help greatly to reach the first of these objectives. It will become easy to pack enormous data-processing capacity into small spaces, at relatively low cost.

Developing the software is the harder part; but the industry's increasing adeptness at devising "expert systems" will speed this process. An expert system for educational use is a computer program that packages a huge amount of accumulated knowledge on a given subject into a form of question-&-answer routine, leading the learner through a logical progression to a correct answer.

COMPUTERIZED CLASSROOMS

These are the expected strengths of computer-aided education (CAE):

▶ It can present a vast knowledge base patiently and uniformly—the rote kind of teaching that teachers find boring and that kids usually hate. Computers can make it interesting.

▶ It can help students put things together—the rote learning combined with other materials—to achieve practical results. For example, multiplication tables applied to solving a problem.

▶ It can help manage the educational process by testing, recording and interpreting test results and developing individual student profiles, along with remedial prescriptions where needed, tailored to the individual. It can do all this with a benign impartiality, perhaps more than any teacher can maintain.

▶ Most of all, computer-aided education can make learning an intriguing adventure, by drawing on the almost unlimited possibilities computers offer for weaving together graphics, sound and enormous amounts of information.

Many educators see this as the breakthrough needed to lift American public education out of the slough of mediocrity. And they think it will be the answer to the problems of bilingual education (which will continue to be a growing issue in many parts of the country) and of adult illiteracy.

But not all educators are so delighted. In fact, according to enthusiasts of CAE, the chief obstacle to its spread is tradition—fear of change. Many teachers, and especially their unions, are hostile, fearing displacement and downgrading. And many early experiments with computers in schools have gone badly, usually for lack of proper teacher training and software support.

Most of all, school boards and the voters in general will have to be convinced. This may be only a matter of time. Change may come by attrition, as older teachers retire. And enrollments will be dropping, as the Baby Boom "echo" of the mid-'80s passes through and disappears. Taxpayer revolt against the high cost of schooling will force a search for new methods, and labor is nearly two-thirds of that cost.

CAE will begin to look better as it becomes clear that its costs may be less than hiring new teachers at the salaries it will take to offset the lure of well-paying jobs in industry and commerce. This will be especially true in the disciplines, such as math and science, that will be in highest demand.

A new generation of parents, many of them already computer literate, will take a different view of education than their own parents did. After all, today's 16-year-olds will be 30 in the year 2000. CAE may seem a familiar and comfortable concept to them ...one well worth trying, especially if it holds promise of better education for their children.

NATIONAL PRIORITIES

Education will assume growing importance among all sectors of the population, as the surge for national excellence expands and the U.S. seeks to earn a more mature and knowledgeable profile among the civilized countries of the world. More will be spent on the upgrading of schools and colleges, most of it coming from state legislatures rather than Washington. And there will be a stiffening of standards in curriculum, teaching and materials.

Schools will have to prepare youngsters for a future in which they face the probability of having to relearn constantly (as many professionals already have had to do for years) or of retraining for new kinds of work every several years as technology changes and develops.

The struggle for education funding could become a politically polarizing issue, far more than it is now. The aging population in many states will be mainly white, while the majority of youngsters crowding into schools will be black or brown. Minorities, including Asians, will be majorities in 53 major cities by 2000. Bearing the cost of their schooling—including remedial schooling—may provoke some hot confrontations.

And some districts will have to follow the example of Los Angeles—at least as an interim measure—and put schools on a year-round basis in order to handle a rising "clientele" without putting up new buildings.

Schools will become more like community centers. Classes will be smaller and hours longer. Kindergarten may start at the age of three or four instead of five (in part to accommodate working parents). In the evening, schools will be learning places for parents who want to keep up with their children or who are planning career changes. Families will be made more responsible for helping their children learn. You can expect much more stress placed on order in the classroom.

Use of TV and other audio-visual aids to learning will stage a comeback, impelled by improved delivery techniques, better software and access to far-flung programs via satellite and cable. Teacher training will benefit too. Summer seminars may be eliminated for teachers in favor of on-site learning.

Math and science instruction will be beefed up under new federal legislation that is just now coming into effect, and more and more state legislatures are undertaking curriculum reforms to emphasize these subjects along with English. Non-academic courses in practical living skills, such as driver's education and cooking, will get pushed aside by more rigorous pursuits.

Basic computer courses will become common even before CAE does. Should you insist that your children become "computer literate"? Yes, at least to the extent of getting used to computers, getting over any feelings that computers are a threat.

But by all means beware of concentrating on computers to the exclusion of other learning, the humanities and social sciences in particular. Computer jockeys will be needed in great numbers, yes, but they may turn out to be the auto mechanics of the future.

The people running the company upstairs will be far more broadly educated; to them, computers will be just another management tool.

The status of teachers is going to change... slowly; it will take time to overcome inertia and union opposition. But a monolithic system is cracking. Uniform starting salaries, uniform increments over time will no longer be the rule. Pay for merit is on the way, whatever the problems associated with making it work. More systems will experiment with attracting liberal-arts graduates to teaching, bypassing schools of education and formal certificate requirements. One effect of this will be to end the shortage of teacher talent, as more young people realize that teaching jobs are opening up. This will call for higher pay for the better teachers, but that's part of the price of better education.

OUTLOOK FOR UNIVERSITIES

Universities have long since ceased being islands of academic detachment, if they ever were, and will increasingly be tied in with government and private research. Ties between major universities and the Department of Defense in particular will be of growing importance. But other government agencies also will rely more heavily on them for research and development in many other areas, mostly high-tech but not entirely.

And universities will be actively courting industry support with research and consulting contracts, donations for purchase of new plant and equipment, exchange of faculty and executives—an active partnership, which is sought and welcomed equally by industry.

These trends will intensify and by 2000 should be dominant features of university governance. Faced with slackening enrollments well before that time, higher education cannot get along solely on tuition and support from endowments and state appropriations.

Whether these trends are good or bad is endlessly debatable and probably beside the point. They are inevitable, given the nation's need for a strong higher education establishment, industry's need for advanced research capabilities, and colleges' need for sources of revenue besides tuition.

At the same time, universities are under growing pressure to reemphasize the humanities and social sciences as a basic part of higher education. The pressure comes from governmental and privately funded commissions, independent critics, educators and—perhaps most importantly—from business.

Our own interviews tell us that American corporations are increasingly concerned with the need for college graduates who are not simply trained in some specialty, be it business administration or engineering, but also capable of growth and change—able to accommodate, to relearn, to grow into new assignments and new specialties. This capability calls for the kind of broad background and open-mindedness that liberal arts are supposed to confer. Their value as a potential meal ticket is rising.

ABOUT VOC ED

Vocational education is undergoing massive change. It is moving out of the public classroom and into the corporation. This is due in large part to the failure of voc-ed to keep up with the changing needs of American industry, due primarily to low funding. Now industry is waking up to its own self-interest in the field.

The coming pattern, one we expect to be well established in the '90s, is of closer cooperation between employers and school systems in the design of preparatory courses, along with elaborate in-house training programs run by companies themselves. These will take in not only entry-level beginners but also longtime employees in need of retraining for new technology or upgrading for new responsibilities. This is probably the most dynamic educational field of the future.

The point we made above about liberal-arts education bears repeating here: Corporations prefer to do their own training but also prefer young people who know math, can speak and write clearly and aren't afraid to crack a book. These attributes will count for more than time spent practicing in an outdated machine shop, especially as we move into an era when fewer and fewer blue-collar workers will ever get grease on their hands.

These workers in coming years will need to understand how to access and load data; how to load the machines, how they function; how to deal with safety issues; the ins and outs of quality control and spot-checking and the basics of hydraulics, pneumatics and traditional machine skills.

Junior and community colleges already are doing a rising share of training and retraining for the new requirements of industry, and this share will keep growing. Also rising is the average age of community college enrollees, now roughly 30. More and more adults will return to them periodically for refreshers and retraining. And states that offer well-thought-out and well-funded training programs will have an advantage in attracting new investment, particularly if federal training programs stay at a fairly low level.

Industry, however, will have to do a better job of forecasting its human-resource needs. To some extent just now, employers are inhibited by proprietary concerns; they don't want to telegraph their production plans to competitors.

THE RISK OF DELAY

But companies may have more to lose by hanging back. Business and industry will be moving into training and retraining in a big way, even more than in the past decade or two. In the next several years they will employ thousands of instructors to provide a range of courses from entry level through professional retreading. There are estimates that outlays for training will exceed 10% of payroll by the mid-'90s. The speed of change in high-tech, the introduction of new techniques and equipment will require brush-up courses at many levels in the average corporation—including upper management.

Computerized training systems will play an increasing part in this, with "expert systems" to help guide classes and individuals through intricate new technical material. Systems of this kind already have become a major factor in military training and skill upgrading, and would play a large role in any new government programs for training the displaced and unskilled in the labor force.

A final observation on the importance of computer education to society and especially the business community: Some degree of knowledge and understanding about computers is essential to any student these days and will be more so in the future; computers will be part of the sea he will swim in as an adult. But more than that, we all have a growing stake in the use of computers in education. They will ultimately reduce illiteracy, crime and social dependency by helping create the kind of skilled labor force we are going to need for the new century and new boom to come.

27

Best New Careers

In a computerized, high-tech era, many of the exciting new jobs will be in technical and scientific fields like computers, biotechnology, optical communications and the like. But not all, not by a long shot.

There will still be plenty of room for people whose inclinations and aptitudes take them in different, more conventional directions. And there will be rewarding careers to be built in nontechnical fields—some of them considerably MORE rewarding than the run-of-the-mill job in high-tech.

This chapter will lay out some of the guideposts that will be handy for youngsters looking beyond school in the decades just ahead, as well as for adults considering career changes.

In our interviews with dozens of educators and corporate executives we found a consistent theme in comments on what it will take to build a successful career in American business: A solid grounding in the humanities and social sciences, not just technology, and particularly in skills that create a competent generalist...writing and talking skills, a sense of history and familiarity with economics. This may come as a surprise to those who believe that some technical specialty is the only key to advancement in the high-tech society ahead. But not so.

A typical comment: "We (in business) need people with the ability to communicate clearly, both verbally and in writing, and who can understand and act not simply on orders from above but on the strength of their own observation on the job. We need people who are adaptable, who are not upset by change but are ready and willing to ride with it. This is going to be especially important because things will be changing so fast. No line of work, no important job will be immune to change. There will be new things to learn, new specialties but also new wrinkles in a field or profession where we used to think a college education—especially an advanced degree—had you fixed for life.''

So there you have Rules One and Two on any list of things to build into a career plan: Learn to open and use your mind, and be ready to accept or even welcome change; see it as an opportunity, not a threat.

Careers in business are just as affected by these trends as any others. New high-tech firms will continue to spring up all over the place in years to come—some fading, others fattening—and all will need business smarts to keep them afloat. A typical pattern is that of the bright inventor or technologist who comes up with a salable idea but can't handle the business end of it. Venture capital won't flow his way if investors can't see a clear business plan. Enter the management-trained business graduate.

Business schools around the country are rebuilding curricula to fit this new scene—to prepare people for fast-moving, high-growth management challenges. They're also training them to become entrepreneurs themselves.

Major corporations will continue to need recruits to move up their management ladders too, but the bulk of such job creation may be among the new smalls. And in either case, we've picked up repeated warnings to this effect: Don't think computer skills are the chief tool you will need. The fact is they may rank well below others, including the communications skills mentioned previously.

Computers ARE and will continue indefinitely to be an essential business and management tool, but that's not the point. The point is that over-concentration on them can become a sidetrack or even a dead end. As one executive put it, ''Sometimes the computer jocks wind up on the sixth floor grinding away at their consoles, while the all-around people who studied humanities and management—along with computers—are up on the top floor running the firm.''

COMPUTER JOBS

Just the same, demand for skilled computer experts will grow indefinitely and will provide vast opportunities for young workers skilled in programming. These needn't be dead-end jobs and probably won't be, not for the individual with a broad enough ambition and education to back it.

Computer software is probably one of the most dynamic growth fields in the future economy. There already IS a flood of software, but that's part of the problem: Finding the program that fits becomes increasingly a grope through a maze. And very few of the commercial, off-the-shelf variety are a perfect fit for every firm; most need some tailoring.

That's where programmers and system designers come in, whether free-lance or as part of a service organization. There will be constantly growing demand for people who can help find the right software, adapt and refit it as needed, and in particular help in designing the data-processing system that's best for a firm.

Consultants in business machinery and communications also will be in demand. Everything in the office will be changing faster than most owners and managers can keep track of. The variety of equipment options already is bewildering. People who can act as guides through the jungle of options will find plenty of clients.

Computers are important at levels well below this sort of upper-scale professionalism. Just about every job in tomorrow's America will involve some degree or another of computer smarts. It will be important—no, essential is the word—to have some grounding in and receptivity to computers. This may not amount to much more than an ability to type and a readiness to learn how the computer console operates, which as designs grow simpler will be no more difficult than learning to drive a sports car.

Executives high in a corporation will have plenty of computer talent available to tackle tricky jobs; but none will be able to function without knowing how to use his or her own terminal. In fact, each will have a positive need to know, for the terminal will be the information fountain.

The same applies to, say, teachers in computerized class-rooms, musicians whose composing is likely to be done on a computerized keyboard, workers in automated and robotic factories, all kinds of appliance and computer repair specialists, auto mechanics, sales managers, accountants and bookkeepers, architects, designers and artists, journalists and authors (this book was written and edited on computers, as we've said), physicians, lawyers, health-care technicians and chefs. Chefs? Sure; food-preparation managers will use computers to check menus, recipes, ingredients on hand, available work force and so on.

This degree of fairly casual computer competence can be picked up easily; learning to type will probably be the hardest part, and anyone can learn to type (even though some of today's executives think it is beneath them). The typical keyboard may turn out to be simpler for tomorrow's learners. The one in use today is badly outmoded, and an alternative version known as the Dvorak keyboard will probably become the standard before 2000; it's much easier to learn and use.

And don't worry about the term "computer literacy"; it means less than it seems to. It's just another way of saying be ready to use a computer keyboard when it is offered. "Literacy" means being able to read and write, but it doesn't mean you have to turn out novels.

Other jobs in and around computers include selling and servicing them. Despite gains in reliability, computers will continue to need a lot of attention. Manufacturers will need plenty of service reps to keep the customers happy, and more and more independent all-brand service centers will spring up to take care of individual and small-business computer problems.

SECTOR-BY-SECTOR OUTLOOKS

Biotechnology is still a small field, but within the next several years it will begin to grow rapidly. It will need biologists, of course, but also engineers trained in biology and vice versa. And chemical engineers to work on improved processing and filtration systems and to scale them up to production size. Molecular biologists and immunologists familiar with the latest in recombinant DNA procedures (which may be changing faster than universities can track). Biochemists. Microbiologists. Enzymologists, cell-culture specialists. Bioelectronics engineers. Plus a variety of technicians. And all of these will be crosscutting a number of fields, from human DNA cloning to plant biology and materials processing.

Communications will need scientists and engineers in specialties so new that many schools aren't even offering them as yet.

Fiber-optic technology is a good example. With the emphasis in communications turning to the use of light rather than electricity, electrical engineering is undergoing a quiet revolution. Students will come from such specialties as radio engineering and semiconductors. But universities will have to devise new curricula for the field.

Engineering in general already is dominated by electronics and will continue that way indefinitely. The long-term U.S. defense buildup is one major factor in this, but there are others. New developments in robotics, including variable-speed electric motors to replace hydraulics, will call for design, production and managing engineers.

Commercial activities in space will also call on the profession for a number of specialties, including some new ones. New power-generation and storage techniques will create engineering jobs. And the entire range of engineering specialties will be affected by computer-aided design in which much of the routine, digging-with-a-stick work will be automated.

Health care will create escalating skill needs at professional and technical levels, with growing emphasis on geriatrics as the older segment of the population expands. But a surplus of doctors and dentists is at hand, and in the years ahead new entrants may have to lower their aspirations. Big-city practices will be harder to break into, and more and more physicians will wind up working on salary for someone else.

Still, opportunities will open at least at the replacement level and in rural and small-town areas where family practitioners and some varieties of specialists will be needed. Inner-city areas are short of doctors too. Technicians as well as physicians will need advanced training in many new kinds of instrumentation, and the frontier of medicine will merge with that of biotechnology to create new specialties. In the field of mental health, new emphasis on brain chemistry will work important changes.

The law is overcrowded already, but this won't stop the flood of starters into the law schools. Beginners would be wise to look for special niches created by new technologies, find ways to be useful to both producers and consumers of new kinds of products and services. Careers in corporate law will be harder to come by due to the competition, and more attorneys will find themselves engaged in fairly routine, second-rung kinds of legal work. Government employment of lawyers will sag at the federal level but may grow in the more prosperous states. And the rise of prepaid legal-aid plans may create jobs for some.

Teaching opportunities are affected by demographics, and there are lead-and-lag effects that make planning difficult if you don't pay attention. Right now, high-school and college-level teaching jobs are declining because enrollments are; but that fact conceals serious shortages in several specialties such as math, science and engineering, especially computer engineering. Competition with industry where the pay is better accounts for this shortage, but some school districts and universities will be upping their pay with corporate help in years ahead. So more opportunities will open.

Grade-school teaching jobs will expand in the late '80s and into the '90s, as the current baby boomlet sends children into the systems. We expect the birthrate to slow in the '90s. But heavy immigration and higher birthrates among immigrants will create grade-school teaching jobs in many parts of the country in the '90s. Language skills, especially in Spanish, will be needed. Vigorous growth in teaching slots will occur in industry, where more and more firms will be setting up their own training and retraining programs. They'll hire more teachers than the public schools.

Office jobs will be plentiful too, but also undergoing changes that wipe out many of the least skilled, such as file clerk and typist, and call for people ready and able to handle sophisticated gadgetry including word processors and computers. Communications within offices and companies among people AND machines will be a growing field; individuals who know how to handle networking will be in demand. Toward the end of the century, automation will swallow up many routine jobs and create new ones at higher skill and pay levels. People looking ahead to office work had better be ready to go with the flow; and it is picking up speed.

Construction won't expand its employment much but will require new skills. The usual trades will be required—masons, carpenters, pipe fitters, cement finishers, etc.—but the up-&-comers will be those who know how to handle computers and computerized equipment. Various kinds of robots and semi-robots will be turning up in heavy construction to do more of the earth-moving, materials-handling and erection work. These will eliminate some jobs but create others, and skilled people will be needed to program, operate and service such gadgetry.

The drive to hold down costs in building will put a premium on people skilled in designing the flow of a job and eliminating wasteful delays and practices. Good foremen and supervisors who know the new technology will be sought after.

Factory job opportunities are shrinking, due to automation. The shift to robotics will be gradual but will pick up speed, and production-line work will slowly diminish and disappear in large plants. New, smaller flexible manufacturing plants will need a relatively few highly skilled operatives to supervise and service the equipment.

Vocational schools in some areas are coming around to this kind of instruction, but most skills will have to be learned on the job. A good grounding in math, an understanding of how to use computers and, above all, an alertness to change and an eagerness to learn will be prime items on a job application. Children who follow fathers (and mothers) into factories in the years ahead will find that reading and writing count for more than simply following orders.

Retailing will continue to need large numbers of people, but much of this inflow will be at the replacement level. Although shopping by mail and by computer is still only a small part of overall retailing, this will grow and will cut into the need for salespeople in the stores. But while clerical jobs may shrink or stagnate, openings for creative marketing and merchandising specialists will grow. Retailing will need bright new ideas to adapt to changing markets and demographics.

Finance is in much the same kind of transition—from labor-intensive to automated. Banks will need fewer humans on the main floor and even upstairs, but those they do hire will need considerable understanding of new equipment and systems. And there will be a lot more banks and other kinds of financial houses.

The investment end of the business will expand and should provide more job openings, especially as "brokerage" becomes anybody's business and is available in more and more nonfinancial retail settings. Insurance will always need salespeople, but a slower rise in population probably means opportunities will also slow down. Real estate is a growth field as far ahead as anyone can see but also an increasingly sophisticated and competitive one. The big action will be in the Sunbelt.

Personal services is a catch-all label for kinds of enterprises that self-employed or would-be capitalists will develop into a spreading group of prosperous businesses in years to come. The rise of singles, single-headed households, working couples and the elderly points to a need for services that they may lack the time or energy to provide for themselves. These can run a wide gamut—from dog-walking, housecleaning services and shopping to investment management, lawn service, health counseling and interior design. Chief requirement for entry: ingenuity. The key to success will be starting a firm in which your employees, not you personally, will provide the service.

Human resources is a small but important segment of business management and deserves a paragraph to itself. It used to be called "personnel" before employers began to realize—often under the prodding of federal anti-discrimination laws—that work forces need special attention and massaging to keep productivity healthy. The field now encompasses employee counseling, job evaluation, hiring and firing, training and retraining, employee-complaint response, administration of wage and benefit systems and union relations, although this last is a diminishing aspect.

It is a field increasingly open to women, who often turn out to have the special compassion it calls for. Now recognized as a quasi-professional field, HR won't have a huge number of new openings but most of them will be interesting.

TAKING AIM

This survey covers only high points, of course, but these are the ones that we feel should be kept in mind by all career planners. Today's high-school students will be in their 30s by 2000, and the great majority will probably have undergone at least one change of career direction and interest. Some of those who went out into the world of work without a clear objective will have developed a specialty of some kind through on-the-job training. That's not a bad idea for some, but it is risky, and we wouldn't recommend it above a solid round of schooling.

A high-school education is a minimum "must" for anything but low-end jobs, and a growing number of new immigrants will be competing for those. More and more factory jobs will require at least some post-high-school education. Lack of education is already a pair of cement shoes for anyone who hopes to swim in tomorrow's job pool.

28

Regional Growth

Regional differences in growth, very pronounced over the past two decades, will slowly diminish towards the year 2000 as the mainstream of national growth broadens.

What this means is that the Sunbelt, led by California, Texas and Florida, will continue to grow more rapidly than northern regions at least until the year 2000, but the *differential* in rates of expansion between the Sunbelt and the rest of the country will shrink over time.

What looks like an emptying out of the "older" part of the country in favor of the "newer" isn't really that at all. The Sunbelt *is* growing faster, both because of in-migration and because the earlier waves of arrivals are now raising their own families and have a birthrate above the national average. But the Northeast and Midwest, as entire regions, are not actually losing population; they're growing, too, at a slower pace but on a larger base.

The intensive churning-around of the '70s is quieting down, both because economic opportunities are rising in most parts of the country, removing some of the incentive to strike out for new territory, and because the population itself is growing less rapidly.

CORPORATE MOBILITY

Regional growth in population and jobs is dependent, quite simply, on business expansion. In an era of rising competition at home and abroad, business is going to be increasingly cost-conscious about location from now on. There are many key costs in business, including state and local taxes, energy prices and environmental controls, but wages and salaries are the biggest factors for most businesses. As has always been the case in this country, capital will flow to areas where business can be conducted less expensively and more profitably, and the people will follow the jobs.

Fast-moving advances in telecommunications and related high technology will make it possible for many kinds of firms to set up shop almost anywhere. Nearness to raw materials, suppliers, and end markets is less crucial in a high-tech setting, while availability and cost of labor supply will gain importance as growth in the labor force begins to taper off.

Ease of business mobility will continue to hurt the older, high-cost cities of America. Old downtown areas will still be attractive to some firms that must do business face to face with their customers. And many companies have too large a stake in their downtown properties—and civic pride in their cities—to give them up lightly.

Yet the pull of technology will lead to further dispersal of business operations in the future. Computer nets and enhanced communications capabilities will draw functions away from the inner cities if there is no compelling reason to keep them there. Any number of functions that are technical and fairly mechanical (i.e., electronic) in themselves can be carried out almost anywhere without loss of central control if well planned.

Commuting patterns will have a good deal to do with locational decisions as well. Barring a totally unforeseen reversal in the energy outlook, decentralization is likely to continue, spurred by such considerations as ease of access, convenience to employees and lower overhead costs. Face-to-face contact with employees will still be important to management, but improved teleconferencing techniques can take over some of this.

Labor availability and quality will continue to favor the suburbs and smaller cities versus the large, inner cities in the future. The latter will have plenty of surplus labor, but it will be largely unskilled or semiskilled, while the suburbs will be rich in clerical and other classifications of workers, including housewives and retired persons available for part-time work. Smaller cities with good universities will continue to attract high-tech firms to specially designed research and development industrial parks.

Vocational training programs could improve the labor supply in the inner cities, but firms will not find these economical until labor force growth slows in the '90s. Government-funded programs aren't likely to fill the gap before then.

Proximity to large consumer markets ranks down the list in locational decisions behind labor force and operating costs for most firms outside retailing. In retailing, market concentration is still the chief lure. Sellers want to be stumbling over consumers everywhere they turn, and in many Sunbelt areas these densities are yet to be found—outside a few booming metropolitan areas. But this too will change as population continues to flow that way, filling in and spreading out.

The same information technology that allows other kinds of business new freedom in site selection will probably work in retailing's favor as well. "Teleshopping" via computer links will spread out into more thinly populated parts of the country to bring them closer to rivalry with the densely packed eastern seaboard and midwestern states in overall retail sales.

HIGH-GROWTH CITIES

Many big companies are likely to decentralize as time goes on, even more than they already have. Various operations can be spun off to lower-cost locations: data processing and invoicing, for example. Numerical operations performed at the end of a fiber-optic cable can be done as efficiently across a continent as they can next door, if there are savings to be had in wages, rents and local living costs.

One effect of corporate decentralizing will be the growth of second- and third-tier cities everywhere, but especially in southern, southwestern and western states. A mixture of attractions will account for this shift. Cities of, say, under a quarter of a million inhabitants may offer lower living and business costs and, in many cases, better quality-of-life attractions than either large cities or rural areas. Mostly, they will offer job opportunities. And more investors will be looking to them for new possibilities—and new markets.

In terms of percentage growth of new jobs created over the next 15 years, as ranked by the National Planning Association, these will be the top ten metro areas, varying in annual growth from just over 5% to 3.5%, for a group average of about 4%:

▶ Ft. Pierce and Ft. Myers, FL; Austin, TX; Ft. Lauderdale-Hollywood-Pompano Beach, FL; Anaheim-Santa Ana, CA; Tucson, AZ; Brazoria, TX; Reno, NV; W. Palm Beach-Boca Raton-Delray Beach, FL; Boulder-Longmont, CO.

Here are the 30 large metropolitan areas that will lead in absolute numbers of new jobs created (not growth *rate*) in the next 15 years. These will see average annual employment growth of about 2.4%. Because they are already the largest labor-market areas, their increases in jobs will bulk heavily in the economy:

▶ Houston; Anaheim-Santa Ana; Los Angeles-Long Beach; San Jose; Dallas; Denver; Phoenix; Washington, DC; San Diego; Boston-Lawrence-Salem; Atlanta; Tampa-St. Petersburg; Ft. Lauderdale-Hollywood, FL; Minneapolis-St. Paul; San Francisco; Austin; Miami-Hialeah; Orlando; Oakland, CA; Nassau-Suffolk, NY; Seattle; W. Palm Beach-Boca Raton; San Antonio; Baltimore; Tucson; Ft. Worth-Arlington, TX; Portland, OR; Riverside-San Bernardino, CA; Raleigh-Durham, NC; Oklahoma City.

TROUBLED OLDER CITIES

Many older, larger American cities are in for more rough going unless they can somehow bring down the cost of doing business within their boundaries. Growing national prosperity will be good for economic development practically everywhere, including within their own metropolitan areas, but these center cities will be out in the cold.

They're the ones caught in a kind of endless loop of bad luck and questionable public policy. High taxes and high wages, plus deteriorating downtown conditions, have helped speed an exodus of tax-paying businesses and residents to the suburbs or to smaller nearby cities. This, in turn, has worsened the conditions that brought on the exodus in the first place.

The problem is as much political as economic. The future of such cities could brighten if more federal and state assistance were channeled to them. But that's not the way things are headed; federal aid is shrinking under pressure of the federal budget deficit, and even revenue sharing is ending. State legislatures, too, will be looking for better payoffs in growth areas where the votes are, rather than in the deteriorating inner cities.

Another 1960s-style urban renewal wave doesn't seem to be in the cards for the rest of this century—which may be all to the good considering the damage done by the last one. Many cities, down to medium-sized ones, still have wide, empty expanses downtown, the legacy of "renewal" that petered out after the wrecking crews departed.

So it looks like stagnation for some years to come, with exceptions, of course. New York, for example: For all its difficulties, it has the critical mass to somehow make do and will continue to enjoy the fruits of its eminence as a financial, import and cultural center. And a number of already prosperous metropolitan areas will become even more so, as noted in the high-growth list above.

But other inland metropolises outside the Sunbelt, like Philadephia, Cleveland, Chicago, Detroit and St. Louis, are in varying degrees of trouble that won't be substantially corrected any time soon.

Most cities, but especially those facing further loss of tax revenues, are going far out of their way to offer inducements for new investment. So are state governments. But increasing corporate mobility may make economic-development recruiting campaigns less effective. A firm that found it easy to move where the pickings looked good may find it easy to do so again when it gets an even better offer, leaving behind a fresh wound in an already crippled city economy. Another problem in luring new businesses with tax incentives is that it can alienate existing local businesses, undercut the revenue base on which city services are funded, and—most important of all—may not produce lasting results.

As many as 50 eastern and midwestern cities may have black majorities by 2000, and political support for be-kind-to-business campaigns will be harder to drum up, even though it often leads to more jobs. It's certainly difficult now; most black elected officials are more preoccupied with consolidating their power than with courting business these days, and the constituencies that voted them in have their own agendas, including more public assistance from all levels of government.

The gentrification trend that has rehabilitated old neighborhoods in many cities is cooling along with a slowdown in formation of new households. It won't disappear in the years ahead, but its future will also be affected by the kinds of services and life-support systems cities can provide. And so there will be great variations from place to place. For example, most state-capital cities will do well. And in the better-off cities (and their close-in suburbs), builders will press for changes in zoning regulations to allow more "in-filling" on underused land.

Cities with a waterfront may be able to drum up support for redevelopment projects that bring in tourists and brighten the area. Baltimore and Boston are good examples of what can be accomplished with a mixture of public and private investment. But Baltimore's Harborplace and Boston's Quincy Market, as successful as they are, haven't done much for the rest of those cities.

To make ends meet, more city governments will turn to contracting-out of certain basic services such as trash collection and even fire and police, in the case of smaller ones. It will be cheaper for cities whose pay and pension scales have grown out of hand. State and municipal unions will fight the shift, but it's probably a losing battle. Taxpayers will vote to hold taxes down any way it can be done, so long as services are at least maintained.

This already is a small but growing trend in the operation and maintenance of jails and other detention facilities in many parts of the country—more so among smaller jurisdictions, but likely to spread to larger ones as time goes on.

TROUBLE IN PARADISE

In the past two decades, migratory patterns brought increasing population and prosperity to the South, Southwest, and Far West at an unprecedented rate, with slower growth almost everywhere else. That pattern is likely to continue indefinitely—certainly past the turn of the century.

But the net rate of migration to the Sunbelt states already is slowing, while growth has picked up in New England. The Midwest is gaining only slightly but at least is holding its own.

Among factors that will slow the southwestern movement of the population, the theoretical center of which will be somewhere in Arkansas by 2000, are overcrowding in the most desirable areas of the Sunbelt and improving economic conditions in the Snowbelt. As a whole, the Sunbelt has plenty of open space left—more than can be filled in for many years to come. But several of its major metropolitan areas already are close to being too big for comfort, and it is these that tilt the overall statistics.

Problems with the quality and availability of water will have to be faced in coming years. And providing enough water for industry, agriculture AND population growth is going to add to the cost of living and of doing business in many parts of the Sunbelt toward the end of the century. (For details, see our chapter on the water outlook.)

But while migration from other states into the Sunbelt is slowing, immigration will remain strong, particularly from Mexico, and keep the region's population growing at a fast rate.

Although the western part of the Sunbelt gets most of the attention, the fact is that growth currently is about the same in the south-central and southeastern states, although on a smaller base, and will probably continue to be. High costs—housing and wages, in particular—will dampen the appeal of California to many individuals and businesses.

The south central region, anchored by Texas, will be the second most rapidly growing one in the country in terms of employment, which is expected to rise by some 45%. Growth will be greatest in professional and technical and service occupations.

Oklahoma and Louisiana will be experiencing problems similar to those of Texas in the decline of oil and gas revenues. Water resources will be strained in the western part of Oklahoma. It and Arkansas will continue to draw in-migrants although at a slower rate than recently. Arkansas especially will continue to attract retirees to the long shorelines of its lakes backed up behind power dams.

THE WEST

The Pacific region will be sharing in the general pattern of growth and prosperity we see for California, and its economic growth will be two or three times faster than the national average.

The West as a whole is the fifth most powerful economy in the world, with higher proportions of educated professionals and singles than other regions. It also has the highest share of college graduates and upwardly mobile families. Which helps account for its readiness to try out new trends in goods, services and behavior, setting the pace for the rest of the country.

It has the highest percentage among the regions of households with annual income of $40,000-up, and even its "Baby Boom Echo" generation—children of grade-school age today—will be growing while it declines in other regions. Its economy is likely to be the healthiest in the foreseeable future, with new kinds of highly profitable and more stable light industry taking over from lumber, defense contracting and mining.

Growth will be uneven in the West. The Mountain States have been attracting net in-migration from everywhere, but their share will decline as business conditions improve faster elsewhere. And no new energy boom seems likely in the next couple of decades to revive the heavy inflow of job-seekers the region saw in the '60s and '70s.

The Northwest may turn out to be the next hot spot for the '90s and beyond, pulling in population and business with its attractive living conditions, labor supply and low labor costs.

The Pacific States will go from a lower share of gross national product than the South Atlantic in 1980 to a higher share by 2000, equal to about 15% of national GNP. Employment will rise over 50%, the largest absolute job increase of all the regions in the country.

Highest growth categories will be professional-technical, clerical and services, with declines among crafts, factory workers and unskilled laborers. The region's employment pattern, in other words, will be close to that of the country as a whole.

THE SOUTHEAST

The South Atlantic region will be paced by tremendous growth in Florida. The region as a whole, extending up to the Virginias and Delaware, will grow at about or slightly better than the national average in the next decade or two, ranking roughly with the Pacific region.

Still, the region's overall population growth will slow down substantially from the 20% increase registered in the '70s... perhaps by as much as half.

Fastest growing lines will be communications, electronics and construction—but the first two are coming up from a relatively small base. Construction, however, will boom as more and more people move in to take advantage of lower-cost living conditions and job opportunities. Many of the latter will be tied in one way or another to investment in, and expansion of, high-tech lines associated with Research Triangle in North Carolina and other area universities.

There also will be continued growth in recreation and leisure spending by vacationers and retirees, whose influx will rise as the national population ages.

Two old-line industries are in trouble—tobacco and textiles. The former is threatened by growing health consciousness and potential congressional revolt against federal support and by 2000 may be in serious decline. Textiles continue to lose place to lower-cost imports and to American investment moving to off-shore production facilities. But the industry is deep in a wave of modernization and automation; at least a modest turnaround is in store before 2000.

Growth will continue to be uneven within the region, with Kentucky, Tennessee, Alabama and Mississippi lagging behind. But water problems in the Far West may make cotton farming more profitable again in Mississippi, and all these states are busily courting high-tech and other lines of business.

NEW LIFE UP NORTH

At the same time, the Frostbelt will be revitalizing, with the most improvement among smaller cities with less severe social problems than the giant cities. New England, and northern New England in particular (New Hampshire, Vermont and Maine), already is pulling in new investment, much of it in high-tech lines attracted by a well-established infrastructure and a skilled labor force. Massachusetts's population will grow about 18% by the year 2000, according to a National Planning Association estimate, and this gain of 1.1 million people will be fifth in the nation, after California, Florida, Texas and Arizona.

Even the industrial upper Midwest, the region hardest hit by the recessions of the early '80s and by the decline of old, labor-intensive lines, is showing signs of a similar recovery, although continuing to lag behind. Its situation will improve, along with that of the entire country, as the high-tech boom ahead spreads its benefits around. And its skilled labor surplus may begin to lure substantial reinvestment if average wage levels are competitive. The sharp decline in union power in the region points in that direction.

POSTSCRIPT: THE AMERICAN FRONTIER

For all this talk of growth, it's good to keep in mind the vastness of this country's totally undeveloped space.

The American frontier was "conquered" and "closed" nearly a century ago, the historians tell us, yet roughly a fourth of this country is still essentially empty—with an average population density of less than two persons per square mile.

"The high growth rate of many western cities and towns masks the fact that they amount to burgeoning urban outposts scattered across the far larger, sparsely populated frontier," says Resources for the Future, a Washington research organization whose data we drew on for this report.

Much of this frontier land has never been surveyed or even fully explored. All of it, as you might suspect, is in the West and Alaska, and most of it is uninhabited, for good reason: It's arid or mountainous or otherwise inaccessible and not fit for much of anything civilization might care to do with it—except exploit underlying riches. Alaska alone has hypothetical coal resources estimated to equal those of all the lower 48 states, plus proven oil reserves equal to at least a third of theirs.

Ninety-six percent of Alaska qualifies as frontier. Ditto for hundreds of counties scattered through the Northwest, Nevada, Utah and the Great Plains from Montana to Texas. Even California has two such counties, accounting for 10% of its area.

Improved water technology might extend civilization and agriculture over more of the empty areas, but not in the short run; just now the problem is making do with fast-diminishing water reserves, and farming is at best marginal and likely to be severely curtailed.

What ultimate good is all this emptiness, other than something to fly over? Perhaps none, in any short-run economic sense. But in a larger sense, it is a reminder that this country's greatness was based in part on the unique opportunities presented by abundant riches and space enough to live one's own life, and there is plenty of both left.

In another sense, it is a reminder of how large this country is and helps keep alive a sort of folk memory of what the West used to be.

29

States: The Big Three

California, Texas and Florida will continue to be the fastest growing states as far ahead as anyone can see, but probably at a somewhat slower pace than in the past couple of decades. These, along with Arizona and North Carolina, will account for roughly half of national population growth between now and the year 2000. Here are detailed outlooks for the top three:

THE GOLDEN STATE

California is riding a new wave of U.S. trade with the Far East, much of it funneled through the state; most of the export side originates within it. Asian countries are setting up banks, in California. Japan owns the three biggest non-American banks, and over a thousand Japanese-owned companies are operating there.

Japan alone has enormous pent-up reserves in pension funds, which California banks and consultants will be managing in growing volume—a continuing source of investment capital in America. Southeast Asia will be growing into a strong market for California exports of goods and services over the next several years, and the number of American-owned plants in the area will expand, along with joint ventures.

Population: California will be the most populous state in 2000, as it is now...close to 32 million people, up 5.4 million from now. The bulk of this growth will be in the south—Los Angeles, San Diego, Orange, Riverside, San Bernardino counties, with San Diego County the second most populous behind Los Angeles.

Over half the state's population and households already are in the southern part.

But population is migrating inland at the same time, a trend likely to continue through the century as more people find themselves being priced out of the coastal areas and move on in search of affordable land and housing. Much of this trek is eastward from L.A. and Orange counties into San Bernardino and Riverside counties. Some go over the Tehachapi Range into the San Joaquin Valley, where the climate isn't so comfortable but there is land available for development. The Sierra foothills will continue to attract urbanites seeking escape from the congestion and high living costs of the coastal areas.

In San Francisco, there will be continuing movement of corporate support services into less expensive East Bay locations, maintaining headquarters in the city for the prestige of the address. And high-tech companies in Silicon Valley, Santa Clara County, will do most of their expanding elsewhere—even outside the state—to escape the Valley's soaring costs, particularly in housing. One of the in-state areas to benefit is that centered around Sacramento, which will become a prime high-tech location. Its population will swell for years to come.

These and other concentrations of population growing up around the state will help revive the shopping center construction business in the '90s. Just now, California has plenty; older shopping centers will be upgraded in coming years to match the new competition. And in housing, builders will be trending to smaller units as a way of reviving demand choked off by escalating house and apartment prices: More developments farther out from urban centers, with recreational facilities attached or nearby.

Energy: Fuel cost and availability won't put any limits on growth. California is tapping such energy sources as solar, wind, cogeneration (use of surplus heat from manufacturing processes), geothermal in both north and south, plus hydropower and nuclear. All these on top of oil and gas, supplies of which should be more than adequate well into the next century.

Water: This is a different story. The time of pinch in southern California is nearing, and before the end of the century painful political decisions will have to be made. The most logical source of additional water is the northern part of the state and, despite entrenched and growing opposition there to further transfers to the South, southern California will have the population and the votes to swing it.

Job opportunities: They will be greatest in fields serving a huge and growing population—retailing, personal services, health care (particularly for the elderly), finance, insurance and real estate. High-tech will also be creating jobs for both professionals and assembly-line people as biotech and communications expand along with computers and microchips. But little job growth is ahead in aircraft and space; farming and related services and logging and lumber mills will be doing less hiring.

Labor force: The state's ethnic mix will continue to shift toward Asian and Hispanic minorities. Within several more years they will outnumber native whites in the schools by about 25% and, given their higher birthrates, will outnumber blacks in both the state and the country as a whole early in the next century. In southern California by 2000 the proportion of Hispanics in the population will be about equal to whites—around 42% each. For the state as a whole, the total of white non-Hispanics will fall below 60%.

The impact on California's labor force will be even more striking. The bulk of new entrants will be Hispanic or Asian. The forces behind this trend include the fact that their immigration numbers are rising along with their birthrates, while the number of young white labor-force entrants is declining and so is the inflow of white job seekers from other parts of the country. California already is experiencing a small net decrease in the white component of its population, due to out-migration to other states, particularly Arizona.

A hefty low-skilled labor supply will help avert a flight of some low-pay industries. But California will have more of such job-seekers than it will have jobs for, while it will need more upscale people to take jobs in its high-tech and service industries. And it may have difficulty attracting them if job opportunities are expanding around the country—as they will be in the '90s and beyond.

Training programs would help, but how these might be financed is an open question. And efforts to give a leg-up to immigrant populations will be resented by native blacks, many of whom could use some help themselves in retraining for better jobs. Signs of this kind of backlash are already apparent, and some Californians worry about inter-minority troubles ahead.

Immigration: Within the next decade, California—along with neighboring states and ultimately the country—may be facing the biggest influx of Mexican immigration it has ever seen. Ominous signs are building up. Mexico's population will nearly double by 2000. It is producing working-age youngsters at roughly double the rate of jobs for them, while suffering a dramatic decline in oil revenues. The government is targeting development increasingly on high-productivity, high-capital lines and skimping on those— like agriculture—that might employ these youths. Even this level of investment is threatened by falling oil prices and the burden of rebuilding after the 1985 earthquake.

Sometime in the early '90s these trends could reach a critical mass. Immigration from Mexico—legal and otherwise—is impelled by two forces: poverty on one side, the hope of betterment on the other. And in a kind of human osmosis, the pressure differential causes a steady flow across a border which, for all our efforts to control it, is a highly permeable membrane.

There will be increasing proposals to "close" our border, which is easier to talk about than accomplish without massive commitments of money, technology and manpower. There are also worries about what might happen inside Mexico if such an effort were to succeed—fears of political upheaval, even rebellion.

Much of today's immigration from Mexico is short-term; people come and go as they accumulate enough cash to return to their families. But if Mexico's job situation turns as sour as it may, more of this cross-border traffic will become one-way, which would put additional burdens on an already heavily laden social-service structure in California and other states. Most illegals don't dare apply for any kind of public assistance for fear of being picked up by "la migra," as they call the Immigration Service, but some do pay taxes via withholding; and their children attend school. Overall, they probably are a major part of the "underground economy," perhaps as much as a third. So far, the above-ground economy—California's included—has absorbed rising immigration without major disruption; some claim it has even benefited from it.

Heavier commitments to assisting economic development in Mexico could be one U.S. response to an impending explosion across the border. Another could be heavier pressures on the Mexican government to allow U.S. capital to build more plants along the border and in the interior of the country. The Mexican political climate is cool to this idea now, but we think it will grow warmer in the next decade or so.

THE LONE STAR STATE

Texas will see its population grow at a rate sharply higher than the country as a whole through the turn of the century, gaining four to five million residents and passing New York to become the second most populous state (behind California) before 1990.

While oil-related problems are easing the influx from other states, Texas will continue to gain from in-migration, and its natural increase will exceed that of the U.S., due to the fertility of its younger population. Immigration from Mexico will be up—perhaps sharply up, for the reasons outlined above—and will bring all of the problems faced by California and other southwestern states.

The fastest growing age group between now and the early 2000s, both nationally and in Texas, will be the Baby Boomers themselves, moving into the 45-to-64 group, which will go up an average of 3% a year. Growth will slow down by some 16% among school-age children and by a bit less among adults 18 to 44. The over-65 crowd will be up by nearly 20%.

Down off its energy high, Texas is moving ahead into new industries that will reduce its dependence on oil, oil products and energy services. Overall economic growth won't match that of the past couple of decades, but will still be better than the national average.

Resource-based output—products of agriculture and the oil and gas fields—will drop by about half as a share of the state's total product in the next couple of decades, while the proportion represented by manufacturing, construction and services will rise. In the latter category, the biggest growth producers will be computers and oil-drilling equipment, especially as new high-tech techniques are wedded to older processes in exploration and production. Apparel and textiles and printing and publishing will also see growth, but at lower levels.

Energy: The shrinking role of oil and gas in Texas' future is more than just a matter of declining world prices. Much of Texas' petrochemical industry, producer of agricultural and other chemicals and feedstocks, is going overseas to joint ventures between Texas capital and Middle Eastern oil-producing countries. This will create new competition for Texas refining and petrochemical firms, which will turn increasingly from commodity chemicals to specialty items, including new and improved plastics. If Mexico decides to open its doors to foreign investment, its own petrochemical complex might also attract heavy investment from Texas.

Declining energy production in Texas will soon stabilize through new recovery methods, perhaps later to include biotech-recovery systems. (See our chapter on biotechnology.)

High-tech and services: With oil and gas playing a smaller role, Texas will be going through a major transformation in the years just ahead. More than half of its gross product is from services, and this share will rise by at least 20% before the end of the century.

Texas already has a substantial high-tech industry, and its leaders in government, industry and finance are working hard to attract more. Its state university system has recently been handed a substantial chunk of cash raised by local donors to endow new professorial chairs in science and engineering, on the recognized principle that strong ties with academic researchers are vital to high-tech growth—a principle already demonstrated by the decision of the computer industry to place its new joint research-and-development effort in Austin, seat of the University of Texas. Another example is the advanced robotics center recently established by the University of Texas/Arlington. Biotechnology and biomedical research, some of it associated with space exploration, will play a major role in several cities, including Houston and San Antonio.

Regions and cities: Houston is in the early stages of transition to other lines. The city could walk away with honors as a leading medical technology center, given its present base, once it shakes its dependence on energy. Commercialization of space should also be good news for the Houston area.

The Dallas-Ft. Worth area has a strong research and development base and is fast becoming an international financial center. San Antonio has a large labor force and prospers in part from the rise of investment along the Mexican border.

The 12 Texas ports on the Gulf of Mexico are expected to show continued growth in traffic over the coming two decades or so, although at a somewhat slower rate than in the early '80s.

Water supply: It's going to be a problem for parts of West Texas. Even though supply is more than adequate in East Texas, there will be special problems there too, chiefly in stemming land subsidence and salt-water intrusion in coastal areas. In the high plains portion of West Texas, the prospect is for a shift from irrigated agriculture to dryland farming as ground-water supplies fall below the economically recoverable level later this century. The net result will be a shrinkage of agriculture in the state. Dallas-Ft. Worth and El Paso may have some expensive supply problems to meet as well.

THE SUNSHINE STATE

Florida will have some four million more residents in 2000 than now, for a total of 15 million—a rise of about 36%. It alone will account for 10% of national growth in employment between now and 2000, the National Planning Association estimates. People are flooding in at an average of 5000 a week.

Employment growth: Note a major switch: The bulk of the newcomers will be job-seekers from other states, not retirees. Although the latter will still be an important part of the state's population, the attraction of Florida as a center of industry, services and high tech is going to be the principal lure.

This marks a considerable success for the self-help efforts mounted by the state government and leaders of industry and finance. The objective has been to diversify—lessen the state's dependence on vacationers and retirees while doing nothing to discourage them.

Business lures: A major high-tech push is underway and will continue well into the next century, tied to the state's enhanced educational facilities, the commercial offshoots of NASA's space programs and a favorable business climate.

The state is transportation-rich. From the center of Florida near Orlando, goods can be trucked to any point in the state in a day or less, and Florida shippers have ready access to northern markets via the finally complete Florida interstate. Major ports around the state are being improved. And there are plans, which may not be realized until early in the next century, for a high-speed rail system linking Miami with the central and northern parts of the state.

Boom areas: Growth will be strongest in Orlando, Tampa-St. Petersburg, Ft. Myers-Cape Coral, Ft. Lauderdale and Boca Raton.

Miami will expand its role as a major financial center and as the northernmost outpost of Latin America. Although predominantly Cuban and South American, the Hispanic population's Mexican component is likely also to grow in the next 15 years or so. Despite the best efforts of the law, Miami will probably continue to serve as the chief conduit for drugs and drug money moving between Latin America and the U.S. Much of the money is laundered there and helps account for some of the city's growing affluence.

Construction: Given its outlook for population growth, the state will need more than two million additional homes and a good deal of expansion in its facilities aimed at retirees.

There is plenty of land still available for development... in the northern part of the farm belt, for example, where growers discouraged by recent crop reverses and encouraged by rising land prices will put large areas on the market. Citrus growing will move farther south into large undeveloped tracts east of Naples.

Not all the development represents housing for newcomers; much of the healthy expansion anticipated along the Atlantic coast above Palm Beach reflects the movement of upscale economic refugees from the crowding in the Miami-Lauderdale area.

But Florida isn't gobbling up growth the way it used to; there are rising concerns about overdoing it, and the state is beginning to tinker with "growth management." Just what that means isn't yet clear, but it probably will put more of the cost of development on the developers themselves through user fees and "impact fees.'' Florida is worried about ground-water contamination and encroachment on wetlands and the aquifer itself.

Builders will be required to provide more municipal-type services such as water, sewer, power, fire and police, even schools—either directly or with higher fees and taxes. This will mean higher housing prices as builders pass on costs to buyers. It won't pinch off growth but will certainly slow it in the '90s. Unbridled expansion is a thing of the past.

30

Water: Scarce Resource

The news about water is that its cost will be going up from now on, faster than the cost of living—and in some areas, double the rate of inflation. The rise will be steep enough to bring dramatic changes in the economy and ecology of large stretches of the United States by the year 2000.

As with all commodities as they get scarce and expensive, water shortages will stimulate new supplies. The rising cost will bring conservation and eventually high-tech methods of recycling and desalting now-unusable water sources. Ultimately, the supply of water will be limited only by the vastness of the oceans, but large-scale desalinization is a long way off—well into the 21st century—unless there is a dramatic breakthrough.

But as land disposal of wastes increasingly pollutes drinking water supplies, the oceans will be eyed not just as a source of water and nutritional substances, but as handy dumping grounds for wastes, too.

The most severe problems of water shortage will show up earliest in several western areas, where present farming methods are already becoming uneconomical. Other states and metropolitan areas, the East included, also will feel the squeeze, which will come as a nasty surprise to people who still think of water as a virtually inexhaustible resource.

Long-term climatogical trends will contribute to western water problems. If well-established patterns hold up, the West can expect another drought in the mid to late-'90s. Dry periods seem to recur on a roughly 20-year cycle, for reasons thought to tie in with sunspots and other solar activity. The next one may be no worse or even less severe than the previous drought in the '50s, but it will hit large areas already plagued with falling water tables and other symptoms of growing shortage.

Even worse, scientists believe the so-called Greenhouse Effect will begin to take its toll around the turn of the century. The earth's atmosphere is on a long-term warming trend, due to the rise in carbon dioxide. One of the first measurable effects, they say, is likely to be a shift in rainfall patterns: Dry areas will get drier, wet areas wetter.

Manufacturers of water-using appliances, like dishwashers and laundry equipment, may find themselves up against stiff local ordinances on recycling and conservation; some already are preparing designs for this eventuality. And businesses in general, along with communities, will be looking for ways to recycle water rather than simply let it flow away. (One fast-food chain already has begun installing water-recycling equipment in some of its big-city outlets, rather than take its chances with price and supply from local systems.)

Biotech research is turning up ways to help with recycling: Benevolent bacteria that eat up pollutants—a technique that municipal water systems will be able to use.

THE HIGH COST

For the next couple of decades, water use in many places will have to be rationed by cost, and some uses—such as intensive irrigation in the West and High Plains—will be priced out of the market, a process that will begin in a few years and probably be complete around the turn of the century.

Meanwhile, other areas that are brimming with water will find it increasingly expensive to maintain the quality they need for human consumption. On the Gulf Coast of Florida, for example, a number of desalting plants are already in use to combat the infiltration of seawater. Several Eastern Seaboard cities, like Boston, will eventually face extensive modifications and repairs to their water systems, due to either leaky plumbing or ground-water pollution or both. Cities like Denver, whose ability to draw on water from across the Rockies is about used up and where water is probably already more expensive than oil on a fully costed-out basis, will have to scuffle for ways to reprocess waste water.

Although water problems differ widely, they all stem from pretty much the same cause: Overuse. In and around cities like Houston and Los Angeles, for example, urban sprawl and zooming population have pushed water consumption far beyond rates that would allow for natural recharging of the source.

Coming scarcities of water will be met in a number of ways. In Arizona, the Central Arizona Project will divert enough Colorado River water to take care of Phoenix and Tucson well into the next century. But their gain is Los Angeles' loss, and that city will now have to look elsewhere for additional supplies—specifically, to northern California, where voters so far have been able to stave off "raids" from the southern part of the state but may not be able to much longer.

The Texas Panhandle will begin converting to dryland farming—wheat and sorghum or rangeland instead of irrigated cotton and corn. This conversion may spread northward throughout the High Plains and Oklahoma, Kansas and into Nebraska, where wells keep getting deeper while the Ogallala Aquifer on which they depend dries up faster than natural forces can replenish it.

Intensive conservation measures can stave off the transition for a time—perhaps for many years—through such techniques as drip irrigation and improved equipment. And coming biotech developments may bring new drought-resistant strains of crops. But the former must be done on an area-wide basis to be effective, which is a political problem, and the latter won't turn up in time to prevent a wholesale shift.

Rationing by cost means that in many regions water will be diverted to urban and suburban development, which can always pay more for water than agriculture can. Which raises a Catch-22 dilemma: As development expands, so does water use.

But problems of this kind aren't likely to stem the tide of migration to the Sunbelt. Metro areas will scramble to accommodate growth, and civic boosters will pooh-pooh scare talk about water. But living costs will begin to rise in the worst-hit areas, and a lot of homeowners may discover they no longer can afford to keep their lawns sparkling green in the midst of a cactus-covered countryside; moreover, local governments may not let them even try. Businesses heavily dependent on a good supply of water will have to crank these considerations into their decisions on where to locate.

THE SALT PLAGUE

The rich soil of the Central Valley of California is increasingly tainted by the buildup of salts from waste irrigation water that can't percolate through the clay underlying the top layer. This threatens to poison either the land or the area's wildlife, if the brackish runoff is piped somewhere else. Some of the land is being taken out of irrigation, which will return it to desert. The fate of the rest remains uncertain.

Techniques for purifying salty water are going to become necessary in many areas of the country, particularly on the coasts. Drinking water in several areas, including some in the Midwest, already is failing to meet federal standards.

Desalting is expensive, but the real cost is coming down as methods become more sophisticated and the price of water climbs. Reverse osmosis (RO) systems produced in Japan and the U.S. already are in use in several places; they can treat brackish water at prices now too high for farming but reasonable for other uses. The world's largest RO plant is being built in Yuma, Arizona, under terms of a treaty guaranteeing Mexico that we will keep down the salt content of the Colorado River as it crosses the border.

Converting seawater via "flash distillation" is a tougher, more expensive problem. It's being done on a large scale only in Saudi Arabia, where energy is cheap. In this country, it is unlikely to be widely installed until either the need grows severe enough or a low-cost energy source is developed.

SWAPPING WATER

Moving water around on a large scale from areas of surplus to areas of shortage is an attractive idea whose time has passed: Too expensive. Congress won't go for any more mammoth public-works programs of this kind when budget pressures are so intense. Besides, the surplus areas won't go along. The Great

Lakes states have banded together to fight any such transfers, and Canada is with them, refusing even to talk about moving water from its share of the Lakes or its western provinces. And Congress has made its mood clear by voting to ban funds for any such planning.

But western delegations in Congress haven't totally given up hope of further federal assistance for local water projects. They see the chance to do some old-fashioned logrolling: Their support for federal aid for rebuilding obsolete water systems in the urban East in exchange for eastern congressmen backing more water projects in the West. Whether this can fly in the next decade is doubtful; it probably would have to overcome a presidential veto.

In the meantime, the buying and selling of water rights is becoming an increasingly lively business in many parts of the West and Great Plains. Water rights entitle the holder to divert a certain amount of water from streams and reservoirs for his own use. More and more marginal farmers are finding they can make a better living by selling these rights to upstream or downstream municipalities, developers and industries than they can by farming.

This process is part of the accelerating conversion of land to ranching and dryland farming of winter wheat and the like. It will help underwrite the continued expansion of Sunbelt cities and industries, unless and until Congress moves to put on the brakes. But there is no sign of this happening in the foreseeable future. The issue is still viewed as essentially one of state and local jurisdiction. And any moves to inject new federal regulation and spending programs in the arena would run against the grain of current and prospective attitudes in Congress.

As water-treatment costs rise in coming years, politicians all around the country will be searching for ways to lessen the pain. Local water-users, homeowners in particular, will squawk if water bills get too high—a legacy of the days, now ending, when water everywhere was looked on as practically "free." (New York City doesn't even have water meters.)

You will certainly see an increase in water rates in coming years, but not enough to cover all costs. The rest will be hidden in taxes. The trick in many areas will be to keep water-driven taxes from getting so high that it discourages the development that is causing the water problems in the first place. For some, however, there may be no other way out. People and firms will ultimately pay whatever it costs to get dependable water, but that doesn't mean they won't look for places where it costs less.

OCEAN DUMPING

The rising pollution of groundwater, caused in part by land burial of wastes, has reawakened scientific interest in ocean disposal of wastes. The National Academy of Sciences has under study proposals to weigh the economic and ecological tradeoffs between sea and land disposal.

It's going to be a red-hot battle, and how it comes out is anybody's guess. But the worse that pollution of groundwater resources becomes, the more the balance of public opinion may turn toward ocean disposal. Scientific opinion already is beginning to move that way, although it is by no means a mass movement as yet. Still, more and more marine biologists and land-based ecologists are beginning to believe that dumping or burning at sea is likely to be the lesser evil.

Biotechnology will eventually help ease the waste-buildup problem on land, through systems employing gene-tailored bacteria that gobble up the gunk and render it harmless, but this won't come soon enough to avert the donnybrook we're now heading for.

The U.S. depends on ground-water reserves for about 50% of its drinking water, and these are becoming increasingly polluted by insufficiently treated waste, chemical runoff from farms and fields, seepage of oil and gasoline and of chemicals in waste dumps. Continued disposal on land heightens the risk to human health, and we are running out of usable sites. In fact, several hundred dump sites are awaiting urgent cleanup. This leaves the oceans, where vast amounts of waste could be disposed of by dumping or incinerating on special ships, if properly treated beforehand. (New York and Los Angeles are already dumping at sea, but with minimum pre-treatment.)

The very thought of expanding this, of course, outrages environmentalists and scares many members of the public who have been conditioned over the years to regard the oceans as delicately balanced ecosystems in which any tampering can bring disaster to marine life.

But, says one ocean scientist, "This is tragic and essentially anti-science. It ignores the very dangerous fact that underground water is being polluted and very seriously so. The real issue is subjective: What are the tradeoffs, the limits to which we can safely go? Take southern California, where we are disposing of the wastes of 11 million people at sea with the loss of, say, five percent of sea life on the bottom. Is that acceptable? What are the alternatives? It may take a real catastrophe, a tragic episode of some kind, to turn people around on this issue. The public needs to be reeducated."

The danger of "real catastrophe" is what the other side of the debate will rely on to fight ocean dumping—the threat of serious depletion of marine life by the same poisons we are trying to contain on land.

Somewhat oversimplified, it boils down to people vs. fish. Scientists admit they don't know what the score would be if ocean dumping were to spread. But they believe that it would take a lot of dumping to have a serious effect, and they argue that careful research and experimentation should begin immediately. Funding could be provided in part by the federal government but also by states and universities, and perhaps even by some kind of industry-supported "superfund," like the one established to finance cleanup of existing hazardous waste sites on land.

Wastes would be at least partially treated to make them more biodegradable before ocean dumping. Acids would be less of a problem, because they are neutralized by seawater. Dumping sites and schedules could be carefully coordinated via regional agreements to avoid over-concentration in any particular place. The 200-mile limit the U.S. claims off its shores would provide ample room for reasonably safe disposal, pro-dumping scientists assert.

Roughly half the U.S. population—though not necessarily the same 50% that relies on underground water—lives within 50 miles of a seacoast, if you count the Great Lakes. Trucking or rail shipment of treated wastes from urban concentrations to coastal disposal points would be a big job, but not by any means an impossible one.

And what about the fish? Market mechanisms could provide one kind of answer: seafood rationing by price. If the price goes high enough, consumption will fall, which may already be happening. And the higher prices go, the more encouragement there may be for commercial seafood farming—fish and shellfish cultivation in bays, pens and lagoons along our coasts. Shrimp cultivation along the coast of Ecuador on the Pacific already has produced a boom in exports for that country. No reason it couldn't be done here and elsewhere in the world. But will it, and will it succeed? No answers now, probably none for some time. But by 2000, the economics of seacoast farming may be more compelling.

NUCLEAR WASTE

One other kind of ocean-disposal battle may turn out to be a preliminary event to the fight over municipal and industrial waste and may influence its outcome. It's the battle over nuclear trash, the waste of atomic electric generating plants.

Proposals to dispose of it in the ocean have so far been blocked by environmental and other groups. But there may be as much as 45,000 tons of the stuff piled up in temporary storage sites on land by the year 2000, and the risks this poses could begin to counterbalance those involved in ocean disposal.

Techniques have been developed here and abroad—Australia included—that might greatly lessen the risk of radioactivity leakage. Wastes would be fused at very high temperatures into tough glass-like blocks, which then would be encased in durable metal—say, copper or stainless steel. The blocks could then be dumped in ocean trenches, some of which are miles deep, where they would sink into thick beds of silt and remain impervious to corrosion and leakage for centuries, or until swallowed into the earth's interior by subduction of the tectonic plates that creates the trenches. So go the claims for this technology, which remains untested, unproven.

The alternatives are clear enough: continued burial on land or stowage deep within natural caves and salt mines. Of course, no one wants such a site in his own state, much less his own backyard, but one proposal recently made by the U.S. Energy

Department calls for a billion-dollar processing facility at the Oak Ridge nuclear installation in Tennessee which, when completed in the late '90s, would hold up to 15,000 tons out of the 45,000 or so tons of high-level waste expected to have been generated by then. The facility would prepare the waste for permanent disposal in deep-rock mine sites not yet chosen.

If and when this issue comes to a head—and it probably will within a decade—an important precedent for ocean dumping may be set.

31

The World Market

In today's fast-changing world, no one country will enjoy lengthy domination of the world economy comparable to England's 100-year Victorian reign or America's 30-year leadership from the end of World War II until the mid '70s.

Without continued innovation and cost control, one country's advantage in a certain kind of technology or manufacturing will evaporate as quickly as it appeared.

In the coming several decades, every country will be increasingly dependent on the stability and prosperity of all others—whether industrial or undeveloped, lender or borrower. The era of the insulated domestic economy is long gone. The producer nations need strong customers to accept their exports. The lender must help keep the debtor nation strong enough to honor its commitments.

There will be no cataclysmic Third World debt crisis—no massive defaulting on loans from western banks, no collapse of the international credit system. Instead, we will see a constant rolling over of past loans at whatever terms—extended repayment, lower interest rates—are necessary to accommodate the current finances of the borrowing nations and the demands of the lenders. This will result in the progressive writing down of loan value on the books of American banks, and it will hurt the profits of some. But the system will keep clanking along.

America will continue to be the world leader in industry and trade, showing by example what other nations can accomplish. But high tech knows no national boundaries any longer, and staying ahead of the pack will require all the ingenuity and productivity we can muster, into the indefinite future.

This country's worried preoccupation with its imbalance of payments will persist for some time to come, but by 2000—if not much sooner—the concern will have faded away. It may even seem rather quaint by then, in light of the enormous growth in world trade and our share of it that will ensue.

The dollar will remain high indefinitely in relation to other currencies—albeit at lower levels than recently—and this factor alone may keep our balance of payments in deficit for some years. But the high dollar will be a token not of trouble but of strength ...a reflection of the respect the rest of the world has for the profits to be made in our markets and the growing competitiveness of our economy in world markets.

Which is another way of saying that much of the "excess" of imports over exports will continue to be foreign investment here, both debt and equity capital. This is a vote of confidence, no matter how you look at it. By giving foreigners a rising stake in American growth and stability, this investment will be a factor encouraging further domestic growth, which will be needed to pay off all that foreign debt.

Even with lower American interest rates, the boom in American productivity and profitability will continue to attract foreign capital. (Japan, for example, has enormous pension-fund reserves that will increasingly become a source of investment capital here.) It will be fueled by American high-technology research and its products. These, along with other services such as communications and data processing, will be our major exports—very high-value-added exports. Even as American exports of farm goods decline as a proportion of our total exports, the export of American agricultural technology will boom.

But at the same time, renewed growth in West Europe and the Far East—fueled in good part by export sales to the U.S.—will also be attracting capital investment, restraining some of the heavy capital flow that has been coming here and keeping the dollar at reasonable levels.

Talk of further tinkering with the system of floating international exchange rates will have quieted. The dollar isn't going to come crashing down, and huge international cash flows—especially into this country—will continue to offset the effects trade deficits might ordinarily be expected to have on exchange rates. This shift has in fact confounded much of the conventional economic wisdom in the '80s.

But the dollar will have to share its world leadership role with a close second—the yen, which, after having been artificially undervalued for so long, will appreciate as Japan gradually opens its own doors to foreign investment. The deutsche mark and Swiss franc also are likely to climb again, as Europe scrambles to catch up with the American and Japanese high-tech boom.

LESS PROTECTIONISM

The U.S. has been going through throes of transition, lashing out in uncoordinated ways at imports that seem to threaten American jobs. But a turn to outright, extensive protectionism is not in the cards, and by the turn of the century, we will be operating in a far more open world market. Other countries will follow our lead or risk loss of access to our markets, the world's largest.

More and more U.S. firms are becoming multinational—taking on foreign partners here and overseas, buying or producing parts and components on the world market wherever they are cheapest—"global sourcing," it's called. A growing number of American jobs will depend on this kind of internationalism, a lot more than could be temporarily saved by artificial respiration for inefficient industries.

The noncommunist world will become a more open market for trade and investment in spite of the discriminations and protectionist devices most of it still resorts to. These are going to diminish in impact in coming years, while the largest organized proponent of protectionism here—the labor unions—will no longer be much of a political force.

The opening-up of markets is bringing about an intensity of competition in price, design and innovation quite unlike anything seen before. It is putting a growing premium on management skills: American productivity vs. the rest of the world's lower labor costs.

But technology, our comparative advantage, is spreading around the world. Even the communist world is involved in this; it hungers for our products—the bidden and the forbidden. And it

284 • THE NEW AMERICAN BOOM

is potentially a huge market in itself, if trade and political relations open up between the U.S. and Russia. In the meantime, Japan and West Europe will continue to bid to supply advanced technology to the entire Soviet Bloc.

The world is being flooded with communications, particularly that originating in the U.S., in the form of radio, TV and data transfer as well as print, and as this flood grows it can have dramatic effects on populations and governments.

One of the effects is a rising hunger for U.S. and other Western goods, but more than goods, for lifestyle and the kind of freedom that goes with it.

DEVELOPING NATIONS

The Third World will industrialize—unevenly, some parts of it rapidly, others perhaps never catching up. But one way or another it will take over more of the mass production, high-labor-content industry we are phasing out or sending abroad. This process will boost incomes and demand for our exports in developing countries.

Yet it won't be smooth sailing for most of them. The modernization of the Third World will require vast amounts of capital, both loans and equity, and it's unclear where it will come from. Many developing countries, fearing corporate colonialism, have restrictions on direct equity investment by foreigners, and large private lenders—once burned, twice wary—are pulling back, confining their Third World lending to the absolute requirements of debt rescheduling.

All of which may require the creation of new kinds of lending institutions in the '90s to supplement the activities of the World Bank and similar international organs. These might turn out to be a separate class of quasi-governmental banks regulated almost as public utilities—enjoying government backing but with close government supervision.

This won't be enough by itself. Ultimately, the Third World will have to turn to private foreign investment for its salvation, and a rising recognition of this prospect is beginning to produce some interesting changes of attitude. There are signs of a new mood, still tentative and fragile; radical movements could easily upset it in countries where population expansion is leaving less and less time for compromise.

Perhaps the best example—because it is the most surprising—is that of mainland China, whose communist government has turned its back on Maoism and is embracing aspects of capitalism as fast as its creaky economy and top-heavy bureaucracy can be pulled along.

China is acting on what must be obvious if unadmitted elsewhere among socialist governments: Socialist-style central planning has been a flop—in agriculture, a disaster—and growth is the property of the market-oriented, capitalist-road countries.

The success of this experiment will be watched closely everywhere in the world but no more so than in the Soviet Union, where it is viewed as a threatening heresy, and in the Soviet satellites, where it probably is a point of envy.

But other nonaligned nations also are watching, and it is among these that the changes may occur. More and more, these countries are in a mood to question if not abandon the failed god of central planning. Having nowhere else to turn—the Russians having long since shown that their "help" is usually worse than the problem—these countries are demonstrating a new interest in direct foreign investment. India is an example to watch; it is boosting its imports of technology from Japan and the West and relaxing its restrictions on foreign ownership.

Not that the capitalists, here or elsewhere, are falling over themselves to rush in—not until there are much firmer proofs of a change of heart (and of laws and regulations). But the time is ripening for such change and we see it coming.

Whether it will come in time in a number of countries is an open question. Large parts of Africa, reeling under decades of inept and corrupt government management, may already be beyond help; today's basket cases may be tomorrow's disasters. Explosive population growth in many undeveloped and semi-developed countries may continue to outstrip the best that investment, technology and improved agriculture can do.

Yet the alternatives are hard to fathom; this country's enthusiasm for new large-scale international financing schemes is at low ebb. We have our own budget and deficit problems to settle first. And even then, the political climate may be unreceptive to further extensions of public credits to countries that won't play by acceptable rules. Against this must be weighed the need to nurture foreign markets for our own exports.

How quickly Third World governments will move to welcome foreign private capital will vary widely among them. But one international banking authority tells us: "At no time since the mid-19th century has the psychology at the top been more receptive to private enterprise, and it runs the gamut from government bureaucrats to trade union leaders."

At the same time, a number of developing countries are awakening to their opportunities for moving up from suppliers of basic commodities—at the whim of world markets—to producers of intermediate goods where they can earn profits that formerly belonged to importers and processors. The best current example, one that will be typical of changes to come, is the way Middle Eastern and other oil-producing countries are getting into petrochemicals.

Saudia Arabia, Indonesia and Mexico have seen the advantages inherent in converting essentially "free" feedstocks into semi-finished goods. Gas that used to be flared for want of a market is now going into petrochemical complexes built by or imported intact from Western producers. This development will help cushion oil-producing countries against the blow of declining oil prices. And it will challenge West Europe's and our own petrochemical industries, which may now have to turn to the production of higher-value specialty items. Similar trends are likely in aluminum and some kinds of plastic feedstocks, while the West moves to less energy-intensive kinds of production.

CONSTRUCTION ABROAD

The American lead in construction technology, particularly in design and development of new methods and in software and robotization, is being challenged, notably by the Japanese.

American heavy-construction firms face loss of overseas markets to foreign competition. The shrinkage is not yet severe but it is growing. More and more Third World countries are developing their own capabilities in heavy construction, and competition is rising from firms in other industrial or industrializing countries such as South Korea.

U.S. firms will probably need some government help to combat this shrinkage. Congress in coming years may ease up further on double taxation of American corporate earnings abroad, and possibly of personal income earned abroad, too. But the industry will also seek further assistance in the form of more liberal government financing to help meet and match the preferential aid foreign competitors are getting from their own governments.

The construction costs of foreign competitors, of course, will rise in coming years, but not enough to greatly narrow the gap with the U.S. By 2000, the American role in foreign construction will be chiefly that of supplying advanced design, technology and management of complex projects. Local firms or joint ventures shared with U.S. firms are probably going to do most of the actual building.

TO THE PACIFIC

This country's attention meanwhile is going to turn more and more to the Pacific, to the Asian Rim nations that are becoming both industrial competitors and lively trading partners on the Japanese model.

Taiwan, South Korea, Singapore, Hong Kong (which will revert to Chinese control in 1997), Indonesia and Malaysia are on a growth curve, and all of them are rising competitors for Japan in such things as electronic assembly and production of small consumer goods for export, and some big-ticket items as well. Growth in all these countries is proceeding at rates of 5% or 6% a year, well ahead of Western Europe, though of course on a smaller base.

China is on its way to becoming the dominant power in Asia, with an outside chance of catching up with Japan—or nearly so— early in the new century. More so if Japan begins to lose its preeminence to other Asian Rim industrial or industrializing countries.

The emerging industrial giants of Asia will be strong competitors to the U.S. in high-tech and manufactured goods. South Korea, for example, is already shipping cars to us and Europe. Before much longer, so may be Taiwan and mainland China, among other developing Asian nations. And U.S.-owned or joint-partnered firms in Pacific Basin countries also will be shipping goods here. But these countries also will be attractive markets for U.S. technology, communications and banking— especially the latter.

These countries will increasingly demand our attention in political as well as economic issues. Washington may have some delicate balancing to do between these interests and our relations with Western Europe and with Latin America. The Asian Rim nations have a long way to go but are moving ahead rapidly.

And by 2000, it will be a different ballgame with more and better players. World trade will be booming.

INTERNATIONAL BANKING

Growth in worldwide banking and financial services will play an enormous part in the coming acceleration of trade. Twenty-four-hour global investment markets, for example; via either their own computers or financial-service firms, Americans will be able to buy and sell U.S. and foreign securities around the clock if they're up to it.

Transactions will be cleared in various currencies—whatever is appropriate to the occasion—but mostly in dollars, and confirmations and closings will be automated. There will be no shortage of brokerages for wheeler-dealers; they'll be springing up all over the place.

At the same time, there's a great swirling going on in the banking business—U.S. banks opening branches abroad, foreign banks opening branches here. There's nothing new in the basic principle; it has been around for generations. But what IS new is the volume of such movements and the potential it holds for knitting foreign economies together with ours and for doing business abroad, which may become almost as easy as at home.

New York, London and Tokyo will be the leading exchanges and clearing centers but may in time be rivaled by others in Asia.

Broad-scale access to banking and brokerage services will both ride on and help stimulate a growing wave of international investment. Several hundred foreign securities already are traded here, and there will be a lot more of them as time goes on. Foreign investment in our securities markets, already high, will zoom as overseas money swarms in to profit from our coming boom.

Meanwhile, U.S. banks operating abroad will be getting deeper into foreign economies via a range of services taken for granted here but less familiar in most other countries: Consumer loans, competitive corporate finance, assistance in mergers and takeovers and the like.

OPEN SECURITIES MARKETS

All this blending will have side effects on securities markets and interest rates here and abroad—some good, some not so good. Currency flows will increasingly run independently of central banks, and these, including the Federal Reserve, will find it harder to manipulate interest rates and to influence domestic financial markets. Free-moving investment across national boundaries, made all the more mobile by the revolution in communications, will flow to wherever the potential for earnings is greatest.

U.S. corporate treasurers will rely on automated cash management techniques to keep them constantly up to the minute on the status of their companies' financial resources everywhere in the world and to handle the movement of funds needed to clear accounts.

Arbitrage—the art and science of making a profit out of finding the best place to park cash at any given moment—will blossom amid myriad new opportunities to make a buck. High-capacity computers linked to financial markets around the world will take over most of the job of finding and cashing in on even tiny and short-lived variations in interest rates.

Fortunes will be made and lost this way, and corporations here and abroad will play the same game with their cash. Such a system offers vast opportunities not only to abitrageurs but also to saboteurs, and governments everywhere in the Free World will be concerned with the security of their international financial communications. Theft via computer is one problem; terrorism directed against capitalistic transactions is another. Solutions will have to be sought on an international basis.

The same goes for controlling and taxing cross-border flows of financial data—an increasingly valuable "commodity." Governments of a number of developed and developing countries are imposing restrictions in the form of tariffs and preferences for their own domestic data-processing and financial firms that exclude or hamper U.S. and other foreign companies. It will take some hard bargaining to resolve this tangle.

A related issue is that of policing investment markets for conformity to domestic law and regulation by foreign investors. In this country, the Securities and Exchange Commission already has launched an effort to make sure that foreign access to our exchanges is conditioned on automatic acceptance of its requirements. It's intended also to close off the possibility of domestic market manipulation via insider trading and the like by Americans using foreign intermediaries.

Third World countries in dire need of investment capital will turn increasingly to ours and to other Western financial markets to raise developmental loans and equity investments.

CREDIT CARDS ABROAD

American travelers will find it easier than ever to spread money around overseas. International credit cards based on "smart card" techniques (see chapter 15, "The Money Business") will provide instant cash and credit just about everywhere; perhaps even within the Soviet Bloc sometime in the coming century.

And to return to the long-term effects of the revolution in international financial management: Large institutions here and abroad not only are becoming multinational but also will acquire increasing power to influence the money stock and national monetary policies. This implies great political power. "If they ever acted together," says a recent congressional study, "they would very nearly constitute a world government."

This has potential for good as well as evil. Working in coordination with domestic central banks and international financial institutions, the world banking community could act quickly to counteract dangerous imbalances and to monitor overexposure by lender and debtor countries alike. The other side of the coin is the question of how this power will be used and according to what rules.

That congressional study we mentioned also had this to say:

"The growth and integration of the world economy in the long run may well be the most significant force for world peace. It could be the source and wellspring of the gradual development of a world political order based not on unenforced charters or on military power, but on the economic self-interests of the nations of the world."

32

National Defense

Amid the dizzying economic changes of the next 15 years, one thing that isn't going to change is the basic nature of U.S.-Soviet relations.

The two superpowers will continue to be essentially what they are today: adversaries locked in a potentially deadly competition—primarily military, but also political, economic and technological. Both sides will devote a lot of desperate energy to keeping things from heating up to the flash point, but there are bound to be tense times as well as breathing spells.

Meanwhile, the American defense buildup will continue, but at a slower pace. Its objective is to fill the gap that opened when the Soviets took off with their intense armaments programs during the 1970s, while our own defense spending was slackening. Our best estimate is that the gap will continue to widen until the mid-'90s, due to Soviet momentum and our own slow start.

Even with smaller defense budgets expected over the next several years, imposed by deficit reduction guidelines, military contract work will continue to be big business, with a lot of opportunities for small and medium-sized firms, especially in computers, software, and electronics. But due to a broad perception of waste during the rapid defense buildup of the early '80s, there will be tough new cost controls that will pare down contractor profits.

SOVIET WILL

Soviet military policy is in a groove. Its objectives are to maintain a wide lead in nuclear weaponry while continuing to promote Marxist takeovers through the developing world—in Asia, Africa, Latin America. These dual objectives are clearly linked, because the Soviets are gambling that if their nuclear superiority is great enough, the West will cave in to one encroachment after another. This is more than policy; it is doctrine. It would be stretching hope to the point of absurdity to expect it to change any time soon—not in a country governed by ideology, never mind how cynically.

Given these facts of life, is there any chance of slowing the arms competition and stabilizing relations with Russia? Sure, some; but don't bet the farm on it just yet. There's a lot of ground to be covered before that sort of plateau heaves into sight, if indeed it ever does. And first, we've got some more rearming to do ourselves.

There will be a dip in defense budgets for a couple of years, then a return in the '90s to annual growth roughly in line with inflation. Pentagon spending will account for about 6% or 7% of GNP in a typical year (roughly the current level), depending on the international climate and who's in the White House. For reference, defense's share of GNP has been higher than this during most years since the end of World War II; it was 10% of GNP under Eisenhower.

In absolute money amounts, this is roughly on a par with the current rate of Soviet spending, though they have a head start. Since their economy is only half the size of ours, however, their defense spending is at least twice as big a share of national product—15% or so. The Soviet consumer is paying for weaponry by settling for shoddy goods, services and housing—and not enough of any of them.

Despite our buildup, the Soviet lead in overall weaponry will be maintained to at least 2000 and probably beyond. We simply aren't spending fast enough to close the gap all the way.

ARMS IN SPACE

Now there are other cards on the table in the so-called Star Wars space defense against missiles—the Strategic Defense Initiative, as it's called formally. If SDI continues on the path originally envisaged for it, our spending will come much closer to the Soviet level and might even surpass it toward the end of the century.

But that is an unlikely prospect if there can be agreement with the Russians to curtail some of their largest intercontinental ballistic missile programs in exchange for our downgrading Star Wars to the status of a long-range research program. And while research continues, both sides might agree to a general ban on weapons testing that would include SDI.

Would the Soviets go along? SDI has ruffled their feathers mightily. Though they lead in brute military strength, they lag far behind us in technology, despite many years of intensive research on anti-missile systems. What they fear in SDI is that if we launch full blast into such a program they are likely to be left behind in a competition they cannot win without stealing the blueprints.

But there are some problems with the SDI concept. To be effective, it must be able to destroy Soviet missiles shortly after launch—before they reach the upper atmosphere and fire their multiple nuclear warheads in our direction—because hitting hundreds or thousands of these relatively tiny warheads in space is probably impossible. Smacking down a fat missile is considerably easier.

Yet orbiting satellites armed with laser guns—the probable SDI mode—are themselves easy to hit. The Russians probably could manage that without too much trouble.

Thus we are left with a dilemma: Is SDI truly defensive, or is it unavoidably part and parcel of a preemptive, first-strike capability? Would it be used as the prelude to such a strike—that is, knocking out the other side's own defenses so that ICBMs could then take out the opposing missiles in their silos?

In this arcane what-if game that arms-control experts play, it doesn't matter whether our side has any such aggressive intention or not. The controlling point is that it COULD work out that way. And that is the point on which the entire concept pivots.

Experience so far has shown that while the U.S. has generally been the first in weapons innovation, the Soviets have been ahead in pouring out the weaponry.

And each escalation of technology has heightened the risk to one side or the other without giving either a lasting advantage. For reasons such as these, Star Wars is not only wildly unpopular in the Kremlin, but given the internal problems it confronts, it also scares some folks in the Pentagon. We think you can put your money down on this bet: Star Wars will remain in the research phase indefinitely.

HIGH-TECH CONVENTIONAL WARFARE

Not so fictional, however, is the oncoming rush of change in the way our forces will be equipped for other forms of war. The same wave of technological innovation that is about to transform our civilian economy is going to have enormous impact on our military. And these are innovations we will NOT bargain away in Geneva or anywhere else.

Improvements in so-called conventional warfare is essential, because regional wars of varying size will be a permanent part of the future, flaring and receding even as the superpowers are locked in nuclear stalemate. The U.S. and Soviets have been fighting each other through proxies ever since World War II, and this isn't going to change. Whether the equipment is manned by Americans or the soldiers of governments we're supporting, the equipment is going to get fancier with every conflict.

By the mid-'90s and beyond, tanks, planes, ships and other military equipment will be on the way to becoming highly computerized and robotized. The kind of advanced technology that can run a mining machine deep in the earth from a control console on the surface can do the same for combat. Using ultra-sensitive feedback loops combined with television, operators of such equipment will be able to "feel" the controls as though the intervening computer didn't exist; it will become "transparent." Remote-control combat vehicles will become common, reducing the number of troops directly exposed to combat while gaining firepower.

"Expert systems" will assist controllers of such equipment as well as go along with pilots to help them in combat, navigation and general emergencies. That is, computerized programs loaded with acquired knowledge about combat conditions will with lightning speed react to emergencies and either tell the pilot what to do (computers already can talk) or take over the controls themselves.

The same remote-control principles described above will lead to a great increase in the use of unmanned planes for bombing, battlefield missions, reconnaissance and the like. Ditto for guided missiles and other "smart" weapons, including shells. And there will be huge advances in accuracy and effectiveness.

Warships will undergo similar refitting. Computers will take over much of the work of controlling a ship's position with minimum human input; ditto for control over other ship systems such as winches and refueling equipment that has always had to be manhandled by large working crews. The same goes for naval armaments; guns and missiles will increasingly be computerized.

Precision-guided weaponry has the potential of restoring the balance between conventional weapons defense and offense in Europe—for example, offsetting the Soviets' lead in tanks, which ought to help cool any ideas they may have about launching an invasion of the NATO countries—something they could do now in full expectation of making it to the English Channel in a few days.

The U.S. will continue to depend on satellites and electronic intercepts for the bulk of its intelligence. The Soviets can't quite match us there but are well ahead in old-fashioned human espionage. Curbs on exports of U.S. technology will be maintained unless and until there is a substantial easing in relations; even then, some restrictions will remain. American companies will chafe at them, and the Russians will get around them any way they can—which won't be difficult, given the eagerness in West Europe and Japan for trade.

The spread of technology in the military won't come swiftly. It's too expensive; and a lot of developmental work remains to be done, to say nothing of all the extremely complicated computer software that will have to be written. But it WILL come, no doubt of that.

TERRORISM AND NUCLEAR PROLIFERATION

The scariest wild card in the future of world order is not the American-Soviet relationship. At least these two powerhouses act with a certain rationality and predictability. The greater problem is terrorism, the proverbial loose cannon on the deck.

Terrorism is used broadly by regimes of both the right and left today, but much of it is aided and abetted by the Soviet Union to destabilize non-socialist governments.

World tolerance of terrorism is waning, but its inherent advantages over direct military action will keep it alive forever, posing continued risks to world stability and especially to the safety of Americans abroad.

The more terrorism extends its bite, the greater the number of governments that will become involved against their will. And this will make it harder for those that now turn the other cheek, or just look the other way, to continue doing so. Out of this may yet emerge some sort of broad consensus to take concerted action.

But sometime in the next two decades, we are likely to see the first use of nuclear blackmail by terrorists, because of the increasing availability of nuclear fuel and the technical knowhow for fashioning crude atomic weapons. This threat will be the ultimate test of the resolve of civilized nations to curb terrorism, and it may take the detonation of a terrorist's nuclear device to achieve the solid front that has eluded us so far.

LABOR NEEDS

The technological advances in warfare described earlier will have a favorable impact on our military's manpower needs. Warfare will be less labor-intensive, and fewer but better-trained soldiers will accomplish more.

The military will not have to resort to a draft, even though the number of youngsters in eligible age groups is declining. But it will have to attract more women to meet its needs, and more women will make it into officer ranks. The military will also have to do even more schooling of recruits than it does now, which is considerable.

The services, the army in particular, can look forward to increasing change in their ethnic mix. A growing proportion of recruits will be from racial minorities, especially Hispanics, as their numbers rise in the population. Many will lack the schooling needed to handle technical equipment; many may not even read or write English well. Computer-aided education and training, in which the army has been something of a pioneer, will take on added importance. And simplicity will have to be engineered into battlefield and other equipment to compensate for skill shortcomings—another challenge to hardware and software designers.

Personnel and related costs will be a rising share of defense budgets for years to come. It will cost plenty to attract recruits; pay will rise to levels more nearly competitive with the private economy, and benefits will be upgraded. Congress will sweat and fret over the expense, but the prospect of a peacetime draft in the foreseeable future is not politically inviting.

Mitigating the labor cost escalation somewhat will be the tight supply of low-skill, entry-level jobs in an increasingly high-tech civilian economy, making military service an attractive first job for many young adults seeking practical training.

The cost of fighting past wars—that is, taking care of yesterday's warriors—is still rising. The Veterans Administration faces a zooming case load that in some respects will double by 2000. It will need a two-thirds increase in the number of nursing-care beds to handle the coming influx of aged veterans of World War II and Korea. Its budget may have to rise by two-thirds or so by the year 2000 to keep up with this growth. It will need a lot of new facilities—hospitals, equipment, nursing homes, etc.

By 2000, the number of veterans 65 or older will double to about 9 million, representing two-thirds of the entire male population in that age range. The number of female vets over 65 also will almost double by 1990; the VA is going to need special facilities for them. VA wants to build a network of geriatric facilities, but current budget stringencies have delayed a start. Some future administration and Congress will have to face up to the costs this will entail.

Meanwhile, veterans will wind up paying more of the cost via means tests that determine who gets how much care and at what level of fees. Private insurance and Medicare/Medicaid benefits will be tapped to help offset VA costs. A start in this direction goes into effect in 1986.

There probably will be far more stringent limitations on the treatment of non-service-connected disabilities. Congress may also require the VA—the biggest but not the most efficient medical service in the country—to tighten up its act. More of its functions may be contracted out, including some kinds of nursing-home care. But some of these economies may be offset by cuts in Medicare benefits, which would tend to push more veterans into VA institutions.

But the picture isn't all bleak. The VA's load will begin to slacken after 2000 and will continue to decline—except for a brief bump around 2020 when aging Vietnam vets hit the system in large numbers—and by 2030 may be down to a level not too far above recent years.

GORBACHEV'S GOALS

The NATO alliance is going to come under severe strain in the years ahead. The new generation of leaders taking power in Russia will in many ways be tougher adversaries than their predecessors, and NATO will be one of their chief targets.

Gorbachev and company will seek to undermine NATO by cultivating Western eagerness to believe in the possibilities for long-range detente, and by blaming the U.S. for the failure to achieve arms control. He in particular can play to these wishful thinkers by presenting a more "reasonable" face to the West, by offering expanded opportunities for trade and cultural exchanges, and most of all, by raising hopes for a relaxation of the tensions that have pushed defense budgets to their limit.

Soviet leadership has its own stake in a relaxation. It needs to modernize the sluggish, muscle-bound Soviet economy, and this is being forestalled by its perceived need to maintain a crushingly expensive military expansion. The situation was already bad before the recent downturn in world commodity prices, especially oil, on which the Soviets are dependent for generating foreign exchange. It's going to be even harder for them to finance an economic transformation in the coming years.

There will be severe restraints on Gorbachev's freedom to maneuver, no matter how quickly and well he has moved to nail down his own power base in the Kremlin. One is the danger of allowing expectations to rise too quickly at home and especially among the Soviet Bloc countries, every one of which is hungry for a crack at Western technology, goods and lifestyles.

Another is the powerful streak of conservatism, Soviet-style, among the party bureaucrats who really run Russia (particularly the military) and who have much to lose if he means business about cracking down on corruption and inefficiency.

Clearly, while Gorbachev may look and sound like a fresh new breeze in the Kremlin, he is very much a product of the Party and will have neither the freedom nor probably the inclination to change things rapidly. Which suggests several possibilities:

▶ A tougher, more aggressive foreign policy for at least a while, to placate the hard-liners while he consolidates power.

▶ Then a change to more restraint in supporting puppet regimes on our doorstep, as a way of lowering the sound level a bit in future dealings with American administrations.

▶ Continued pressure on Afghanistan, where the Soviet military is deeply committed; but also renewed efforts to maneuver the West into some sort of face-saving international agreement that would confirm the Soviet conquest.

▶ A fast build-up of Soviet investment in domestic industrial and technological development, favoring West European and Japanese companies over American—in effect inviting American firms to lobby Washington to make a deal with Moscow.

▶ Limited moves to improve Russia's human-rights image among Western opinion-molders, such as renewed emigration of Jews and some let-up of restraints on artists and writers, etc.— steps that would cost little but might have a substantial foreign payoff.

Gorbachev is clearly more imaginative than his predecessors. The West has a formidable new adversary on its hands.

This is the reason we have serious concerns about the future of the NATO alliance. There will be growing demands, from both Americans at home and European allies, for a reduction in our troop and other commitments to NATO, and these will mount with the *appearance* of a lessening of the Soviet threat, due to arms-control agreements or other conciliatory moves.

Our judgment is that NATO will survive in at least its present form—as will its communist counterpart, the Warsaw Pact—but by 2000 each will be undergoing basic changes which, if detente is in place by then, may substantially reduce their scope.

If there is to be a warming trend, it will probably lead to some kind of delicate "normalization" in relations. But long-term objectives won't change—on their side or on ours. We can expect an indefinite continuation of the testing and probing that has gone on in the past.

It's a good idea to be realistic about any hopes for fundamental change in Russia. The Italian writer Luigi Barzini has put it this way (in his 1983 book the *The Europeans*):

"The Russian Revolution exaggerated the worst traits of czarist autocracy: secret police, mass exiles to Siberia, forced labor camps, the concentration of all the economy in the hands of the state. The Soviets dedicated the largest percentage of the national income to armaments and starved the peasantry, as had been done in Russia for centuries. In the end the communist regime turned out to be a caricature of what had existed before."

33

Political Clout

Political power in this country will continue to shift towards older Americans and the southern and western regions, reflecting demographic and migratory patterns.

And the ideological trend will continue to be rightward. If having more to conserve is what makes for conservatism, future American voters will have ample reason to steer toward the right side of the political road.

Rising incomes are likely to keep most voters in the moderate-conservative range, particularly on economic issues. Americans have never gone in for wide ideological swings. If we stray as voters, it is only slightly to one side or the other of a broad middle range. We foresee nothing in the next couple of decades to change that.

Which means that Americans will persist in the current trend toward economic conservatism: no big new social programs, increasing emphasis on incentives for free enterprise, selective deregulation to promote competition, and so on. On social issues, however, we see a continuing liberal trend towards laissez-faire tolerance and individual freedom of choice. Despite the recent successes of activist social conservatives, Americans will remain tolerant of diverse lifestyles, in keeping with the increasingly diverse nature of American society.

Despite the rise in anti-big-government attitudes, we doubt that government will decline much more in size or influence, even though its growth will level out. Complexities of the high-tech era we're heading into may even require regulation in new, more specific policy areas—such as individual privacy in the super-computer age, genetic engineering, and medical technology.

If the country can stay out of wars, the major issues in forthcoming campaigns will be economic and to a lesser extent social. For example, coping with the transition to the age of automation. Gray Panther issues, most of them economic, will gain importance as the older segment of the population grows.

Women will be a larger and faster-growing force in politics. A woman as vice president is no longer farfetched. And perhaps a woman will appear at the top of the ticket before long, but the first woman president is more likely to be one who succeeds to the office from the vice presidency. The voters of 2000, the youngest of whom are only three or four years old now, may not find this challenge to tradition so upsetting as it might have been to their parents.

The role of unions in national politics is certain to shrink in coming years. They will keep their special, influential status within the Democratic party as long as they remain its single largest organized power center. But union leaders face the same problem as Democratic leaders: figuring out where the membership is heading and finding a way to get out in front of them. It is fairly clear that union members' loyalties don't extend much beyond the plant door. With union clout ebbing inside the plant, there's little reason to expect it to grow on the outside.

Third parties will come and go, and voters will become more independent, tending to split tickets and casting ballots on personal preferences rather than party discipline, which has been slipping for years.

POWERFUL OLDSTERS

Important demographic shifts are taking place in the electorate. Only five or six years ago, 18-year-olds outnumbered people aged 35 by three to two. By the end of this decade, it will be the other way around and then some: The 35-year-olds will outnumber the 18s by close to one-fourth. By the mid-'90s, this disparity will grow to nearly 40%.

The significance of this shift is that a much higher percentage of older people actually vote than those at the youngest end of the scale. Records show, for example, that twice as many people aged 35 vote as those aged 18.

In the next three presidential elections, about half the electorate will be under 45. But by 1992, about one-fourth of voters will be in their 30s, compared to 18 percent in 1976. As this aging process moves up through the population, the under-45 age group will decline as a percentage of the electorate and by 2000 will be a minority.

These aging Baby Boomers will be concerned with social security—theirs and that of their parents. And this will have a strong bearing on politics and policy.

But for the next 10 years or so, the bulk of the electorate will be people concerned with economic opportunity—their own advancement—and they will be more accustomed to change than their parents are.

SUNBELT POWER

In the meantime, the center of population will continue moving west and south. A Sunbelt-dominated electorate will lean more to the right of center on issues of federal intervention in the economy and society. Transfers of wealth from the newly rich states to Frostbelt states with high social-service costs won't be any more popular than it is now.

And Republicans seem favored in coming presidential elections into at least the start of the next century if they keep their noses clean and the economy remains healthy—as we expect it will. They will be thrown out only if there are major scandals or precipitous economic downturns on their watch.

For the Democrats to benefit from demographic and geographic power shifts in America, they will have to rebuild along new lines. The shift of 1984—voters in the South and West casting a majority of electoral votes, for the first time—will be accelerated after the 1990 census and the reapportionment that follows. A Democrat—most likely a westerner—might still make it to the White House, but his party carries a mounting handicap because of Republican presidential strength in the West and South.

We expect this Sunbelt surge to continue indefinitely; certainly into the beginning of the new century. Part of the continuing southward and westward shift of political heft is the rising numbers and influence of Hispanic (chiefly Mexican) and, to a lesser extent, Asian voters in those parts of the country. These will make themselves felt in issues of national scope—response to communist intervention in our hemisphere, for example.

ELECTORAL COLLEGE

Talk of an all-in-one-day national presidential primary will boil up every four years and get nowhere, but there will be some success for efforts to consolidate primaries on a regional basis, as several southern states plan for the fall '86 elections. State caucuses will eventually fade away.

The big "sleeper" issue is reform of the electoral college, which is either an anachronism or safeguard, depending on your point of view. Most politicians feel it is a nuisance at best and a potential time bomb at worst. And one of these years it will blow up—when it fails to elect the candidate who has won a majority of the popular vote. It almost happened in 1960 and again in 1968, not to mention the still-debated election of Rutherford B. Hayes over Samuel J. Tilden in 1876.

When the crunch comes, Congress will have to act quickly to find a way out of the fix, while the losing side whips up anger over frustration of the popular will. Congress will fish around for compromises, perhaps challenging enough electoral votes to throw the election to the popular candidate. But even this won't be easy; the Constitution does not bind electors to vote for any one candidate.

In any event, one such crisis will be enough. Congress will propose a constitutional amendment instituting direct election; a sufficient number of states will ratify it in due course, and everyone but the loser will heave a sigh of relief.

Such a critical juncture might also be the time when proposals for a single six-year presidential term are taken seriously, along with—alternatively—demands for repeal of the Twenty-Second Amendment limiting presidents to two consecutive terms.

GETTING ELECTED

The business of politics will continue to ride the leading edge of technology. Campaign committees will invest heavily in the latest electronic gadgetry to work up mailing lists, specialized appeals and personalized letters to every conceivable voter segment. These, along with sophisticated TV and radio spots for wide distribution, will make it easy to target both narrow and broad audiences.

But all this will cost money. Despite the furor over the staggering cost of campaigning in America, the role of private funds in federal elections will not diminish. We will probably not see public funding of congressional elections, with major candidates getting a campaign allowance from the federal Treasury. Why not? Incumbents won't want to give their opponents free money to unseat them. PACs—the political action committees of corporations and unions and causes—will assume an even larger role in campaign finance.

Congress may even *loosen* rules on campaign finance that restrict the amount any one PAC or individual may give. Improved computer data bases will make it easier for the press and public—and rival politicians—to find out who's giving how much for what. This publicity may impose some discipline of its own.

TV is now permanently in place as the prime campaign medium. Televised presidential debates will continue to be the accepted routine even for chief executives running for a second term. Reagan saw to that with the precedent he set in accepting the 1984 debates when he didn't have to.

ON CAPITOL HILL

After many years of White House accretion of power, Congress' power—especially the negative knack of blocking presidential will in foreign policy—has been expanding at the expense of the presidency, and we expect this trend to intensify. Successful presidents will continue to be those most adept at both stroking and pressuring Congress. Not even election by landslide will be enough in itself, as several recent incumbents have found out.

Congress, after all, has the ultimate source of power—control over spending. And it will continue to upgrade its own capacity for study, analysis and forecasting, equipping members and committees to go head to head with the bureaucrats "downtown" in the executive branch.

In fact, a sizable and still expanding bureaucracy has grown up around the members of Congress themselves—hundreds of staff assistants with an amazing range of expertise. These staffs, backed by the resources of the Congressional Research Service in the Library of Congress, help arm legislators for their crusades and are the source of many of the ideas and investigations that pepper every session. Even the Pentagon has long since found that the armed services committees and their myriad subcommittees are rubber stamps no longer. Now they bristle with their own expertise and often differing views of security needs.

So the net of it is that the legislative branch swims in its own computerized sea of information and is no longer dependent on the executive for advice and counsel. This independence will continue to grow and to make for lively political theater in the years ahead.

But while Congress has a mind of its own, it also usually has MORE than one. Maintaining order and party discipline will continue to give the nominal leadership fits for as far ahead as anyone can see. Regional caucuses, caucuses on a bewildering variety of special issues, proliferation of subcommittees to the point where virtually every member can find or fashion a platform from which to spring to fame—these trends will continue to frustrate all efforts to turn them around, no matter how hard the leaders try.

Nor will there be any significant cessions of power from the legislative to the executive branch, despite all the pleadings of future presidents for more neat and orderly procedures; Congress will continue to be too rambunctious for that. No grant of the line-item veto, for example, which would allow a president to choose among provisions of an appropriation bill, accepting those that fit his program and shucking off those that don't.

But Congress WILL try to shape up its budget-making procedures. These in recent years have become increasingly chaotic, with annual end-of-session cliffhanger dramas culminating in "continuing resolutions" to keep the government running on near-empty. Pressure is growing for a two-year budget cycle, since one year clearly isn't enough. But even this is likely to include a lot of annual revising and tinkering and is no guarantee of smooth sailing in itself.

The new "automatic pilot" approach to deficit reduction, embodied right now by the Gramm-Rudman-Hollings law, will survive in some form or another, because it enables members of the House and Senate to go on record for fiscal restraint without having to be recorded in vote after embarrassing vote in which they actually cut spending for particular programs. Despite the recent challenges to the constitutionality of this particular mechanism, ways will be found to preserve the concept of across-the-board spending cuts.

Erosion of the once-mighty congressional seniority system won't be reversed in the foreseeable future, but the search will continue for ways to restore at least some of the clout of congressional leaders that was lost in the reforms of the '60s and '70s. That wresting of power from "The Establishment" is largely responsible for the fractionalizing and confusion typified in Congress by the annual budget donnybrook.

In any event, the House will experiment with leadership by ad hoc committees, hoping to struggle back toward creation of consensus on difficult issues. The Senate has a different problem ...modernizing its archaic rules—especially the use of the filibuster by a determined minority—without giving up its role as a brake on excesses by the House or the executive. This will simmer along indecisively until an impasse develops on some issue of sufficient national importance to cause a storm of public outrage. What will provoke it and when, no one can say; our guess is the showdown will come before 2000.

TV will help prod the Senate along, however. Now that the Senate has moved to follow the example of the House and allow its peculiar and often somnolent proceedings to be televised, significant changes may not be far off.

Limitations on the length of Senate debate will emerge stepwise over the next several years—say, by lowering the number of votes required to shut off filibusters; creation of a more orderly mechanism for steering bills onto the floor and keeping them moving; even an electronic voting system like those used in most state legislatures and in the House. Upcoming generations won't cherish the Senate's 19th-century ways as the 21st century nears.

The average age of members of Congress will stabilize at just under 50 before long, which is younger than it has been in a long time. There will be enough new members in their 20s and 30s to keep things stirred up, poking at the hierarchy for more power-sharing. But few of them will be in it for the money; congressional pay, while fat by national median-income standards, will continue to lag well behind what an unusually bright, ambitious person can earn in the private sector.

THE PRESIDENCY

Ideas on ways to reform and improve White House operations will continue to turn up—many of them simply visionary, such as the recurring proposal for election of additional vice presidents to take over various administrative duties. Any meaningful change is more likely to come via technology rather than constitutional tinkering of that sort.

The power of computers and of quick access to information can make an increasing difference in the White House, extending the reach and grasp of the presidency. Some future president, perhaps the next, will order work begun on a government-wide "command and control" network, a civilian counterpart of the Pentagon's. And then the ability to track complex operations and monitor agency actions—and spending—will be more centralized and effective. Budget-making, the process that forms the hub around which all government revolves, will become more orderly, sensitive and realistic.

But there are limits to what improved technology can do for the process of leadership. For all its authority and pomp, the executive office of the president is still powered more by personalities and politics than by computers. Each new president quickly discovers the limits of his power, not simply in Congress, but also in the vast bureaucracy that supposedly is his to command.

Sweeping powers to reorganize the government are sought by one president after another but are granted only seldom and grudgingly by Congress. Every so often it agrees to the creation of a new Cabinet department—Energy, Transportation and Education being postwar examples—but has yet to kill one off.

Some future president will appoint a blue-ribbon commission to draft a plan for modernizing the federal government, and parts of its recommendations are sure to be adopted as we move into the new century, particularly those dealing with reform of the budget process. But while the president may propose, it will still be Congress that disposes; any and all reforms will have to win its support first. There won't be any broad grants of reorganization power to the chief executive.

The power to fill federal court vacancies gives some presidents an extraordinary opportunity to influence the future. Richard Nixon got this chance, replacing nearly half the Supreme Court in less than three years, leaving a conservative legacy that endures long after his departure from office in disgrace.

Ronald Reagan has got this chance, too, and he's seized it in appointment after appointment of conservative jurists to federal district and appellate court positions. Due to the waning health of several elderly associate justices of the Supreme Court, Reagan may get a chance over the next two years to leave his stamp on the High Court for a generation to come.

Which brings us back to our starting point: It looks as though the U.S. is firmly on a conservative political course well into the next century.

34

Some Parting Words

The theme of this book is growth and change in an America undergoing a transition into a new kind of economy, a new population mix and a new relationship with the rest of the world.

We've outlined for you the ingredients for what will be one of the strongest and healthiest booms our country has ever experienced. Healthy, because of relatively low inflation made possible by big increases in productivity, which themselves will result from the high technology in which the U.S. will continue to lead the world.

And we have tried to show how synergy—the linkage among technologies—will produce an effect greater than the simple sum of the parts: a growth curve that will take off in the '90s and keep going into the new century.

None of this happens automatically. As individuals and as a body politic, we shall have to make the right choices at the right times. Mistakes no doubt will be made, and there are bound to be times when the short-term outlook seems to darken, and growth slows or stops. That's normal; the business cycle won't go away.

But preoccupation with the short run can be seriously misleading. Our research and reporting convince us that it would take a series of enormous misjudgments to derail the coming boom. We would have to reverse course almost totally in government and in the economy—away from a market-oriented, enterprise society to something else. The something-elses of this world have all been tried, and they're not working very well.

Here in the U.S., we've outgrown illusions about central planning and "fine-tuning" an economy too enormous and too vigorous even to be described in simple terms, much less "managed" in detail.

The rest of the world seems at times to have more confidence in the American economy than we do ourselves. While our editorial pages agonize over fleeting signs of slowdown or threats of inflation, governments and peoples abroad increasingly look to us as the model for what they long to achieve.

Harold Macmillan, former prime minister of Great Britain, now the Earl of Stockton, spoke of this not long ago. The U.S., he said in the House of Lords, has regained its "natural buoyancy" and is exploiting new technologies and building new industries that will produce jobs at a time when Britain, and by implication other countries, are still tinkering with the old machinery and ignoring the future that is bearing down on them.

SOME PRACTICAL ADVICE

Our objective in describing the changes ahead has been to help you get ready—preparing to both protect yourself and profit from them in personal and business affairs.

To be taken advantage of fully, these judgments and forecasts must be translated into concrete business and personal investment decisions that meet your individual needs.

Certain general investment strategies emerge. Keep these guidelines in mind: a long period of generally low inflation and high real growth in GNP, with the greatest growth in high-tech fields. No serious recessions over the next 15 years. Interest rates trending gradually lower.

These predictions are most hospitable to a combination of financial investments—the equity and debt instruments of growing corporations. The most innovative firms will grow at a brisk clip; there won't be severe inflation to erode their profits.

Stocks: Look for the industry leaders in the high-growth fields we have listed in several chapters of this book. Try to spot companies with high research and development spending as a percentage of revenue, but with price-earnings multiples that haven't yet been pushed through the roof by prior market speculation. Don't be afraid to hold good stocks for a long period.

To get a breadth of ownership within a particular sector, look for specialized mutual funds that invest in high-growth categories, such as health care, telecommunications and biotechnology. The less adventuresome investor can participate in broad market advances (and also declines) by buying so-called index mutual funds, composed of stocks in the Dow Jones or Standard & Poor's indexes.

Bonds: If interest rates trend lower over the long haul, you're not going to take a beating on the value of the bonds you buy now, and you might even enjoy some modest capital appreciation. In the meantime, you'll benefit from locking in today's rates. But keep in mind that bonds will be a conservative investment compared to other ways of participating in the boom we foresee.

Real estate: It always does best when high inflation batters financial instruments, so we don't see real estate *in general* outperforming the stock market by a wide margin over the next decade or so. But fine real estate investments abound for the serious investor who's willing to plan his purchases carefully and use the leverage of borrowed money wisely.

Keep in mind that opportunities for the greatest appreciation will be raw land in the path of development in high-growth areas, which will tend to be found mostly in the Sunbelt. But raw land, which doesn't produce current income or generate income-sheltering tax losses, is the trickiest of all real estate investments; it's not for the novice.

Rental buildings, both residential and commercial, also require plenty of expertise, and the economics of most deals are highly dependent on rents being boosted by inflation or high demand in a growth area. Those rent increases won't be coming easily either, at least on office space. Because of generous tax write-offs for new construction, many American cities are extremely overbuilt in office space, and this glut of capacity will depress or at least restrain rents for several years to come. The next several years should see a lot of distress selling—a good opportunity, but only for the very skilled investor.

Tangibles: Gold and other precious metals make sense to those who foresee economic disaster—which we certainly don't. As a hedge against an unexpected resurgence of high inflation, gold can be a good small ingredient in a balanced investment portfolio, but we don't recommend that you take a heavy position.

If you want to dabble in collectibles like art, gemstones, antiques, or rare stamps and coins, keep in mind their drawbacks as investments. You'll be up against such risks as no current income, changing fashion, insurance and security costs, slender resale markets, high transaction fees through dealers and auction houses—all of which add up to low liquidity. Nonetheless, the very finest and most rare items in virtually every category will tend to appreciate handsomely over long periods.

KEEPING YOU POSTED

We hope that you will reread this book from time to time, with special attention to those sections that bear most directly on your own future.

For more than 63 years The Kiplinger Washington Editors have been serving readers with advance alerts on developments of importance in personal and business planning. The judgments set forth in this book are our own but are based on extensive research and dozens of interviews with people deeply involved in making the future come true.

Forecasts as far-reaching as these will need updating. We'll have more to tell you in our weekly *Kiplinger Washington Letter*, monthly *Changing Times* magazine, and our specialized newsletters on tax policy, agriculture, and the economies of California, Texas and Florida. We'll be glad to hear from you if you have questions.

Index

V

Venture capitalists, 91, 151, 207
Veterans Administration, 298
Virginia, 259
Voice of America, 71

W

Wall Street Journal, 192
Warsaw Pact, 300
Washington, 25, 63, 121, 170
  baseball, 170
  fiber-optic technology, 63
  price supports, 121
Washington Post, 192
  conventions and conferences,
    137
Water, 272–280
  agriculture vs. development,
    274–275
  biotech research, 273
  climatological trends, 272
    Greenhouse Effect, 273
  high cost, 273–275
    Central Arizona Project, 274
    conservation measures, 274
    desalting plants, 273, 275
    rationing, 273
  high-tech methods of recycling,
    272
  nuclear waste, 279–280
    temporary storage sites, 279
    U.S. Energy Department,
      279–280
  ocean dumping, 277–279
    biotechnology, 277
    chemical runoff, 277
    National Academy of Sci-
      ences, 277

salt plague, 275
  converting seawater, 275
swapping water, 275–276
  water-treatment costs, 276
West Germany, 88, 132
  highway controls, 132
  space stations, 88
Western economic system, 2
Women
  fashion and style, 196-197
  in labor force, 27–28, 226
  in sports, 170
  needs for appliances, 180
  rising educational levels, 159
  shopping, 201
  working, 228–230
    comparable worth, 229
    teleshopping, 230
World Bank, 19
World trade and finance, 4, 281–
  291
  construction abroad, 286–287
    government financing, 287
  credit cards abroad, 290–291
  developing nations, 284–286
    corporate colonialism, 284
    population growth, 285
    quasi-governmental banks,
      284
  international banking, 288–289
  international exchange rates,
    282
  less protectionism, 283–284
    global sourcing, 283
    Third World debt crises, 282
  open securities markets, 289–
    290
    automated cash management
      techniques, 289
    high-capacity computers, 289
    Securities and Exchange
      Commission, 290